Behind the Mirror

Behind the Mirror

Inside the World of Big Brother

TARAN ARMSTRONG

sourcebooks

Copyright © 2025 by Taran Armstrong
Cover and internal design © 2025 by Sourcebooks
Cover design by Pete Garceau
Cover images © checha/Getty Images, ikuvshinov/Getty Images, liangpv/Getty Images
Internal design by Tara Jaggers/Sourcebooks

Sourcebooks and the colophon are registered trademarks of Sourcebooks.

All rights reserved. No part of this book may be reproduced in any form or by any electronic or mechanical means including information storage and retrieval systems—except in the case of brief quotations embodied in critical articles or reviews—without permission in writing from its publisher, Sourcebooks.

No part of this book may be used or reproduced in any manner for the purpose of training artificial intelligence technologies or systems.

This publication is designed to provide accurate and authoritative information in regard to the subject matter covered. It is sold with the understanding that the publisher is not engaged in rendering legal, accounting, or other professional service. If legal advice or other expert assistance is required, the services of a competent professional person should be sought. —*From a Declaration of Principles Jointly Adopted by a Committee of the American Bar Association and a Committee of Publishers and Associations*

References to internet websites (URLs) were accurate at the time of writing. Neither the author nor Sourcebooks is responsible for URLs that may have expired or changed since the manuscript was prepared.

All brand names and product names used in this book are trademarks, registered trademarks, or trade names of their respective holders. Sourcebooks is not associated with any product or vendor in this book.

Published by Sourcebooks
1935 Brookdale RD, Naperville, IL 60563-2773
(630) 961-3900
sourcebooks.com

Cataloging-in-Publication Data is on file with the Library of Congress.

Printed and bound in the United States of America.
MA 10 9 8 7 6 5 4 3 2

For anyone who's been unable to explain their obsession. Hope this book helps.

Contents

INTRODUCTION ... IX

Chapter 1: Adaptations ... 1

Chapter 2: The Evil Doctor ... 17

Chapter 3: Influences ... 36

Chapter 4: Community ... 56

Chapter 5: Twisted ... 78

Chapter 6: Do Not Assume ... 98

Chapter 7: The Evolution of Strategy ... 119

Chapter 8: Controversy ... 143

Chapter 9: The Renaissance ... 166

Chapter 10: Cancellation ... 199

Chapter 11: Cracking the Code ... 225

Chapter 12: The Cookout ... 261

Chapter 13: The Rules of the Game ... 293

Chapter 14: The Sword   319
Chapter 15: The Mirror   351

NOTES   361
ACKNOWLEDGMENTS   389
ABOUT THE AUTHOR   393

Introduction

It's 3:00 a.m. on a Saturday night. A group of sixteen strangers have all left their regular lives behind and have been herded into a sound-stage dressed to resemble a house sitting on the edge of a studio lot. Some of them will live here for the next one hundred days.

From three thousand miles away, I watch them sleep.

For the last ten years, I've turned this into my job. But I've been doing it for far longer than that. On the screen in front of me is a grid of four camera feeds, glowing with the green of infrared night vision. Each of the four feeds shows a different angle from inside this "house," and on each one is someone sleeping. These aren't the only cameras in the house; there are ninety others placed strategically to capture every movement of the people inside.

On the bottom-right feed, I see someone shift in their bed. This might be it.

I'm not the only one watching. Thousands of people from all

corners of the country are staring at the same four camera feeds. Many more are fast asleep themselves and will catch up on what happened on this lot in Studio City in the morning. Not me though; I need to be here for this.

My eyes glued to the bottom-right feed, I watch as someone quietly gets out of their bed. My stomach drops. It's happening.

I pull up my notes and start typing.

Named after the classic *1984*, *Big Brother* premiered on CBS twenty-five years ago with the absurd concept of putting twelve strangers in a house and streaming the live feeds of them online for anyone to see. It's a fitting idea for the early days of "reality" TV back in the year 2000, when that word actually felt like it should mean something. There's an almost naive optimism to the idea that access to the actual footage of a show wouldn't compromise the storytelling ability of its editors. Yet, here we are twenty-five years later, and the live feeds for *Big Brother* remain a cornerstone of its hardcore fan base and an essential part of the show's longevity.

It's easy to take *Big Brother* for granted. It's a silly show with silly marketing and silly challenges. *Survivor*, its sibling show, takes itself much more seriously and tends to attract an audience that isn't *quite* as ashamed to admit they watch it. Despite its colossal success, in a world where reality TV is considered popcorn TV at best and trash TV at worst, *Big Brother* struggles to keep its reputation out of the bin.

And that's before you tell people about watching the players sleep.

I promise I'm not a creep. Or maybe I am. I suppose that's for you to decide. Before you do, let me make a case for myself and for this silly reality show that's come to define my life in ways I never could have imagined. Because behind that silly exterior lies a rich landscape of social strategy, real human moments, relationships, and game theory; ultimately, it is a distilled reflection of the society in which it exists. I genuinely believe there is no other piece of media that has as much to say or teach as *Big Brother* does, silliness and all.

For a decade now, I've made covering *Big Brother* my career. It started with recapping the episodes and has expanded into daily coverage of the live feeds from the house. Every morning, thousands of people tune in to have me fill them in on what's been happening in the game while I give my commentary and analysis on the strategy of the contestants.

Three months at a time, my life becomes dedicated to monitoring the daily lives of the people on this show. I watch them as they meet each other, judge each other, come together, split apart, open up, lie, betray, and vie for power. It's the ultimate character study as the layers peel back on how the players operate in this high-stress environment where trust is a scarce resource.

While I may have turned this voyeurism into how I make my living, I'm far from the only person who falls into the rabbit hole of *Big Brother* and the live feeds every summer. The show's dedicated fan base has kept the show alive and well into its third decade on the air, with no signs of slowing. In fact, *Big Brother 24* boasted the highest viewing time of any streaming series in the months that it was airing. Because the feeds run 24/7, discussion about the show is constantly dominating online spaces like Reddit and Twitter to the point that many fans keep themselves caught up with the events on the feeds through social media alone. Popular contestants from the show can expect to come out of the house with hundreds of thousands of followers, offers to go on other shows, like *The Challenge* or *The Traitors,* and, if all else fails, a career selling Flat Tummy Tea on Instagram.

The *Big Brother* community is intense and fierce. Even the more casual viewers of the show still tend to tune in to the three-episodes-a-week schedule that the show sets on CBS. It's a show that invades your life with its overwhelming presence. The game never stops, and something exciting could happen at any moment. Your favorite player might have just won over a crucial ally or been thrown to the wolves. All you need to do is check Twitter or listen to the latest *Live Feed Update* podcast to find out. Better yet, tune in yourself and maybe you'll be there when something happens that changes the whole course of the game.

There's a darkness to all of this, of course. Parasocial relationships flourish in this kind of environment, and many players come out of the house to an onslaught of people who feel like they know them. What are you doing buying that kind of car? Don't you know this would suit you better? Why are you hanging out with this person? Don't you know what they said about you on day 47 in the house? While the show is not in the business of streaming people going to the bathroom, or changing, or yes, sometimes hooking up, that doesn't mean that players aren't going to come out of the house to a slew of screenshots of them in compromising or embarrassing situations. And that tends to be the least of their worries.

Many of the players I've spoken to over the years have described themselves as having symptoms of PTSD after playing the game. For some it can take years to adjust back to their regular lives and learn to trust others again. A hundred days is a long time to spend completely cut off from the rest of society, living in a reality where one wrong move can lead to your demise (in the game). Even the successful players have talked about the difficulty of getting out of the headspace where they're meant to be tricking and manipulating people who they've come to care about on a daily basis. And this is before all of the scrutiny they undergo from having millions of people watching their every move for months.

It's not all bad though, at least in comparison to other reality shows. While live feeds can mean more scrutiny, they also mean more truth, more actual reality. It's an open secret that going on a reality show means giving up the ability to control your own narrative. Editors can make you into America's sweetheart just as easily as they can make you a pathetic villain. The live feeds are a layer of defense against this; they hold the *Big Brother* producers and editors more accountable than they would be otherwise.

One of the best recent examples of this is Taylor Hale from season 24. Despite being a former Miss Congeniality and one of the most popular players the show has ever seen, Taylor Hale was picked out early on in the game as a house punching bag and was bullied, targeted, and made to believe that her own attitude and actions were the cause of her harassment.[1] At first, the show didn't seem to know how to portray the situation. Every person in the house seemed to back up the narrative that Taylor was a terrible person who deserved what was coming to her. Most shows would take that easy narrative and run with it, playing some dodo music and just dunking on the person for cheap laughs. *Big Brother*, however, facing pressure from the live-feed audience, was forced to take the more difficult approach of showcasing more of the nuance of the situation.

"My stomach churns when I think about living in that house without 24/7 live feeds. I am genuinely afraid anyone could have a similar experience to me, and not be believed leaving the house. Sunlight is the best disinfectant. Live feeds are the sun."

Taylor Hale, *Big Brother 24*[2]

Whether this is more a defense of live feeds or an indictment of reality television as a whole is another story. After all, there has to be some level of complicity in the awful behavior that we watch for our own entertainment.

In recent years, more and more scrutiny has been leveled at players for racist or misogynistic behavior in the house. Debate has raged among the community about how to handle it. In 2020, CBS set a casting mandate that 50 percent of all casts in their reality shows must be Black, Indigenous, or other people of color. This had an immediate impact, as the first season to air under this rule made history with an alliance of Black players dominating the game and managing to get every one of their six members to the end.

Social issues have always been a prevalent feature of the show whether the producers like it or not. Power dynamics, threats of violence, outside interference, and real-life events outside of the game have all impacted various seasons of the show. A clip of Houseguests discovering the results of the 2016 election went viral during *Big Brother*'s "Over the Top" live-feed-only spin-off season. Going all the way back to the show's second season, they had to tell the Houseguests about 9/11 and people were calling for the cancellation of the whole show as debates raged about whether a show as frivolous as this should even be on the air.

Should this show exist? In order to answer that question, there are many areas we need to explore. I've seen firsthand the kind of damage it can do to its contestants, the kind of toxic fervor it can stir up in its community. The show is far from the worst in its category, but that doesn't absolve it of guilt. Although there are dedicated psychologists on set, many players have found this resource to be inadequate, feeling as if they were just sent on their way with the advice to avoid looking at their phone for a little while. Then there are those issues of representation: What kind of standards need to be applied to the casting process? How much should the show interfere to protect the players from harmful behavior? It's an incredibly complicated line to walk, made more difficult by the fact that the producers can't hide most of it away behind an edit.

There's a story to tell here about a Dutch man named John de Mol, a biosphere experiment that took place in Oracle, Arizona, and of the ways that, for better or worse, *Big Brother* and reality TV took the world by storm and changed popular culture forever. There are the people who make the show, acting as gods in their own version of *1984*. Then there are the players who actually lived in this alternate reality and came out the other side, changed. I'll be pulling from the hundreds of hours I've spent interviewing contestants and speaking to fans in my time covering the show, including many interviews conducted specifically for this book.

Finally, there's me, and every other member of this community who fell into the rabbit hole of *Big Brother* and never found their way out—a community of people who huddle around a screen at 3:00 a.m. on a Saturday night watching someone sleep because if he doesn't wake up soon, the impending revolution in the house might be called off. There's nothing more compelling than seeing these moments play out in real time. It's *raw*.

This book will explore all of these issues, telling the story of this show and its conquest over our culture while trying to convey what it's like to have been hooked on something that feels impossible to explain.

My love for the show goes deeper than the entertainment value. It goes back to being a shy kid who felt like he didn't belong anywhere. I can't remember a time *Big Brother* wasn't in my life, shaping the way I saw the world. As I navigated the difficulties of childhood, the show became my constant companion, a staple of my summers that exposed me to a whole new way of thinking.

As I grew older, my obsession deepened. I started looking for the mechanisms behind the social strategy in the game, hoping I could learn from these strangers on the other side of the country. Then somehow, this obsession turned into a profession as I was able to connect with an audience that was as eager to decipher these insights as I was.

Seeing a reflection of society condensed and made into a game was a revelation to me. In real life, when someone has power over you, there's usually not much you can do about it. If you play *Big Brother*, the tools are right within your grasp. The power can shift every week. You can win a competition or sway people to your cause and upend the social structure of the house.

It's an intoxicating fantasy with an immensely broad appeal. Anybody who ever had to navigate the social hierarchy of grade school or deal with workplace politics or any power structure in their life can relate to the game of *Big Brother*. More than that, everybody plays their own game of *Big Brother* every day of their lives. Everyone can find something to connect to in this show because it's just *us*.

1

Adaptations

"I know some people out there are not happy with how this show went down, and they blame that on me. But the simple fact of the matter is, if you're not happy with this show, maybe you're not happy with reality based–TV in general. And if you're not happy with reality based–TV, maybe you're not happy with...with, as the name suggests, reality."

Dr. Will Kirby, winner of *Big Brother 2*[1]

As summer turned into fall at the turn of the millennium, CBS had a $20 million problem on their hands. *Big Brother* sucked. Everyone knew it. The fans hated it, critics panned it, the producers were all making excuses, even the hosts hated it and thought it was going to ruin their careers.

"I know the show sucked. And still does. I look back at my six weeks on the lot at CBS and BB with a mixture of relief that I got out relatively unscathed," said Ian O'Malley[2], the short-lived cohost to Julie Chen on *Big Brother 1*. He was let go shortly into the season, but Julie Chen wasn't so lucky. In writing about season 2, Andy Dehnart of Reality Blurred remarked, "Julie Chen, apparently deciding that her career was over anyway, will return."[3]

The biggest issue with season 1 of *Big Brother* was as simple as it was deadly to a fledgling show: It was boring. Dreadfully boring. The premise, which saw ten strangers enter what they called the "*Big Brother* compound" to be completely cut off from society and monitored 24/7 for eighty-eight days, *was* interesting to the U.S. audience. It premiered to a tremendous twenty-two million viewers. But as subsequent episodes started airing, much of the audience quickly lost interest.

The ten contestants were to vote to nominate two of their fellow housemates for "banishment" every week. The Houseguests who received the most votes would then face banishment from the audience as the viewers voted for one of them to leave the house. This would continue until the end, when the audience decided among the final contestants to pick the winner of the show, who would receive a $500,000 cash prize.

The *Big Brother* premiere leaned *heavily* on the concept for its entertainment value. We tour the house with an unenthused Ian O'Malley, who seems like he's being held hostage and forced to list off facts about the house like he's presenting a book report. He explains through a pained smile that yes, there are cameras in the bathroom and shower, but they'll be used only if contestants use the area for purposes other than going to the bathroom or showering. "Whoa, that's wild," proclaims cohost Julie Chen in what is now probably the only memorable sound bite of the season for how unbelievably awkward it is. The rest of the episode is dedicated to introducing the contestants before sending them into the compound. Set against a backdrop of a crowd of hundreds of onlookers cheering them on, the contestants entered the big red door one by one, turning around to wave to the crowd. "Yeah! Yeah!" yelled Will Mega, the final contestant to enter before the door closed behind him.

What would they get up to on the inside? You'd have to wait until episode 2 to see more than some cursory introductions. "Wow, that was intense," says Chen in a statement sure to cause some cognitive dissonance in the viewer. If you were one of the unlucky viewers who tuned in to episode 2, you were greeted with a minimally narrated collection of clips as the contestants explored the house while the cameras followed them around and they introduced themselves. There was no real structure, no real story, and very little drama or excitement.

Will Mega brought the most drama to the show, claiming his strategy was to entertain the audience so they'd keep him around. Unfortunately for him, both his fellow contestants and the American public weren't keen on his brand of entertaining antagonism, and he was the first one banished from the show. The rest of the "exciting" cast included Karen, a forty-three-year-old mother missing her kids; "Chicken" George Boswell, playing up his goofy shenanigans; and winner Eddie McGee—one of the only contestants to actually admit they were there to win the money. Things got so bad that production tried to entice the contestants to leave the show with $50,000 so that they could replace them with a more interesting cast member.

None of them took the offer.

The bad reviews quickly started rolling in from those who managed to avoid nodding off during the six drowsy episodes that aired each week. As an eight-year-old enthralled with *Survivor*, I'd often insist on staying up to watch the Wednesday-night episode of *Big Brother 1* that followed the weekly *Survivor* episode only to be lulled to sleep by the cheesy transition jingles that played in between the disconnected clips being aired. Over its twenty-five-year run, many new fans have found *Big Brother* and gone back to binge older seasons. If you ask these fans what they think of season 1, you'll hear one of two answers: "Oh, I didn't watch that one" or "Yeah... I couldn't finish it."

These tend to be the kindest things that anybody has to say about the season. Future *Big Brother 2* star Hardy Hill described watching the first season as "watching paint dry. It was very boring." He nearly didn't audition for season 2 because of it.

Despite the dull delivery, *Big Brother* still had a fascinating concept—one that has an interesting origin story of its own. The idea of isolating a group of strangers and observing them as they create and manage their own minisociety might not seem quite as novel nowadays, but at the time it was almost revolutionary. *Big Brother* was a grand social experiment. What kinds of behavior would be revealed from the contestants who were being forced to live with people from another walk of life? What could we learn from the result of such an experiment? Even just the notion of being filmed 24/7 by a small army of unavoidable hidden cameras felt like something straight from *The Truman Show*. These threads are a core part of what makes the show work all around the world even twenty-five years later.

The license to *Big Brother* was a hot commodity in the U.S. *Who Wants to Be a Millionaire* had shaken the entire television industry with its dominance over the ratings, and networks were scouring European television listings to find the next big nonscripted import to introduce to a U.S. audience. After a heated bidding war, CBS came away with the rights to *Big Brother* for $20 million from Dutch media company Endemol. They then watched as the ratings declined week by week, ending with less than half of the viewers it started with.

It was a completely different story internationally. After the show premiered in the Netherlands, Dutch cocreator Paul Römer described his life as a roller coaster[4] as the show instantly became a massive hit and expanded to Germany and Spain to equal success before coming to the U.S. all in less than a year. In America, though, the show did not see the same kind of growth.

Maybe the American audience just wasn't as interested in reality TV? Well, not if *Survivor* had anything to say about it. *Survivor: Borneo* had premiered just a few months prior to *Big Brother* to fifteen million viewers and more than tripled its numbers by the finale.

TV Guide Insider wrote that *Big Brother* had "possibly the worst reviews in television history."[5] *Entertainment Weekly* had *Big Brother* listed as the third worst show of the year, writing, "No one cared who 'won' *Big Brother*, as long as it went away."[6]

So what happened?

That's the question that sparked a power struggle between Endemol and CBS. Known as the "Father of *Big Brother*," John de Mol was its cocreator and the founder of Endemol. De Mol was convinced that CBS was to blame for the poor performance of the show in the U.S. He blamed the casting and said he'd be insisting on a more exciting cast than the duds on season 1.[7] His Dutch co-creator, Paul Römer, helmed the production of the show in the U.S. and noted that the American audience didn't seem to find the show as controversial as the international audiences did[8] and quickly moved from controversial curiosity to acceptance for what it was: boring.

Les Moonves, head of CBS at the time, had his own vision. He believed that the show needed fixing: "If we can fix the product… we feel there's great potential there."[9] The *New York Times* reported that executives at CBS believed Endemol fell short because it misread both American television and American culture and that they'd want more hands-on control of future versions of the show.[10] *Hollywood Reporter* quoted sources saying that CBS was willing to bring the show back for a second season only if they were able to make significant creative changes to the original Endemol format.[11]

But hold on—what was it that made the show worth saving in the first place? If it was so widely considered to be a failure, why even bother with a second season?

There are actually a few answers to those questions. There's the obvious: CBS spent $20 million on the rights to the thing and built a very expensive set that was just sitting there waiting to be used again. Moonves noted in an interview with *Insider* that giving *Big Brother* a second shot wouldn't be all that difficult because the custom-built house wired with twenty-eight cameras and sixty microphones was still all in place.[12] Then of course there's the fact that *Big Brother* continued to be such a hit around the world—paired as it was with the success of *Survivor* on CBS, they understood that this kind of reality TV still had untapped potential.

Not to mention, *Big Brother 1* wasn't exactly a slouch in the ratings. While they did fall throughout the season, Moonves was quoted as saying, "*Big Brother* did just fine and, in fact, improved our summer ratings and our summer demographics. And, frankly, the last episode of *Big Brother* beat the Olympics, so by any stretch of the imagination, that's doing well."[13]

During all of this discourse about the show's failure and the drop in ratings from week to week, there was also something completely unexpected going on beneath the notice of the critics.

After braving the cacophony of dial-up internet tones, fans were discovering the lifeblood of the show—and the catalyst for my own involvement—the *Big Brother* live feeds. Over the course of season 1, traffic to the hilariously titled official website, www.bigbrother2000.com, steadily grew. That's right: even as TV ratings went down and people were abandoning the show, interest in the live feeds was going up.

With over four million unique visitors in July alone, the embarrassingly named site was ranked as one of the most heavily trafficked new sites on the web that summer.[14] "It's tremendous," said Paul Römer. "In Holland, which is a very small country with only fifteen million people, after a hundred days we had fifty-two million page views. In Germany, we had over 200 million page views. Now in England, I had a report… On the day of the first banishment show in one day they had 9.2 million page views, which tripled the last record. The live streams are doing very well. The Internet success is huge."[15]

If you were a curious viewer back in 2000 looking to dip your toes into the world of internet voyeurism, all you had to do was click on the Live Video tab. You were then greeted with a list of featured archived streams, such as "Karen is upset and guilty over her remarks about George" and "George, Brittany and Eddie share their dislike for William." At the bottom of the page was a viewer advisory statement you could click on that read, "The Web broadcast of CBS/Endemol's *Big Brother* is not intended for younger audiences. Big Brother is not scripted, but is a result of the participants' reactions to their environment and interactions with each other on a day-to-day basis. Life is full of surprises, as anyone will tell you, and the daily lives of *Big Brother* participants are no exception. It's important to realize that the unexpected may happen; by choosing to access this Webcast, you may be exposed to incidents, language or other situations you may find objectionable."[16] At the top of the page were four feeds to click on that represented the four different cameras you could view to get a look at what was happening in the house at that very moment.

This was intoxicating. I still remember the first time I caved and looked up how to access the live feeds. It felt dangerous and taboo. At your fingertips there were people just existing who you could watch on your computer screen. It wasn't always exciting; you'd occasionally tune in to a group meal with some light small talk and quickly get bored. But then as the contestants would drift off into smaller groups you'd start to learn their real feelings about the people who had been sitting around that table. If watching the show felt like seeing a real-life soap opera, watching the live feeds felt like eavesdropping on your favorite characters in unprotected moments never meant for the show. It was unlike anything I'd ever seen before, and it was fascinating.

Nearly a decade before Netflix Instant started experimenting with streaming content on demand and JustinTV began its journey to eventually become Twitch.tv and create an entire industry of live streamers, *Big Brother* was on the ground floor offering something that still hasn't been replicated twenty-five years later. It was nearly unheard of to be live streaming anything in 2000, let alone 24/7, and for that content to be from a professionally produced network television show? It still doesn't sound real.

So while everyone loudly complained about the show, more and more people were quietly venturing over to the website and discovering something groundbreaking. At the end of the season, the *LA Daily News* stated, "Web watchers may have revolutionized reality TV."[17]

It wasn't easy for the producers to understand what they had on their hands at first. After all, if you give away all of your footage online as it happens, what incentivizes the viewer to come back for the televised version? Early on, Paul Römer would try to hide as much as possible from the live feeds, but he eventually discovered that the success of the live feeds wasn't a hindrance to the success of the show at all. In fact, it was the opposite.[18]

In an interview conducted for bigbrother2000.com, Römer said, "I really had to change my mindset on how I produced the show. In the beginning, I tried to keep all the breaking news out of the house away from the Internet. We had a panic button in the house, [with] which we could close down the Internet. The idea was when something special happens in the house, we don't want to spill it to the 'net, we want to save it for the show. Air it on television then bring it to the Web—And then I found out we benefited from all the attention on the 'net. People saw things happening live and they wanted to see what we did with it on television. The moment I would show it on television the Internet side went sky high because people wanted to see what happens now. I learned that there was a mutual benefit. We are not competitors. We were really helping each other, but that's a big change of mindset for a television producer. And that has to happen with all the executives, with all the networks. They all have to have that experience. [It] will be a struggle, but in the end it will happen."[19]

This mindset wasn't unfounded. Research conducted by Lisa Gandy and Lisa McChristian published in *The Corinthian* in 2002 found that *Big Brother* internet viewers were more likely to be regular viewers of the televised show despite having potentially seen some of the show's content already on the feeds. Internet viewers were also found to pay more attention to the show and be more involved as viewers.[20]

So all the pieces were there for *Big Brother*, but it could never succeed if the televised version kept shedding viewers and evoking exceedingly hyperbolic criticism. *Big Brother* was continuing to expand around the world, so Römer stepped down as Endemol loosened its grip and let Les Moonves and the crew at CBS take a crack at making the show work for an American audience.

There was only one man CBS was interested in putting in charge of *Big Brother 2*: Arnold Shapiro.[21] Shapiro was an Oscar-winning documentarian, having made the acclaimed *Scared Straight* and more recently having run the successful docudrama reality series *Rescue 911*. To serve as coproducer alongside Arnold Shapiro came a young Allison Grodner, who had climbed the ranks to producer-director on *Rescue 911*. *Big Brother* wasn't exactly in line with the kinds of projects Shapiro was used to working on, but the idea intrigued him. "I like doing shows that change lives in a positive way. I realize that *Big Brother* is more of an entertainment show—it's not meant to save lives or alter lives like my documentaries are—but it's nice to have a mix," he explained to *TV News Daily*. "I figure after thirty years of doing worthwhile programming to try to improve society, even I'm entitled to one fun project."[22]

Ken Tucker of *Entertainment Weekly* wrote, "CBS has wrested control of 'Big Brother 2' away from its creator, the diabolical John de Mol, and handed it over to producer Arnold Shapiro, who's been busy promoting 'BB2' as containing more conflict and more sex."[23]

More sex was a big part of the changes that CBS wanted to make. I suspect that many of the complaints about casting hid a not-so-subtle complaint about the lack of promiscuity from them in that first season. In Europe, sex was a much more common occurrence on the show, but the American cast was more hesitant.[24]

The promo for season 2 was chock-full of sexual innuendo and imagery. "This summer, come over to our house for the hottest party in America," says the promo, with people in bathing suits popping champagne bottles.[25] After stocking the bathroom with condoms for the season 2 cast, Shapiro said, "We are not directing these people or controlling these people in any way. They are going to do what they want. The intriguing thing to me is if some of that behavior occurs… I don't think the viewers are going to know whether they are doing it out of genuine lust or desire, or whether they are doing it as part of a grand manipulation to win the game."[26] He later elaborated, "I have a feeling that some members of this cast will possibly interpret the pool rules as swimwear-optional,"[27] and "CBS has their blurring machines on standby."[28]

Shapiro's expectations were certainly met. "Viewers have witnessed group showers, hot-tub-based kissing games, and more sex talk than a night out with Kim Cattrall," said Josh Wolk of *Entertainment Weekly* after the first week of season 2.[29] The cast was younger, hotter, and much more open to enticing the more voyeuristic viewers to the show, engaging in what became known as "showmances" that even resulted in a proposal on the finale.

Though critics agreed, sex alone wasn't enough to save this disaster of a show. Shapiro had another idea when it came to fixing the casting issue that *Big Brother 1* faced. This time around he wanted a more dynamic cast, filled to the brim with people that would be making good TV. No more boring people. It was important that they all have an intense drive to win: "We have the most dynamic, competitive, outgoing and, in some cases, outrageous cast that any reality show has had. We were looking for highly competitive people—these people have their eyes on the prize every minute of their waking state."[30]

While then CBS head Les Moonves was disappointed in the casting for season 1 in general, there was also a consensus at CBS that the audience had exacerbated the issue by voting out the most interesting (meaning, the most antagonistic and dramatic) Houseguests first. After all, the first two contestants banished from the show were drama starter Will Mega and exotic dancer Jean Jordan.

To fix this issue, they didn't need to look too far. *Survivor* was the biggest show in the world, and its second season continued to crush. On *Survivor*, the contestants voted each other out. Villain Richard Hatch was able to take control of the game, much to the audience's dismay, and then a record number of those viewers tuned in to watch him win the first season of the show. To this day, the *Survivor: Borneo* finale is one of the most watched episodes of television ever.

The idea to allow the Houseguests to vote each other out ran counter to the existing format of *Big Brother*, but I think Moonves ultimately had the right of it when he said John de Mol and Paul Römer had misread American culture. Reality-based TV having to actually represent reality sounds quaint to modern sensibilities, jaded from decades of reality shows pumped into the culture that make the "reality" moniker come off as satire. But perhaps for the American viewers, so steeped in capitalistic individualism, there's something about the ruthless, cutthroat zero-sum game *Big Brother* became that felt closer to home, a little closer to *their* reality.

The allusions to American capitalism weren't exactly subtle. "Banishments" were rebranded; players on the wrong side of the power structure in the house were now literally "evicted" from the game. That structure was easier to build for players as power in the game was consolidated. The collective vote to nominate two players for banishment turned into a system where the power to nominate was won by just one player. Each week, the players would compete to be named the "Head of Household." That Head of Household (or HOH) would then have the sole power to nominate two players for eviction. At that point, the rest of the Houseguests would have to choose which of those two they would vote out of the game. This process would continue until only two contestants remained, at which point all of the evicted players would return to cast judgment upon the Final Two and vote for which one should win the $500,000 prize and title of *Big Brother* winner.

If *Survivor*'s game structure was supposed to be evocative of our tribal origins, *Big Brother*'s suddenly became a representation of the structures of our own modern society (with some tweaks, of course).

It was brilliant.

Somehow the contrived structure of this game was evoking a raw response from its contestants. The Houseguests of season 1 were often criticized for being far too aware of the cameras, but in season 2 the players got so caught up in the game that the criticism started to vanish from online discourse. The "diary room" was introduced as a private space where players could voice their unfiltered thoughts about what was happening in the game. The episodes were exciting and packed with drama: players let the power of the HOH go to their heads, and the rest of the house revolted against them; contestants started engaging in relationships on the show despite having significant others at home; and real animosity built up (famously resulting in one contestant scrubbing the toilet with another's toothbrush). More criticism started to be levied at the show for its glorification of the manipulative and promiscuous behavior of its cast.[31] But what viewers weren't complaining about was the show being boring.

The new format was also just so damn *relatable*. Cool kids teamed up to exclude the outsiders. People sucked up to those in power at the expense of their friends. Some made concerted efforts to bully and keep others down to maintain their own social status. You'd be hard-pressed to find someone who couldn't see a piece of themselves in at least one of the players as they struggled through the social hierarchy that the game helped create. You could start imagining yourself in that house, wondering how you would handle those situations that seemed so much more familiar than you would have expected from such a contrived scenario.

This was a revelation to me as a young boy. Not only could I see people struggle with the same in-group/out-group situations that I'd experienced, but I could watch as they overcame those boundaries, finding strength in their own numbers and creating their own in-group. Then, of course, as *Big Brother* fans are wont to do, my allegiances flipped and I started rooting for the remnants of the cool kids now that they were the new outcasts and underdogs—especially as I saw the former outcasts let the power get to their heads and become the very bullies they had just overthrown. I was obsessed.

While the show would never fully recover from the damage season 1 did, season 2 stopped the bleeding. Kicking off with eight million viewers (only about a third of the audience season 1 started with), it held on to that number through the first few weeks until, for the first time in the show's history, there was a steady *increase* in viewership, rising up into nine million, then ten million, and eventually finishing the season with over twelve million viewers, beating the viewership for the season 1 finale.

These changes had an immediate impact on the show's ratings, but more importantly they are the foundation for the show's eventual longevity. Despite the success of the international versions of *Big Brother* in 2000, none of them stood the test of time. The U.S. version of *Big Brother* is currently the longest-running version of the show (which isn't to say that other versions haven't found their own enormous success, but we will get into that later).

To this day, *Big Brother* fans completely disregard season 1 as being part of the show at all. *Big Brother* started in season 2; season 1 was some other show that has been lost to time. *Big Brother 2* was sexier, more entertaining, and more *American*. It was a perfect encapsulation of American culture. It was reality based TV.

In the finale of *Big Brother 2*, Dr. Will Kirby stood in front of a disgruntled jury of evicted players he had been backstabbing, manipulating, and lying to for the last eighty-two days. He told them that if they had a problem with how the game went down, they shouldn't blame him but instead take it up with reality—this was reality TV, after all.

His speech is widely considered to be one of the most arrogant and ill-advised pleas to the jury in the history of the show. You're supposed to be buttering these people up, offering apologies for what you *had* to do to advance yourself in the game. Will did none of these things. To this day, he stands as one of the most devious and conniving winners the show has ever seen, and he's still totally unapologetic about it. He is the perfect representation of the change in *Big Brother*. It's almost as if he's speaking directly to Endemol, the American public, and the critics when he says, if you don't like the new direction of this show, take a good hard look at the world around you, because you're living in it.

Dr. Will Kirby ruthlessly cut the throats of everyone on his way to win *Big Brother 2* in a 6–3 jury vote, cementing his place as the first true winner of *Big Brother*.

America *loved* it.

2

The Evil Doctor

"You have to ask yourself. Can anyone take pleasure in watching groups of people get angry at each other and tear each other apart verbally, psychologically, and emotionally? I can, and I sit there and do it every day."

Dr. Will Kirby, winner of *Big Brother 2*[1]

In order to understand *Big Brother*, you have to get to know the Evil Doctor, Will Kirby. The son of a poet, Will grew up in Tallahassee, Florida, where he was named the "wittiest" student in his high school yearbook.[2] He went on to receive a medical degree from Nova Southeastern University College of Osteopathic Medicine just before his stint on *Big Brother* in 2000. In his intro for the show, Will states, "Every day I walk a fine line between confidence and being cocky."[3] After watching him for the next eighty-two days, the audience would discover that the statement proved more true than anyone could have imagined. He was cocky, disrespectful, extremely deceitful, and sometimes cruel as he navigated through this new format for *Big Brother*.

In other words, he was *perfect* for it. Dr. Will Kirby was everything that Arnold Shapiro had been looking for: entertaining, competitive, attractive, and promiscuous.

Joining Will on the cast was another attempt at spicing things up, Kent Blackwelder. Clearly cast to cause conflict in the house with his political views, Kent infamously introduces himself to America in the first episode saying, "We were all kind of searching for the gay guy. It's deviant. It's perverse. And it's a lifestyle that 90 percent of Americans don't want anywhere near their families or themselves. You know, it used to be sickos, weirdos, and freaks. Now it's 'alternative lifestyle.' And it's not cool to not think that's cool. But don't come throw it in my face and try to tell me it's normal."[4]

Fellow castmate Bunky Miller, who took some time to reveal to the rest of the cast that he was, in fact, gay, says to the audience, "Kent said he'd never vote for me [to be evicted]. And I'm like, yeah, wait till you find out I'm gay. Then you might vote for me."[5]

Fans were upset at the blatant attempt to create drama directly at the expense of everyone in the house, especially Bunky. As is often the case with *Big Brother*, opinions changed over the course of the season as Kent reluctantly became one of the more popular Houseguests with the audience. This was largely fueled by a turn that mirrored the one involving *Survivor: Borneo*'s Richard Hatch and Rudy Boesch when Bunky finally came out to Kent and the two became best friends in the house. After all, nothing screams early 2000s television more than solving homophobia through the power of friendship.

After just three episodes, Will entered into a relationship with fellow Houseguest Shannon Dragoo, who had come onto the show with an existing boyfriend. One of Will Kirby's longest-lasting legacies is that he literally coined the term "showmance" for all of reality TV. Straight to the cameras, Will said, "I do have a message for her boyfriend at home. He's out of here! It's over for him; that's completely done with." By then, almost every other player was already sick of him. "Will is being a dictator, and he needs to go," said Bunky during the first week of the game. The audience agreed: "Will is an arrogant ass... He talks about himself as if he is God's gift to humanity," wrote David Bloomberg of *Reality News Online*.[6]

So, how did he win? If his fellow players didn't like him and the audience was against him, why wasn't he just kicked out right away? With Shapiro's genius format changes, the audience was now powerless to stop Will, who could be as unpopular as he pleased and still be fine as long as the people in the house didn't kick him out.

So why wasn't Will nominated by the HOH and voted out by the other players if they disliked him so much? That's where things got a little more interesting.

After the players entered the game in July of 2001, a clique of literal cool kids was quickly formed. Having all chosen to sleep in the bedroom that was a bit on the colder side, they called themselves "Chilltown," a name that would eventually strike fear into even the most seasoned players of *Big Brother*. But back then it was just a rowdy crowd of hot young people hanging out and acting like they were better than the older Houseguests. Apart from Will himself, this crew consisted of a thirty-year-old man who called himself Mike "Boogie"; Shannon (who went on to have a spiteful experience with a toothbrush and a toilet bowl); and finally Justin Sebik from New Jersey, who liked to call himself "Just-incredible." So yes, they weren't exactly crowd favorites, but they seemed like strong competitors. In the very first Head of Household competition, Mike Boogie won the power to nominate two other players, which only served to further bolster the egos in Chilltown.

"It was almost like *Lord of the Flies*," *Big Brother 2* contestant Hardy Hill told me.[7]

Hardy was happy to talk to me about his experience years later. He's long since moved on from *Big Brother* but still remembered the early days of the season. "You had the people in the one area, called the 'hot box,' or The Other People, or whatever. Then you have the other area where it's just cooler temperature-wise, and they call that area 'Chilltown.' It's Sociology 101. People obviously find common ground with those they're in close proximity to. It's human nature."[8]

While sides were forming, another player in the game, Nicole Schaffrich, a thirty-one-year-old personal chef, had gotten off on the wrong foot in the house. A self-admitted control freak, she was labeled by the others as loud and abrasive, and she had particularly gotten on the nerves of one Mike Boogie. "The first person I would nominate is Nicole. The second person I would nominate is Nicole. The thing that Nicole could do to change my mind is…be quiet! Just quiet down. You know, the house is not that big. Just, you know, www.ZipIt.com!"[9]

So with Boogie holding the power to nominate two Houseguests for eviction, Chilltown wanted to find a way to ensure that Nicole would be the one the house sent packing. The problem was that as the HOH, Boogie himself didn't have an eviction vote. That meant that between the two people Boogie chose to nominate, they didn't have the numbers to control who went home. The solution? Boogie shocked everyone when he nominated Nicole up against the most well-liked player in the house, forty-three-year-old Sheryl Braxton. She was the "Hot Mom" of the house and everyone loved her.

This just isn't what you were supposed to do. Everyone knew that you nominate people you *don't* like; people you wanted to see go home. Why would Boogie nominate Sheryl if he had a great relationship with her?

The idea was that she would sit on the nomination chair as a pawn in Boogie's bigger game. By putting up Sheryl, he was ensuring that the rest of the house would be all but forced to vote out his nemesis, Nicole. Because everyone knew that you didn't vote people out that you actually liked. Right?

Well, as people grew more and more sick of Boogie, Will, and the rest of Chilltown, Nicole started to campaign to stay. She ran on a platform of being anti-Chilltown. If she stayed in the game and won the HOH, she'd use it to nominate them. Being targeted lit a fire under Nicole, and the rest of the house could see it. "I am vengeance bitch now. I want to get Will the hell out of here. And you know what? My ass can get kicked out of here the third week, and I will walk out with a smile on my face, just knowing I got Will out of here."[10]

As David Bloomberg put it, "It occurs to me, as we move towards the first eviction, that one of the changes made to this year's *Big Brother* stands out among the rest as having the most impact on the game. Instead of being voted out by the viewing public, contestants are voted out by each other. Now obviously this is a big change—that much is obvious. But what might not be so obvious is what kind of strategic changes the players themselves have to make in the face of this. For example, if the old rules were in effect, Nicole would be dead in the water. Nobody dislikes Sheryl—why should they? There's nothing to dislike as far as the viewers can see. But because the fellow contestants are voting, they aren't just going to go with who they like; they're going to have to factor strategy into it. So because Sheryl is so well liked, this may be the best opportunity for some of the other contestants to boot her out the door."[11]

While Chilltown spent the rest of the week congratulating themselves for such a genius strategy, the rest of the house came together to blindside them at the eviction vote, saving Nicole and upending the entire power structure of the game.

To this day, Sheryl remains a cautionary tale to anyone who is being nominated for eviction. Even players who have never seen season 2 know the phrase its first week spawned: "Pawns go home."

> "I think the biggest difference between everyone else in the house and myself is that I have claimed to be dishonest, evil, and backstabbing from the beginning, and they're all now realizing that that's what they are."
>
> Dr. Will Kirby[12]

Another big change for *Big Brother 2* was less popular, but still hugely successful for CBS. With the live feeds such a draw in season 1, the decision was made to charge for access to them in season 2. While they expected traffic to go down, they opened up a whole new stream of revenue for the show. After the season ended, it was reported that nearly 100,000 people had paid for the live feeds in one way or another. *Variety* reported that "Webcasting of *Big Brother 2* shows Net can be profitable."[13] The subscriber count grew consistently throughout the season, and CBS was extremely pleased. They described the live feeds as having exceeded their expectations.[14]

The new paid format for the live feeds had an interesting impact on the fans of the show as well. With many people unable or unwilling to invest the time or money in following the live feeds, the community began to divide into factions. There were the regular TV viewers and the "live cam watchers." Those watching the live feeds could help fill in the gaps and answer questions for the TV viewers when the edited show didn't provide enough context, and there seemed to be a respect for those who were in the know.

Still, it wasn't exactly something you'd be proud to tell your neighbor about. "What did I do this weekend? I watched a 24/7 live stream of a group of fame-hungry strangers lie and betray each other for money. What's that? Oh yes, there are cameras in the bathroom, but we don't see the footage from those."

When writing about the show for the *New York Times*, Marshall Sella noticed a trend in the people he spoke about it to. "Many claim to have found *Big Brother* a bit repugnant, and take the revealing step of slipping from first- to second-person when they discuss it, as if they weren't obsessed with the monstrous thing." He goes on to quote from one such interaction. "I truly did not like it... But you did watch, all the time. You had to watch to see what would happen."[15]

The live feeders watched as the next few weeks saw Chilltown decimated one by one until they had all either been ejected from the game (more on that later), evicted by the other players, or just jumped ship. All of them except, of course, for the Evil Doctor.

The thing was, Will was terrible at the HOH competitions. Many of them were quizzes about the Houseguests, and he openly admitted to not paying attention to anyone when they talked about themselves. Additionally, people started articulating the idea that was the inevitable conclusion to Sheryl's eviction: if they were voting out popular players because they were more of a threat to win, the less popular players must have been less of a threat to win. And Dr. Will was the least popular of them all. If he held no power because he wasn't winning competitions, and he wasn't likable enough to win the game in the end, he wasn't worth taking out of the game. In fact, he would be the ideal person to bring to the Final Two to guarantee that the jury would vote for you. Because of course everyone knew that you didn't vote for a person you didn't like to win the game.

Will understood this perception better than anyone, so he perpetuated it to his advantage. "The only reason I'm here is because I've incorporated this theory since day one, which is lose everything. No one would ever think of it. It's so ridiculous it would never work. And the simple fact of the matter is I'm here."[16] Will kept up the appearance of weakness, both competitively and socially, which ironically kept him in the game.

That's why he wasn't immediately voted out for his cocky attitude, but it's not why he won the game. "Will has been telling anybody who'll listen that they should take him into the Final Two because obviously anybody would beat him. But will they? Is it really such a lock? Or are the others setting themselves up for a fall if they believe him?" wrote Bloomberg.[17]

Somewhere along the way, the audience started to come around on Will. The revolutionary force that toppled Chilltown named themselves "The Other People," or TOP—a name that underscored their status as outsiders and underdogs. But what happens when the powerless finally rise to power? Power has a way of corrupting, and *Big Brother* is a perfect stage to showcase that tendency. The audience began to bemoan TOP's self-righteousness as they claimed moral superiority over Will and his ilk while turning around and stabbing each other in the back in order to advance their own games. Meanwhile, the audience came to begrudgingly respect Will's honesty…when it came to lying. Bloomberg wrote, "I'm beginning to actually root for the guy, despite what a complete jerk he was early on. He is playing the game well, and even though he has been an admitted liar the whole time, he actually has these fools *believing* him!"[18]

That last part is the key. For all of Will's faults, he had a huge ace up his sleeve: his charisma. The Evil Doctor became the devil on the shoulder of the other players, whispering temptation into their ear. *Use me,* he seemed to be saying; *I'll work with you to take out these bigger threats and clear your path to the end. After all, I'm easy to beat.* He had a way of making the other players feel like they were the only ones in his confidence. *All those other players are lame, but you? You're better than that. You should have been in Chilltown all along. Why are you sacrificing for this group of people when you deserve better? Come on! Do something for yourself for once.* As he corrupted them, the audience became more and more frustrated with them—and so did the players being betrayed.

No player took the brunt of this more than Nicole, the very same person who had flipped the house against Chilltown in the first place and vowed to take Will out of the game. She had developed a close relationship with handsome hunk Hardy Hill, and they had dominated the HOH competitions that season, but Will managed to infiltrate their friendship and convince them he was worth keeping around. "The smartest thing I've done in this entire game is falsely befriend Nicole," said Will as he neared the finish line. She had been convinced to keep Will around for an easy win in the end and had betrayed nearly everyone else standing in her way. But while Will was openly saying things like "I'm the biggest liar in America" and "Anybody that believes me at this point is dumb,"[19] Nicole was still proclaiming that she had played an honest game.

> "Look like a human on the outside, but it's just skin over circuitry and wires."
>
> Dr. Will Kirby[20]

In a small town in Maine back in the early 2000s, I roamed the halls in the middle of a school year with a secret. It was my last day there, and nobody knew. The day before, I had been at the center of the worst fight yet between my mother and father. They'd been long separated and lived in different towns. My mom moved us around a lot, so my dad had been driving me to the school in his town, trying to give me some stability. After this latest fight, that was no longer an option, and just like that, I was to leave my school and friends behind.

I didn't know how to tell them. It was my fault, of course, the fight. I'd been having fun and didn't want to go back to my mom's house that night. Now I'd be leaving my friends, and I didn't understand how to grapple with the guilt of that. So I kept quiet, willing the situation to be untrue by virtue of not speaking it into existence.

Big Brother would eventually teach me that trying to avoid hard truths would almost always lead to failure. At lunch, a teacher came up to me asking if it was my last day. It caught my breath. Nobody was supposed to know. In that moment I tried to hate that teacher for dissolving my illusion. Instead, I nervously glanced at my best friend sitting next to me at the table. I could see the concoction of confusion and pain written plainly in his face as it seared into my memory. In an act of betrayal, I looked back at the teacher and slowly nodded my head.

The following day I roamed the halls of a new school filled with strangers. Feeling like I had been blindsided the day before, I imagined I was the Evil Doctor himself, navigating a new social landscape after losing my allies. I preferred the fantasy of *Big Brother* over the reality of it.

This wasn't the first time I'd changed schools, and it wouldn't be the last time I was shuffled around against my wishes. Watching Will navigate his own turmoil and succeed in the face of overwhelming odds left me in awe. It's no surprise that I was so drawn to *Survivor* and *Big Brother*; the concept of being thrown into a new environment to deal with a group of strangers scratched an itch I didn't know existed in me.

By the time I watched Will, I'd seen two seasons of *Survivor*, and the formula for that show had become clear: to win you create an alliance that's bigger than the opposing alliance, then vote them all out. You won by being in the majority. While there was an appeal to that idea, it wasn't something I could relate to. I was always the one on the outside. Watching Will have so much confidence in himself despite being a social outcast was inspiring. His journey spoke to me far more than any *Survivor* winner could.

I struggle with this. I'm aware of how absurd it sounds to say that a man who competed on a "real-life soap opera"—who lied, manipulated, and said things like "I would stab them in the back and leave them to bleed on the kitchen floor and I wouldn't even clean it up"[21]—was inspiring to a nine-year-old. Maybe more than twenty years later, I've been indoctrinated by what was normalized to me as a child. I am, after all, the guy who has made a career of monitoring strangers 24/7 for months at a time. Maybe it's as simple as saying I probably shouldn't have been watching this show at such a young age, but I'd like to think it's a little more complicated than that. The show certainly seemed to be glorifying deception, catering to some of the crassest forms of entertainment for ratings. So what does it say about those of us who found so much more value in Shapiro's version of the show? These were some of the questions being explored back then as critics and viewers had to face the reality in front of them: *Big Brother 2* was a hit, but at what cost?

> "If you look back at the first series of *Big Brother*, to be honest it was so boring! Because we were so careful. Because we were so afraid to hurt people, to harm people."
>
> John de Mol[22]

"Just-incredible" Sebik from New Jersey was originally part of the Chilltown crew but was ejected from the game before the first eviction even took place. After numerous incidents and warnings with no real action from production, Hardy threatened to walk from the show if they didn't do something about Justin's behavior. They were finally forced to step in when Justin got drunk and repeatedly asked fellow player Krista Stegall, "Would you get mad if I killed you?" while holding a knife to her throat. Producers quickly called for him over the loudspeaker, to which he replied, "Oh, boy. We got problems. I think it might have been that knife to your neck?"[23] Justin was removed from the game, and with him went all of the knives in the house, to be replaced by plastic versions that have become a staple of the *Big Brother* house ever since.

For Krista's part, she initially denied having any memory of the incident. "When Julie asked me about this, I had no recollection of what she was talking about because we were basically joking around," Krista told *The Early Show*. Of the producers, she said, "They blew that completely out of proportion. Justin is just a fun guy. I really don't have the memory of the knife."[24]

She later sued CBS for negligence, claiming they did not do a proper background check on the contestant from New Jersey, who was discovered to have had multiple violent arrests on his record prior to his appearance on the show.[25] CBS indicated that it intended to fight the lawsuit, but the result was never reported. In 2006 Krista did tell the *Daily Advertiser* that while she was unable to comment on the lawsuit due to a disclosure agreement, she looked back at the show as a positive experience and was able to use it to her benefit.[26]

"Last year [*Big Brother*] was well known for being 'boring'—this year it is over the top," *Reality News Online* reporters wrote.[27] "We've already seen increased conflict, but is that necessarily a good thing?"[28] "It may be time to clean house altogether."[29]

ABC News reported that "Poorly screened contestants are par for the course for the new breed of reality shows."[30] This was referring to the infamous *Who Wants to Marry a Multi-Millionaire* special that had been broadcast on Fox the year before. A blatant attempt at ripping off the huge success of *Who Wants to Be a Millionaire*, the premise was to have fifty women compete for the right to marry a "multimillionaire" they wouldn't meet until they married him. After Darva Conger won the competition and was married to Rick Rockwell right there on the spot, it was later revealed that Rockwell had previously been accused of domestic violence, which had gone under the notice of the producers of the special.[31] Conger later had the marriage annulled.[32]

So by the time Justin Sebik put a knife to Krista's throat, audiences were not feeling particularly charitable about CBS's claim that their background checks had been adequate. If Paul Römer had been disappointed in the lack of controversy from the American audience for season 1, Shapiro certainly delivered it in spades for season 2.

> "I hope that everyone has underestimated my potential for just, massive destruction."
>
> Dr. Will Kirb[33]

In the game, things came to a head at the Final Four when Will's lies finally caught up to Nicole and he betrayed her, helping send out Hardy to guarantee his own spot in the Final Three. It wasn't surprising that Will had betrayed the duo—he'd been telling anyone who would listen that he had planned to from the start—but it was still shocking to see Hardy lose.

If you'd asked anyone before the season started who would win, they all likely would have brought up Hardy's name. He was extremely handsome, chivalrous, and competitive enough to be dangerous in the competitions. In *Survivor*'s second season, everyone's favorite mom, Tina, had just narrowly won over all-American cowboy Colby, who had been too honorable to cut her at the end. Right after *Big Brother 2* finished, pretty boy Ethan Zohn was about to take the crown of *Survivor*'s third season with his luscious curly hair and (now literal) million-dollar smile. Even without an audience vote, that's how these shows were *supposed* to go. Not *Big Brother*.

Nicole was distraught. "I am so absolutely flabbergasted and disgusted that Will may place in first or second. The lying, deceitful, satanic asshole…who lost every competition on purpose and thinks it's funny because we're all stupid to him.[34] At this point everybody watching at home was screaming at their television that she should have seen this coming. That she was the one at fault for bringing him this far. The evicted members of the jury watched along at home as well as she reaped the rewards of her labors. After she had betrayed them for Will, they seemed to enjoy watching her pay for it.

When she won the final HOH and had to choose who to bring to the Final Two with her, she surprised nobody with her choice. "I need to take the person I have a chance against winning in the finals, and unfortunately that's Will.[35] Nicole had dominated the entire game, from flipping the house in week 1 to taking charge and crushing the competitions to make her way to the end. But somewhere along the way she had given in to the devil on her shoulder, and it cost her everything.

Will went on to get six of the nine jury votes and forever set the tone for this new, "real" version of the show. Lies and manipulation were the name of the game, and trying to deny that fact was akin to denying reality itself. "Will changed the dynamic of the show. He changed the dynamic of how the game of *Big Brother* is played," Hardy told me seventeen years after Will took home the money. "It was almost like a long con. He's a genius.[36]

That's how Will won *Big Brother 2*, but it wasn't until years later that his *Big Brother* story would be complete.

Big Brother is a fabricated reality, designed to quarantine its inhabitants from the outside world. There are times, however, when that becomes impossible. In the final weeks of season 2, real-life events pulled everything to a halt. There were just three players left in the game: Will, Nicole, and fan-favorite New Yorker Monica Bailey. Just two days before the final eviction was to take place, terrorist attacks shook the nation on September 11.

For a time everything about *Big Brother* was completely forgotten, but after a few days, fans of the show began to remember that there were three people still stuck in that house, cut off from the rest of the world. When fans checked in on the live feeds, they discovered that Will, Nicole, and Monica were likely the only three people in America who didn't fully know about what had happened. "As of Thursday morning, the three remaining *Big Brother 2* Houseguests have carried on in a bizarre parody of normalcy, with Nicole giving Will a haircut, repeated discussions of strategies to win Head of Household, and the trio playing endless games of Monopoly," wrote *Zap2it reporter* Brill Bundy. "This has prompted many fans to question what is happening at CBS and why the Houseguests are not being informed of the scope of Tuesday's tragedy."[37]

It was unclear what the Houseguests had been told about the attacks, but it was clear they were ignorant of the details. After a few days, they started to notice that no planes had flown overhead since Tuesday, and they began to realize that whatever happened must have been really horrible. To make matters worse, Monica's cousin worked at the World Trade Center and had been listed as missing in the wake of the attacks. "We knew a tragedy had taken place involving planes in New York," Will told *Entertainment Weekly*. "That was really the extent of it."[38]

"It's time to end *Big Brother 2*. Events in reality have overtaken reality TV," wrote Susan Schechter in an open letter to CBS on *Reality News Online*. "I am addicted to *Big Brother*. But I look at that show now, and I simply don't care… Let them go home, where they can be with their families and friends… It's time to shut it down. Let them all be winners."[39]

More letters were arriving from all around the country. "I also feel we need to end the show immediately." "The game is over and your audience won't come back." "Do the right thing, Arnold."[40]

Reality News Online reported that the "vast majority" of its readers had indicated that the show should be stopped.[41]

"Obviously the tragedy that happened in America far outdoes anything with the show," Shapiro told *USA Today*. The show's publicist told reporters, "Regarding production, we're still in the process of deciding what the future holds, as is probably the rest of the country."[42]

CBS continued to delay its final episodes until finally on September 18, Julie Chen opened the penultimate episode of the season stating, "The rules of this game require virtually no contact with the outside world—no TVs, no phones, no computers, no news. But the horrific events that unfolded the morning of September 11th forever changed the world. The three Houseguests that remain have been told of the tragic events of the outside world by the producers of this show.[43]

The Houseguests were allowed to contact their families, with production members being used as an intermediary. "What you think, what I think, what the internet thinks, is irrelevant. It's what Will, Monica, and Nicole think," Shapiro told the press after the season ended. "All three are out, and not one has chastised us for the way we handled it. They thanked us.[44]

"What's important to me is that my family is in New York taking care of that business," said Monica. "Whether I leave tomorrow or I stay, if they're not here and they can't get here, that's not important to me. I want them to not focus their energy on me here. Focus everything they got there, 'cause I'm going to be OK.[45]

In light of all the controversies and a real-life tragedy that made the show seem beyond trivial in comparison, the future of the show and really the whole genre remained uncertain. The third season of *Survivor* aired in the fall of 2001 to a less enthusiastic audience. It was no longer the dominating force it had been just a year prior, placing eighth in the overall ratings for the fall season. But CBS head Les Moonves was undeterred. In an interview with *Zap2it*, he acknowledged that viewers' desire to watch unscripted programming may have diminished since the events of September 11 but that he still believed in the shows they were producing. "We were very pleased with *Big Brother 2*, and we're looking very carefully at producing a third season," he told them.[46]

Moonves wasn't alone. Shapiro declared *Big Brother 2* a much better show than the previous year's was, telling *TV News Daily* that he had delivered on his promise of producing "America's best summertime real-life soap opera."[47] Other CBS officials were quoted saying the show was "compelling and interesting."[48] CBS wasn't alone in this assessment. Felice Prager at *Reality News Online* wrote, "Yes, I'm hooked on the show, with all of its bizarre personalities and strange interactions."[49] The ratings were up, the reviews were much more positive. *Big Brother* had finally become a hit in the U.S.

A few months later, *Big Brother 3* was officially announced, with Arnold Shapiro and Allison Grodner returning to produce the show. This time around, Shapiro said, production would be cracking down on bad behavior. Alcohol would be rationed, and there would be a zero-tolerance policy when it came to violence.[50] After having pushed a little too deep into the mess of season 2, it seemed they were trying to clean up their image. Shapiro started to bring the marketing of the show back to its roots, describing the concept of *Big Brother* as "sociologically intriguing."[51]

I certainly don't disagree with him, but it was a bit of a hard sell at the time. Still, season 3 performed exceptionally well in the ratings, surpassing the second season in the show's continued trend upward.

Nobody felt this more than the cast members, who were being treated as celebrities this time around. Hardy Hill described part of his experience to me: "Everyone was really excited to meet me. I didn't understand that. A production assistant asked me if I had any idea the impact I had, and I was like, what are you talking about? He told me that the LA area had a shortage of jump ropes because of me because everyone watched me jump rope on the show… It was bizarre. You go from seeing the same people for two and a half months to having people clamoring around you wanting your autograph and stuff. It was completely mind-blowing."[52]

Whether you liked it or not, *Big Brother* was here to stay.

3

Influences

"We have to be very careful, because if we do this the wrong way, we're playing God."

John de Mol, creator of *Big Brother*[1]

In 1991, surrounded by desert in Oracle, Arizona, eight participants entered a giant white door one by one as a crowd of hundreds of onlookers cheered them on. Sound familiar? This wasn't the *Big Brother* compound they were entering; it was a research facility known as the Biosphere 2, a completely closed-system dome meant to replicate the different biomes of Earth and be completely self-sufficient.

With a retro futuristic vibe, the compound itself was immense and imposing. Made primarily of glass and concrete in different shapes to contain each biome, it's a structure that wouldn't look out of place if you were told it was on Mars.

The participants were scientists, entering the biosphere with the intention of staying there, cut off from the rest of the planet, for *two years* of their life. The whole country watched on the edge of their seat, wondering what would come of this grand experiment. Would it accomplish its stated goal of proving the viability of closed ecological systems for space travel? What else might we learn from something so bizarre, so alien to our regular way of life?

As it turns out, the Biosphere 2 experiment did have a lot to teach us, just not always in the ways that anyone expected.

"I have to say that the whole aspect of living inside the sealed area for two years was the hardest thing about being in there," said participant Jane Poynter in a talk given for Microsoft Research describing her experience in the dome.[2] "Yeah, hunger was kind of a pain. Yeah, oxygen loss was kind of a pain. But the emotional factors, and the breakup in relationships, and the small group dynamics… It got ugly in there, I can tell you."

Despite developing friendships prior to entering the biosphere, over time the scientists divided into factions. "I really thought that we were prepared for going inside this isolated environment. We broke out into two factions of four people…and it turns out that's strangely a very normal occurrence for groups in enclosed environments. It happens in the Antarctic, it happens in space; it's just something that happens. It's incredibly uncomfortable, though, and heartbreaking when it's your friends that are on the other side. And two of the people that were on the other side of this divide were my best friends when I walked into the biosphere."[3]

In the psychology of isolated and confined environments, psychologists have found that small groups in such isolated environments often display a lack of cohesion, usually resulting in either scapegoating or subgrouping. Scapegoating is used as a tactic to increase group cohesion by uniting members against an ostracized individual. Subgrouping occurs when groups find reasons to divide into opposing factions.[4] Of course, both of these behaviors are abundant in your average *Big Brother* house, but the phenomenon extends well beyond the confines of reality TV.

In the case of the Biospherians,[5] the factions formed out of a disagreement about the future of the experiment. It turned out that the self-sufficient dome wasn't quite as capable of sustaining life for the full two years as they had hoped. There were some key details that were overlooked, including the large amount of exposed concrete that had absorbed CO_2 and prevented the anticipated photosynthesis they had expected to be able to produce the oxygen necessary to sustain the Biosphere 2. Oxygen levels continued to decline at an alarming rate, and food production began to slow as well. The eight scientists became starved of both oxygen and food. "We actually were showing similar biomarkers to animals that are going into hibernation," Poynter said.[6]

So began the war between the factions. One group of Biospherians wanted to break the bubble so they could eat and breathe again, claiming that the self-sustaining part of the experiment had clearly already failed and that they weren't doing justice to the other experiments they were conducting in the dome in their current condition. The other group disagreed and insisted that they continue on as planned.

Poynter explained, "Ten months after enclosure, the four of us would huddle at the end of the dining table for lunch, and the four of them would either leave and eat elsewhere or crowd together at the end of the table. Sit-down dinners gave way to people grabbing their food and running to their rooms... As we passed them we hugged the wall and averted our eyes. So did they. That was the way it was for the remaining fourteen months. We never looked at each other in the face again."[7] Later, there were complaints from crew members about being spat at by other members.

Ultimately the faction wishing for more oxygen won out of necessity. The biosphere was failing and needed oxygen to be pumped in. This came at a huge hit to the experiment's reputation in the country as the press was beginning to call it a failure. Or worse, maybe the whole endeavor was fraudulent to begin with. While this was not quite true, there was a reason people were beginning to doubt its bona fides.

If you've been thinking that this all sounds a bit larger than life and hard to believe as a genuine scientific experiment, those are the same instincts that the American public had as more people started to look more deeply into the Biosphere 2 project. You may also be wondering, as I was, what happened to the first biosphere project. Well, Biosphere 2 was named as such because the creators of the project considered *Earth itself* to be Biosphere 1. To make matters more confusing, there was an attempt at a second expedition into the Biosphere 2, making it, I suppose, the Biosphere 2, Part 2.

Rumors began to spread that creator John Allen was less scientist and more cult leader. The *Village Voice* characterized him as "much more the Jim Jones than the Johnny Appleseed of the ecology movement."[8] John Allen had founded Synergia Ranch, where he and his followers lived. You couldn't be blamed if you found footage of their wacky "theater exercises"[9] evocative of the kinds of things you'd see in a cult documentary. It turned out that a frequent visitor of Allen's ranch was billionaire Ed Bass, heir to an oil fortune, who invested $200 million in the biosphere project.

To be clear, there was real science done, and the experiment did provide valuable data, especially when it came to climate change. However, many began to see the intention behind the dome as more of a pet project designed by a cult leader and his billionaire buddy. Desert ecologist Tony Burgess said of Allen, "He had created this whole world. I think a part of him, like any red-blooded male, wanted that god-like power."[10]

Four years later and five thousand miles across the Atlantic in the Netherlands, a forty-two-year-old John de Mol was told about the biosphere experiment by one of his employees, who had read an article about it on a plane. "I was intrigued and kept on asking more and more and more," described De Mol. "And that was the start of *Big Brother*."[11]

John de Mol is a deeply ambitious man. Born into a family with an established dynasty in the world of entertainment, he started his career at Radio Noordzee after the director (his father) hired him when the younger De Mol was sixteen. "I would go hang out at the station after class. I was totally captivated by the atmosphere. [My father] wanted me to go study law or something like that. But my mind was made up, I wanted to be in radio. So I never went to college."[12]

After moving on to work at a pirate radio station that got shut down by the Dutch government, he then started doing jobs for TROS, a public broadcast television station in the Netherlands known for its game shows. It was there he developed his love for TV. "In the first six months working in TV, I hated it. Then one day we were working on a Miss Holland program, and I felt this strange nervousness and butterflies in my stomach and realized that, in ten minutes, five million people would be watching us. That's when the fever started."[13]

He seemed to love the idea of being behind the scenes on something that would reach millions of people, being in control of what they saw and how they reacted without them ever knowing he was holding the puppet strings. Very *Big Brother* of him. John quickly moved up the ranks, becoming a freelance producer and creating his own production company, John de Mol Produkties when he was just twenty-four years old.[14]

After a decade of trying, he finally found his niche when he came up with a show called *Love Letters*. The idea for the show was pretty simple: three couples would compete in a variety of games, and the winning couple would get married right there on the show and have their honeymoon paid for as a prize. The viewers' favorite game was the champagne pyramid, where couples would one by one remove glasses of champagne from (you guessed it) a pyramid of champagne glasses without knocking the whole thing over.

The show was a huge hit in the Netherlands due in no small part to its host, Linda de Mol, John's sister, who sang the endearingly cheesy but earnest theme song and charmed the audience so much that she went on to be one of the country's most famous TV presenters. *Love Letters* premiered in 1990 and remained on the air for fifteen years before Linda moved on. The show was so successful that John brought it to Germany as well, where it ran for eight years and was one of the most popular programs on German TV in the 1990s.

Love Letters was the success that John de Mol needed, and it broke ground in the space of reality television. People were getting married on TV! What next? It would be a decade before American audiences would be greeted with the infamous *Who Wants to Marry a Multi-Millionaire*, something that Linda poked fun at in a special episode of *Love Letters* that aired in 2001. "Welcome to *Love Letters*, the program that is not only very romantic but also groundbreaking because now it's just the thing to get married on television, but *Love Letters* had its premiere in 1990 and I can assure you that it caused a lot of commotion then!"[15] It was a special episode of the show because in 2001, the Netherlands was the first country in the world to legalize same-sex marriage, and in that episode of *Love Letters* it became one of the first television programs ever to broadcast the legal marriage of two men live on air.

De Mol followed this up with a host of other popular shows, including the huge hit *All You Need Is Love*, a heartwarming show where popular Dutch presenter Robert ten Brink would do things like bring loved ones together for Christmas when they were otherwise incapable of doing so. These extremely popular Christmas specials still air every year in the Netherlands. However, De Mol had grander ambitions than just succeeding in the Netherlands; he wanted to take over the world. "We would like to be up there in the top three international production companies," he told the *Independent*.[16]

In the early '90s, there was a big opening for international programming in Europe due to an initiative the European Community called "Television Without Frontiers." De Mol's goal was to fill that opening, but he often found himself competing with fellow Dutchman Joop van den Ende, who had his own production company. Rather than continue competing, the two agreed to combine forces and merged their companies (and surnames) to create Endemol, a name that would make reality TV 'shippers proud. Unfortunately for the two men, the company would struggle to perform for years after the merger, and they both took on personal losses of $20 million to keep the company afloat.[17]

It was at this time in September of 1997 that John de Mol was told about John Allen's ill-fated biosphere experiment. He grabbed Paul Römer (who went on to run *Big Brother 1* in America) and a few others and sat them down for a lengthy brainstorming session. What came out of that session was Project X, the most ambitious television concept in the history of the country and maybe, if De Mol could manage it, the world.

It's important to understand the scale of what they were trying to achieve. Trying to re-create the $200 million biosphere project in TV form was not any easier than you might have thought it would be. In order to monitor the contestants 24/7, they needed not only a huge number of cameras but also a "house" that they would need to build from the ground up, designed specifically to allow for seamless coverage. Special camera tracks needed to be built in between walls and hallways for camera operators to maneuver. "The technology you need does not exist at all. So everything had to be developed to be able to visualize the lives of the residents," Paul Römer said. "Of course we hope that the program will be successful, so that we can recoup the investments by repeating the project. Here or abroad." The show was the most expensive production ever on Dutch television and a massive gamble for Endemol.[18]

The entertainment industry is littered with the corpses of overly ambitious gambles. Twenty years prior, *Supertrain* was America's most expensive production ever after NBC spent at least $7 million building the train sets to film what was meant to be *Love Boat* on a train. For decades the show was considered one of the biggest bombs in television history[19]—not to mention the fact that the biosphere itself wasn't exactly a smashing success.

De Mol found himself struggling to get anyone on board with his ambitious experiment. There were doubts about its profitability from networks, doubts about its ethics from most people who heard about it, and worst of all, doubts from even his own company about the viability of such a show.[20]

"I don't think the program existed in anyone's mind as it eventually became. No one except John de Mol himself expected it to be a success," Rolf Wouters, one of the original presenters of the show, described.[21]

Somehow De Mol was able to see something that nobody else could and was in the unique position to override any and all objections to his grand experiment. Like Frankenstein creating his monster, De Mol was poised to take bits and pieces scattered around the world to create something new and groundbreaking—something that only he had the vision for.

While *Big Brother* and *Survivor* were the drivers of the peak of reality TV, the genre actually had a long history prior to their arrival. *Candid Camera* premiered all the way back in 1948, and many consider it to be the very first reality show, though it certainly wouldn't fit the mold for what we'd consider reality television today. Another show that stakes a claim for being the first reality TV show aired in 1973 on PBS. It was called *An American Family*, showing candid moments from a family living in Santa Barbara, California, over the course of seven months of their lives. The show was a sensation, boasting over ten million viewers an episode.

"During the next hour you will see the first in a series of programs entitled *An American Family*," producer Craig Gilbert describes in the opening minutes of the series. "For seven months, the family was filmed as they went about their daily routine. There's no question that the presence of our camera crews and their equipment had an effect on the Louds, one that is impossible to evaluate."[22]

When faced with criticism over how the show seemed to challenge conventional American values by allowing an openly gay man to be portrayed as an integral member of the family and depicting marital struggles that eventually led to divorce, Gilbert said, "I stand behind every frame of that series. Yet I understand why it made so many people uncomfortable. This was a film about all of us. About how we're all trying, and usually failing, to make sense out of life. That's a truth most of us are unwilling to confront—least of all on television."[23]

In 1991, it was of course the Dutch who innovated the genre and pioneered many of the trappings of reality television that we'd think of as staples today. *Number 28* took seven students who were all strangers and put them in a house in Amsterdam to follow their experiences each week. They were allowed to come and go to live their normal lives, but the show was able to edit together storylines by cutting in confessionals and using music to add flair to the situations it depicted. This style of editing would become more and more possible after Avid Technology released their Media Composer in 1989, revolutionizing the world of nonlinear editing and making it suddenly much more feasible to sift through hours of footage to craft storylines.[24]

A year later in 1992, MTV premiered *The Real World*, which followed a formula that was very similar to *Number 28*'s. So similar in fact, that *Number 28* creator Erik Latour attempted to bring legal action to the creators of *The Real World* for not crediting his show. While he had trouble getting anywhere legally, with *Real World* creators claiming their inspiration came solely from *An American Family*, he still firmly believes that they took the idea from him.[25]

The Real World begins every episode with the famous narration, "This is the true story of seven strangers picked to live in a house and have their lives taped to find out what happens when people stop being polite…and start getting real…*The Real World.*" *The Real World* was a huge hit and became a staple on MTV for decades, though like *Big Brother*'s transition from season 1 to season 2, its spin-off show, *The Challenge*, eventually eclipsed it with its more competitive nature.

John de Mol had these examples to draw from as he crafted what was then still only known as Project X, but his vision was far more ambitious. The inciting idea for the Biospherian concept was the start of it. Isolation was key, forcing the contestants to interact only with their new society within the bounds of the show. The constant monitoring with nowhere to hide would ensure nothing was missed and prevent the contestants from withdrawing from the cameras. If they were *always* being filmed, they would get used to it much more quickly. Then came the competitive part of it: the contestants were to nominate each other for banishment. "That is the strongest soap element—the mean twist, the opposing interest, the betrayal," said Paul Römer. "It has two dimensions. The soap opera level: how do they talk to each other, who goes with whom. But also the psychology of a group; how do people react to each other under such circumstances? I find it surprising that not a single psychologist has reported here to study the project in detail. I wouldn't want to miss a second."[26]

Pitting contestants against one another was a format being pioneered by *Expedition Robinson* in Sweden. The original version of what eventually became *Survivor*, the show saw contestants divided into tribes to vote each other out each episode. British TV producer Charlie Parsons had been shopping his idea for a strategic reality show around for years before Swedish broadcaster SVT agreed to turn it into a full series, a risk that most other networks hadn't been willing to take. *Expedition Robinson* became Sweden's biggest show by the end of June 1997.

Initially the idea was for Project X to confine its contestants for a full year, but that idea was quickly changed to be one hundred days to better suit potential broadcasting needs.[27] The whole show was designed to be a perfectly repeatable blueprint to be sold around the world, and every detail was to account for that fact.

Eventually they landed on a name for Project X: *The Golden Cage*. The idea at that time was that the house would be luxurious, but again that idea was scrapped in favor of something more cost-effective and repeatable.

Another new piece of technology was making headlines around this time. In 1996, nineteen-year-old Jennifer Ringley bought a cutting-edge device called a webcam, intending to take some photos of herself for her web page. But when a friend joked that she could use it to make a fishbowl cam of a person, Jenni's life changed forever.

Zoos were at the forefront of the webcam revolution, recognizing the value of providing a live-updating view of the animals to web viewers. The technology was extremely limited at the time, however. With barely any bandwidth to work with, most webcams resorted to uploading still images at a set refresh rate. A particularly interesting shot for the time was provided by sticking a webcam into a fish tank and allowing viewers to get a live perspective as if they were in an aquarium. Funnily enough, *Big Brother* would later use this fishbowl cam concept on the live feeds, cutting to a camera dedicated to filming a tank full of fish that they'd put in the house whenever they needed to restrict the viewers' access to what was going on.

Back in 1996, Jenni took this human fishbowl idea and ran with it, setting up her webcam in her bedroom to upload a still image every few minutes at www.jennicam.org. At first it was just a few of her family and friends who would check up on her, but after a reporter in Australia heard about the site and wrote an article about it, traffic started to increase at a dramatic rate. Jenni told Alex Goldman of the *Reply All* podcast, "Pretty immediately things went crazy. I got a call from my ISP that I owed them several hundred dollars for bandwidth charges and I'd have to move my site. It was not something I had definitely prepared for."[28]

As people started discovering the site, the question of propriety often came up. Jenni just left the camera on 24/7 and didn't censor anything. She wrote on her site, "Myself, I do not think this constitutes pornography. Most often, pornography is defined as something explicit which is made with the clear intention of arousing the viewer. *Yes*, my site contains nudity from time to time. *Real life* contains nudity. *Yes*, it contains sexual material from time to time. *Real life* contains sexual material. However, this is not a site about nudity and sexual material. It is a site about *real life*."[29]

She fascinated the American public, appearing on *David Letterman* and attracting millions of viewers to her site. "This to me is the perfect idea for the internet," Letterman told her. "This will replace television as we know it now. This will replace television because this is really all people want…

People are lonely and desperate. They're lonely, desperate, miserable human beings and they're reaching out because they want to see life somewhere else taking place." Jenni replies, "I think the thing is you can see wild America and you can see lions and badgers and antelope eating and sleeping and doing what they do but for some reason wanting to see people doing the same thing is sick and perverse."[30]

She was the first of her kind. Over the course of the seven years in which the site was up, she added more cameras to each room of her apartment and improved the refresh rate of the camera, sometimes experimenting with full video streaming.

Over in the Netherlands, JenniCam had caught the attention of John de Mol, who saw the human fishbowl concept as a perfect fit for *The Golden Cage*. Clearly there was a substantial appetite for the kind of voyeurism that this new technology was allowing. With that, the live feeds were born and the final piece to the puzzle was in place for the new show.

For Jenni's part, she didn't seem to be a fan of what *Big Brother*'s version of live streaming came to represent. "I keep JenniCam alive not because I want or need to be watched but because I simply don't mind being watched. Years ago, I had an idea for this experiment, but I was the only guinea pig I was able to convince. I am interested in an experiment that involves real life… Shows with hand-selected people living temporarily in buildings wired for surveillance, competing for popularity and cash, are not real life. What I do is not exactly 'exciting' enough for television. What you'll see is my life, exactly as it would be whether or not there were cameras watching. From minute to minute, it can be tough to see what it's about. The site has existed now for about seven years. As a chronicle, a long-term experiment, the concept becomes clearer."[31]

Despite once saying she intended to keep the cam up until the day she died, Jenni eventually shut the site down and all but vanished from the internet. She was exhausted. In 2000, she had fallen in love with the fiancé of one of her friends. In the spirit of being open about everything, she bared her soul in one of her many journal entries posted on the site. "I vomited repeatedly that day, and every day for two weeks. I was and still am sick with guilt, every single day. But I know there is nothing I could have done. As soon as we fell in love, the damage was done. No way of communicating that would have been gentle or kind."[32]

After the fiancé broke off his engagement, he and Jenni developed a romantic relationship and moved in together, which of course meant that their intimate moments were now being broadcast to millions of people. The *Washington Post* called her a "red-headed little minx" and an "amoral man trapper,"[33] but Jenni persisted. She was in love, and if nobody else could understand that, she'd just have to deal with it.

"I think what really bit the most is when that relationship did start failing… I do think I ended up staying in that relationship for a lot longer than I would have because—I really, really went out of my way to make this happen, so I'm not just going to give up. So I definitely thought there was more of a weight of responsibility on me to try harder just because I had apparently made a huge mistake."[34] On top of that, interest started to wane, Jenni began having issues with payment processing to keep her site afloat due to the nudity on her website, and she decided to leave it all behind.[35]

―――――

With all the pieces in place for *The Golden Cage*, all that was left to do was find the eight cast members to participate in the ambitious experiment. The producers put out newspaper ads looking for candidates with prompts like "Describe yourself in one line" and "What is your life motto?"[36] Basic stuff. From there, some were sent confidential invitations to the John de Mol Produkties studio. In the sea of potential candidates, Paul Römer would appear and tell them they must not have any contact with each other. If anyone's name found its way to the press, the candidate would be removed from selection. He'd give them more questionnaires to fill out and tell them to remember that if they participated in the show they would become famous.

Candidates were then given psychological and medical tests to verify that they were fit to participate, followed by a background check.[37] They were divided into groups and given activities to perform, like building a house of cards, before being pulled into a small room for individual interviews where they were asked deeper questions about themselves: "What's your biggest regret in life?" "What are you most proud of?" After all the grilling, candidates were sent home, and the process narrowed even further. For the first season, the process landed on nine contestants, adding one more to the originally intended eight. Most were in their twenties or thirties, and they included a fashion saleswoman, an account manager, a singer, a civil servant, and a police constable.

One must wonder if John de Mol could, like John Allen, be accused of wanting to create his own biosphere for the sake of obtaining godlike power over its inhabitants. For someone as ambitious as De Mol, I don't think it would be an unreasonable assumption. Yet, his infamous ambition seemed to go beyond the inhabitants of one house.

"*Big Brother* was the ratings cannon and that was what it was about, not about the residents of the house. De Mol was quite ruthless in this regard," said the fashion saleswoman, Sabine Wendel, who went on to become one of the first season's stars.[38]

De Mol only ever seemed interested in tapping into our collective consciousness and creating something that would move us, then taking that movement and using it to propel himself to greater success.

"With reality you can maneuver 'ordinary people' into situations and ask yourself: what would I do? Behavior and psychology is an inexhaustible source for making television," Mark Koster wrote, quoting De Mol in his book *De Mol: De machtigste mediafamilie van Nederland*.[39]

With production ready to begin, the producers made another last-minute change. They ditched *The Golden Cage* for a more immediately recognizable and accessible title: *Big Brother*.

If somehow you've never heard of George Orwell's *1984* or his concept of *Big Brother*, the connection is about as simple as De Mol makes it out to be, with his direct reference to the book's most famous quote: "*Big Brother* is watching you." In the wake of society's ever-growing fears of rapidly evolving technology, De Mol's Orwellian surveillant nightmare of a house was a bit catchier as a concept than *The Golden Cage*. It was a clever name that allowed the public to instantly recognize what made the show unique.

I can't help but love that original name though. *The Golden Cage*. It feels like a perfect description of what the show came to be—the notion that your cage is comfortable and appealing enough that you can't even see or care that you're trapped.

John de Mol and Co. at Endemol realized that they didn't need a luxurious house to be their cage; the allure of fame and fortune was more than enough to trap its participants. To me it goes even further than that. It goes back to the template for a show that was supposed to translate across countries and cultures but failed to appeal to an American audience. It goes back to Arnold Shapiro reshaping the template in the image of American capitalism. It goes back to an audience that couldn't enjoy the show until it was capable of representing the worst of us, and as we decried its descent into the amoral, cutthroat game that it became, we also sat back, grabbed a snack, and enjoyed the view from our own golden cages.

Or maybe it's just me sitting in here, writing about this show that has trapped me so thoroughly.

When I trace all the threads woven into the creation of *Big Brother*, the fact that the show was created seems inevitable. There was (and still is) an insatiable yearning in us to see and understand more of each other. It only becomes an issue when we start to want that in increasingly more extreme and dramatic situations. JenniCam was at its most popular when people thought she was about to be intimate with her boyfriend. *Big Brother* added a game element to facilitate its goal of becoming a real-life soap opera. It only continues to escalate from there.

The show premiered in 1999 to a massive audience in the Netherlands, capturing a 28 percent market share and increasing week to week, ending with three times its initial draw.[40] The website for the live feeds became one of the most visited web pages in the Netherlands.[41] Still, many rallied against the show for its exploitation of the participants and the audience's voyeuristic desire for drama. "The makers have found a television formula to mobilize the desire for the forbidden fruit," proclaimed Marcel van Dam in the Dutch house of representatives. "*Big Brother* exploits intimacy."[42]

Writer Joost Zwagerman reflected on the show, "Why do we watch it when it comes on television? It is a mystery to me. A voyeur wants to see something that pleases his eye… This is a horror film incarnate; this is the Netherlands at its abyss. I think every time we look at *Big Brother* we look at the abyssal emptiness within ourselves. I have no other explanation."[43]

I don't think he's entirely wrong. *Big Brother* was designed to capture the worst of us, then tweaked and fine-tuned to *draw out* the worst in us. That's the cage. Still, I can't help but see its golden hue. The show has meant a lot to me over the years. It's taught me so much and brought people and communities together. It's changed the lives of both its contestants and its viewers. It may bring out the worst in us, but sometimes it can also bring out the best as well. I think it's the capacity for both that has propelled the show to endure as long as it has. But we're not quite there yet.

Back in 1999, De Mol's ambitious gamble paid off, as the show was picked up in Germany, Spain, the UK, and, of course, the massive market in America. "We've been waiting for the right opportunity. I've always known there will come a moment when the American market will open—the viewers won't take it much longer that the fall schedules are announced and you get talk show No. 289 and sitcom No. 374. People want to see something else," he told the *LA Times*.[44]

The meteoric success of *Big Brother* was so enormous that it made John de Mol a billionaire practically overnight. In 2000, Endemol had attracted the attention of Spanish telecommunications company Telefónica, which bought the company for $5.3 billion.[45] De Mol stayed on as creative director of Endemol, continuing to guide *Big Brother* into various countries. He later bought back shares in Endemol, and after a few more mergers and acquisitions, the Endemol Shine Group became the world's largest independent production company. De Mol went on to create a number of other successful reality show formats, including *Deal or No Deal*, *1 vs. 100*, and *Fear Factor*, and got another megahit with *The Voice*. Through it all for John de Mol, *Big Brother* endures as a monument to his ambition, a show that was created from bits and pieces around the globe to culminate in something that turned a mirror on all of us.

"I try to consume as much information as possible about what's happening in the world," De Mol told *Ogilvy Asia*, "because I do believe that even in entertainment, it is a reflection of what's really happening in the world."[46]

4

Community

"My life was pretty bad afterwards... My mom got a ten-page letter telling her how horrible she was for raising me and what a terrible person I was. I got fired from my job... I was scared to leave my house. My dad flew to LA to get me because he thought someone was going to harm me at the airport."

Jennifer Vasquez on her time after *Big Brother 6*[1]

In order to understand *Big Brother* fans, you need to know the story of Jennifer and Kaysar on *Big Brother 6*.

Kaysar Ridha was a twenty-four-year-old contestant that season who was worried about fitting in. "I definitely stand out in this house. I'm different from the other Houseguests. I'm Muslim, I'm Arab, specifically I'm Iraqi."[2]

It was 2005, just a few years into the Iraq War, and America was still reeling from 9/11. For many Americans, Kaysar was the first Muslim person they'd ever seen on television. He explained to the audience that he'd be praying five times a day in the house.

"You kind of have a biased opinion going in for the first time because of the whole...war with Iraq," a fellow contestant said of him.[3] After an intense conversation about the war, another said, "It's so weird talking to him and listening to these stories. It's one thing when you hear it on the news, but he doesn't want any loss of life because these are his people. And I can't really understand where he's coming from because I haven't faced that situation yet."[4]

He did initially have some trouble fitting in, getting nominated for eviction in the very first week. "When I'm not smiling, I'm very hard to approach...and I knew that coming into the game," he said, "But I was hoping people could see past that."[5]

"People might be thinking that you're either being too standoffish or your 'religion' is taking over you and you can't talk and you can't be fun," a well-meaning Houseguest advised him.[6]

He finally managed to gain some footing when he bonded with the "buxom blond" and future superstar of the show, Janelle Pierzina, over their games of chess.

"My father taught me how to play chess when I was a little girl. I do something differently with each guy I play," she told us in a series of diary rooms that introduced America to the woman they'd soon all be cheering for. "I let James win because I don't want him to think I'm really smart. I really want to see who the smartest guy is. That's why I play chess."

"Janelle, she's dumb but she's a nice girl." James said in a diary room, proving that her ploy was working. "She's really hot though."

It was Kaysar who she was the most impressed by. "Kaysar's very intelligent," she said. "He makes very slow and calculated moves in his chess game."

"You're working me," he told her playfully. "It's not going to work on me."[7]

It was an adorably endearing segment for the both of them, while making it clear that they were smart players who would be approaching the game of *Big Brother* with the same deliberate, calculated strategy as in a game of chess.

With Janelle on his side, Kaysar started to make inroads into the social landscape of the house, developing strong bonds while trying to represent himself and his culture as best as he could. "I'm in a unique situation," he said. "I'm an American, yet I'm an Iraqi as well. I feel the pain on both sides... I want to bring the human touch to the war. I want to actually talk to people. And maybe through my voice as opposed to violence, we can reach people's hearts."[8]

Courageous is the word I would have used to describe Kaysar. After making some allies of his own, Kaysar ended up in an enviable *Big Brother* predicament. He had made some good friends in the game but was also being courted by *the* big player in that season, Eric "Cappy" Littmann. Cappy was a firefighter, beloved in the house with a dedicated following. In *Big Brother 6*, Cappy's word was law, and Kaysar had been fortunate enough to get into his good graces. The issue was that Cappy wasn't fond of Kaysar's other friends and allies. It was made clear to Kaysar that if he wanted to get in good with the power, he'd need to drop them.

Kaysar refused. He began tactfully, trying to mediate and offer advice to his friends on how to avoid trouble with Cappy and his followers. But the more Kaysar tried to mediate, the more trouble he got in with Cappy, who issued an ultimatum to Kaysar: he was going to have to choose a side.

The game is riddled with these kinds of decisions. If Kaysar approached the game like a chessboard, the obvious answer to his dilemma was to sacrifice his allies to gain advantage in the game. He wouldn't be the first—and he'd be far from the last—to do so.

It's a situation I deeply related to. After abruptly changing schools years before, I'd found myself rudderless and alone in an unfamiliar environment. Over the first few days, a group of friends had taken pity on me and kindly taken me under their wing. Soon though, I received an invitation to sit with a different group at lunch—the cool kids. I still remember the pitch.

"Why are you sitting with *them*? You should come sit with us at lunch today."

Suddenly, my association with the group of friends that had taken me in seemed shameful—a mistake I'd made. To correct this mistake, I decided to sit with the cool kids at lunch that day.

In a moment that now feels ripped straight from a YA novel, I had to walk by the old table I was now rejecting in order to get to the new one. Before I could get very far, someone from the group called my name—like I'd simply forgotten where I belonged. It was a different kind of shame I felt then. I turned around and sat down with them, unable to carry on to the cool table.

I just couldn't go through with it. It was the "*them*." The judgment I had known was being pointed at a group that didn't deserve it. It scared me. Unlike Kaysar's resistance to Cappy's influence, mine didn't feel noble. It felt more like cowardice, an inability to push myself to meet new and scary people, content to stay with the familiar.

The table I rejected never let me forget it. For years I found myself bullied, kicked, and excluded. But it wasn't just the choice of table that paralyzed me; it was the fact of being new, the crippling depression in the face of my parents' nasty ongoing custody battle. For those years, I no longer dreamed about being Will Kirby, conquering all the challenges in my life. Instead, I retreated altogether. I started reading large fantasy tomes and imagined myself on a different world entirely, filled with magic and destiny. *Big Brother* was too real for my fantasies.

Then there was Kaysar. The courageous Kaysar, who had bravely rejected Cappy's offer and chosen to stick with his friends despite the danger to his game. Cappy and his crew didn't take Kaysar's rejection well, and the situation eventually culminated in a big blowup between the two sides of the house in an infamous scene where the producers had to intervene on the loudspeakers and separate all the players into different sections of the house.

To say that Kaysar was adored and beloved is an understatement. He became the most popular player the show had ever seen. My thirteen-year-old self can attest to the absolute craze that was the Kaysar fandom. I *loved* him. He was smart, respectful, and super handsome, and he played the game hard while being extremely loyal to his allies.

I didn't look up to Kaysar in the same way I'd felt inspired by Dr. Will. I saw Kaysar as a storybook hero, bravely navigating the kinds of real-world scenarios I'd once found myself in. Where I'd seen myself as a coward, Kaysar was daring. He became my avatar as he gave me the courage to return to reality and put myself back together.

These connections were not conscious ones for me at the time. I trudged through childhood with *Big Brother* as my companion, grew up, and moved on without ever giving it a second thought. But my experiences are just one example of the many ways that people find themselves attached to characters on the show. This is not unique to *Big Brother*, but the next stage of the story is.

In the five years I'd been watching these shows, there was never a player I wanted to see succeed more than Kaysar. The episodes alone were no longer sufficient to sate my growing appetite for his success. I scoured the internet and found JokersUpdates.com, where dedicated fans of the live feeds would post "updates" on what was happening minute by minute in the house.

The latest update was posted less than two minutes prior to my landing on the site. It had to do with Kaysar!

7:19PM 07/21/2005[9]:

Kaysar: Here's the thing James, I wanted you to commit before this happened.

James: I don't play by making commitments.

Kaysar: How do I know I can trust you?

What were they talking about? I scrolled farther down. There were countless posts from just that day, detailing the lives and conversations of the players. I catapulted down the rabbit hole, devouring every word.

After the big house blowup, Kaysar was the number one target for Cappy and his followers. Then, the night before I found JokersUpdates, he had narrowly beaten Cappy's closest ally and partner, Maggie, in the Head of Household competition, having guessed one hundred to her ninety-seven in the tiebreaker question. The answer was above one hundred, and all of America exploded in celebration as Maggie solemnly looked down at her chalkboard.

I needed to know what was happening now. I read farther down the page.

12:28PM 07/22/2005[10]:

Kaysar: I'm not asking anything of you. You're a smart player.

Jennifer: You may not believe me, but you and Maggie are the best people in the house.

Kaysar: I get mixed feelings about you, but I'm going to trust my gut. I do think you're playing the game, but at the same time I think there's integrity in you... One day we might have the same interests in mind.
Jennifer: I think we will.

Kaysar was trying to determine who he could trust and how he was going to use this HOH to shatter the political structure of the game. I quickly learned that he had a plan—a secret plan that I was now in the know about before anybody who only watched the episodes on TV. I agonized for days as I religiously checked back in with the forum to get updates on its progress.

This is an origin story that echoes across twenty-five years of the show's existence. Once you get a taste of what it's like to experience these conversations as they're happening, you can't go back. As Kaysar's plan that week took form, I went about my life with a spring in my step, a secret joy that nobody in my real life could take from me. My inner fantasy had been made real, and it was playing out in real time. It didn't matter if I felt like a failure because Kaysar was what I could aspire to be, and seeing him overcome his own awkwardness and ostracism meant that someday I could get there too. His success was my success.

Susan Schechter of *Reality News Online* wrote about her first experience tuning in to the live feeds in a previous season: "Maybe it was a dumb thing to do, to pay $24.95 to watch this... For those who haven't seen the feeds yet, it's pretty simplistic. There are four live feeds you can watch, one feed at a time. There isn't a lot of difference between the four channels. One has two Houseguests in the HOH room. One has a long shot of the bed, and one is from the side. The voice is the same. Earlier today one camera was on Jason brushing his teeth for a very long time. The other camera was on Joshie in the backyard shuffling cards. I guess he didn't feel like playing solitaire... So what is happening in the house, and what is the difference between what we see on TV and on the feeds? A lot. And nothing. It is hard to describe. The live feeds pretty much allow us to be voyeurs—right now as I write I see Marcellas and Gerry doing the laundry in the backyard. It's almost midnight here but it is still sunny there in La-La Land. Marcellas and Gerry are talking about the women being horny—and Gerry makes a comment that would never be on TV... But when that is all said and done, it is strategy—who you are going to vote for, who do you think will get veto... I cannot stop watching."[11]

I wasn't even watching yet, but the existence of the live feeds still impacted the way I saw the show. This wasn't *Survivor*, where they'd filmed the game months ago and we were just waiting to find out what happened. Kaysar was in that house, across the country from me, choosing a path that would make or break his game. I personally wasn't much of an active participant in online discussions, but I loved reading people's discussions about the show and what was happening on the feeds. It was a constant draw to check back in and see if anything had happened. What did everyone think of the decision to trust this person or target this other? It's a level of investment like no other. It lives with you.

Prominent figures emerged in the early days of the online community, either because they offered humorous and insightful commentary on the show or because they were able to provide a great space for content and discussion. One of the most successful and prominent figures was known as "Hamsterwatch" (also affectionately called "Dingo"). Hamsterwatch was a well-known commentator of the live feeds who eventually started her own site to host all of her snarky jokes and quips. It quickly blew up to the point where she was getting twenty-five thousand views a day on her site, and she's still going strong to this day, continuing to provide content about the show.

In a piece Hamsterwatch wrote in 2015 for Reality Blurred, she said, "We hardcore feedsters aren't necessarily proud of our addiction, but the many BB sites, chats, and forums that have sprung up over the years have made us realize we aren't alone, that there are others who hang on every word spoken in the BB house, every deal struck, every lie told, and every personal bad habit displayed by every cast member... We watch for different reasons. Some want to see all the strategic gameplay as it unfolds, some delight in the intentional and unintentional comedy that always happens, some obsess about particular cast members, and some just like watching the eye candy of the mostly young and pretty people who are invariably cast on the show. My favorite part is watching the social interaction develop (and often derail) among a group of strangers who are thrown together to simultaneously get along and compete against each other, especially when cabin fever and paranoia start to kick in—and they always do. I can't get enough of it. Our club includes people of all ages and lifestyles, including many former cast members from the show as well as a number of celebrities who share our peculiar passion."[12]

While *Big Brother* has never been the biggest show in the U.S., its online presence has been a steady juggernaut. The discussion the show can generate is endless. There's *always* something happening, *always* something new to talk about. People developed communities around the show, checking in with each other daily—hourly even.

Friends (and enemies) were made. People like Hamsterwatch were early progenitors of online content creation. She ended up finding success with her website and quitting her job. At this point in my life, I couldn't have known how important that was for my future career and how much it would come to change my own life. At that time, in that week, I was just furiously checking JokersUpdates to feel that rush of success as Kaysar put the pieces in place for his plan.

What a glorious plan it was. If Kaysar was America's hero, Cappy was the villain, seen as self-righteous and running the house with the iron fist of a dictator. America hated him. Ironically, Cappy and his crew were convinced that they were beloved by the audience, which only stoked the flames of audience disdain even further. Cappy's alliance called themselves "The Friendship," and to this day "friendship" remains a bit of a dirty word in the fan base.

Kaysar's HOH win meant that "The Friendship" was about to be humbled in a big way. "I just delivered a crushing blow to the opposition," Kaysar told us in the diary room.[13]

These emotions run deep. I'm watching the clip twenty years later as I write this, and I can still feel it: I'm thirteen again seeing Kaysar best his opponents, putting fear into the faces of his tormentors. Cappy was every bully who had been cruel to you in your life, and Kaysar was the one strong enough and smart enough to stop that bully dead in his tracks. This was real; it was twenty days of buildup for a payoff that was far from guaranteed.

As the HOH, Kaysar orchestrated a plan to gather all the outsiders into one alliance he called the "Sovereign Six" and take a shot at Cappy by putting his closest ally, Maggie, on the block.

Cappy was supposed to be untouchable. The reverence that the Friendship alliance had for him was such that the very idea of him being targeted that week seemed unthinkable. Kaysar let them think as much until the time was right to strike.

With all the pieces in place, Maggie confronted Kaysar, believing that she was the target of his HOH.

"I didn't think I was going to be the target of your game this early on," she said, shaking her head.

Kaysar stared her down. "You're not the target. You're the bait."

"Kaysar, you sealed my fate."

"No. I sealed your partner's fate. I caught the bigger fish."

The plan all along, of course, was to take out Cappy. Maggie was dumbstruck, walking away just muttering, "Amazing... Amazing... Amazing..." in disgust.[14]

I think I might have cheered watching that moment for the first time. The Friendship alliance, now branded the "Nerd Herd" by contestants and audiences alike, was in shambles. After Cappy was voted out, they built a shrine in his honor and mourned him as though he had died, all while spewing hatred for Kaysar and his crew. This was a game of strategy, yes, but it felt like it had become more like a war. With emotions boiling so fervently, the audience engagement soared to new heights.

Big Brother is a show that occupies a permanent position in your day-to-day life more than any other piece of media. It's easy to spend more time with the players being watched on the feeds than any of your real-life friends. Then these people you've spent so much time with find themselves in such heightened situations of life or death in this game meant to resemble the most cutthroat elements of society. Any artist would be envious of the depth of emotion that the show can provoke.

So is it art? Doesn't it feel cheaper than that?

I've seen the friendships and communities that developed through this fandom. I personally know a number of people who met through their fandom of the show, fell in love, and started a family. That's not unique to *Big Brother*, but it is intensified through the existence of the live feeds and their impact on the community.

Maybe that's the best way to describe the show: it intensifies.

It mirrors society, and what's reflected back is a concentrated blast. It provokes more emotional response, more time investment, more community. I've been able to learn so much more through this show than any other. There's just so much it gives. But with more of the good comes more of the bad.

Big Brother contestants in the early days could expect to come out of the house with more websites made about them than your average celebrity. Some were positive. A web page made in 2002 in honor of contestant Lisa Donahue said, "Thank you, Lisa, for sharing with all of us a glimpse of your compassion, your humor, your amazing strength, and the beauty of your heart, body, mind, and soul. May all your wonderful dreams come true!"[15]

Hamsterwatch gave me her thoughts on sites like this. "I have never gotten into any of it to that level," she said. "There's never been anybody on the show that I thought was God's gift. Just no, no. That's not why I'm here. It's like this one's so hot and sexy, and I'm like, well that's not why I'm here."[16]

It's undeniable, though, that *Big Brother* attracts all kinds of people. As with JenniCam, there's always been a draw for the voyeur who's looking for sexual content. Whole communities are dedicated to grabbing screenshots of lewd moments on the feeds, accidental flashes, and all kinds of other things that most contestants would prefer didn't exist.

Hamsterwatch went on to say, "There's plenty of other sites to find your hot and sexy people. That's why I never understood that logic. But it's like you say… We watch these people brush their teeth, we watch them sleep. And it's just a much more intimate connection to each of them than is available on any other show or any other format of any kind."[17]

When researching the early days of the online *Big Brother* community, one thing that became clear to me was that despite its size, it was very fragmented. While today's online world has an isolated little corner for every conceivable niche you can come up with, back in the early 2000s it was pretty surprising to see so many different pockets of community for just one thing.

You had Hamsterwatch and her brand of snarky humor; you could find updates at Jokers, fan pages, hate pages, TV forums, home theater forums, voyeuristic communities, the chat rooms on the CBS site itself, and more. There were even some dark places that contained fans of the dreaded Friendship alliance. All of these different corners of the internet were alive and bustling with activity every day that the show was on air.

For David Bloomberg of *Reality News Online*, the strategic component of the show was always the draw. "Analysis," he said. "Figuring out what people did right and wrong… That's what keeps you coming back. And of course it's different every time because you have different people interacting in different ways… Every season has something that's fresh and new to me."[18]

Bloomberg created a column he called "Why ____ Lost" where he would analyze the gameplay of each week's evicted player and try to figure out where they went wrong in the game. A far cry from some of the other areas of the fandom.

But just because the community was fragmented did not mean the different parts never interacted. Bloomberg accidentally found himself stumbling into a fandom war when writing about season 2 contestant Krista (the woman at the center of the Justin Sebik knife controversy). Those at BanishKrista.com felt she was a liar and should be removed from the house, prompting users to "Go to Justin's Fan Site and tell them how lucky Justin is to have gotten away from the swamp slut!" Meanwhile, some Krista supporters were frustrated with anything that painted Krista in a negative light, writing into *Reality News Online*, saying, "You guys keep quoting from Joker's board. That board has been very biased this year."[19]

With such a wide variety of communities and a vast quantity of content to consume, disagreements run rampant in the *Big Brother* community. For as many lifelong friends who have been made, so have lifelong enemies. Speaking of...

Back in *Big Brother 6*, Kaysar and the Sovereign Six had come down from the high of pulling off their coup against Cappy and his Friendship alliance. It was time for a new HOH to be crowned, and wouldn't you know it, the winner was the very bait that Kaysar used to lure in his big catch of Cappy: his partner, Maggie. She took her revenge that week, and Kaysar was evicted.

Part of what can make moments like Kaysar's HOH week so sweet is the knowledge that it's not scripted, that reality can come for you at any time. His eviction the following week was a sharp reminder of that fact. Well, it almost was.

As if by divine (or producer) intervention, a twist had already been in the works. All of the evicted Houseguests thus far hadn't actually gone home. They'd been sequestered away as the game continued to play out. After a week in sequester, it was revealed to

Kaysar that he had an opportunity to come back into the house. In the end, it came down to him and his nemesis, Cappy. Only one of them could return. And the sweetest part of all was that it would be decided by an audience vote. Kaysar was overwhelmingly voted back into the house by America, and he reentered with a chip on his shoulder and a mandate from the audience: put an end to the Nerd Herd.

Kaysar entered the house to raucous celebration from his closest allies and utter dismay from the Friendship alliance, which had hoped to see Cappy walk through that door on the back of America's vote.

There wasn't too much time to celebrate, though, as they immediately went into the longest, most intense HOH competition the show has ever had: the "Pressure Cooker." The concept of the competition was simple: All of the contestants would stand in a glass box holding on to a button. If anyone let go of their button, they were out of the competition. The last person remaining who was able to continuously hold their button won.

This all played out live on the feeds, hour by hour.

One by one, Kaysar's allies dropped out of the competition, either unable to continue holding on to their buttons or accidentally letting their hands slip. It was beginning to look like all hope was lost yet again and that Kaysar had rejoined the house for nothing. Hours passed as they continued standing with their hands on their buttons well into the dead of night.

Then the Friendship started to falter and drop out while Kaysar held strong. Night turned into morning, and after twelve hours, the only two who remained were Kaysar and Jennifer. They'd been on friendly terms at the start of the season but had drifted apart as they found themselves on opposite sides of the house. But now the two of them held on to their buttons as the sun rose on them and the fates of their games and that of their allies rested on their shoulders.

Here I am, thirteen years old, so relieved that my guy, Kaysar, has another chance, giving me back the hope of returning that pep to my step. When Kaysar was HOH, it was like I had a secret superpower in life, and I wanted that back. I wake up to find that apparently the HOH competition is still going. It's Kaysar versus Jennifer, and she's promising him the world if he's willing to let go and let her win.

You see, there were two sides at war in the house, but *Big Brother* is rarely that simple. Though aligned with the Sovereign Six, James maintained connections on both sides, positioning himself as a free agent to hedge his bets if power shifted. It also turned out that Maggie (Cappy's partner) proved to be a far more dangerous player than Kaysar had realized. During the week that Kaysar was out of the game, Maggie got into the ears of his core alliance members and convinced them to turn on James. She pitched that James was playing both sides and if they continued to let him slide by, it would be him at the end laughing at how he'd played them all. They fell into her trap and took a shot at James and his girlfriend, Sarah. The betrayal backfired when James won immunity, leaving Sarah to be evicted in his place.

So Kaysar comes back into the game and is informed that the two sides have essentially called a ceasefire because James has become the consensus house target.

Why is this important? Because after fourteen hours of holding on to their buttons, Jennifer is promising Kaysar that she will honor the truce and target James with her HOH. If that's what both of them plan to do, why does it really matter which of them wins? Kaysar counters by saying he wants to make sure none of his people end up on the block against James. Jennifer says that she gets that and her alliance members will be understanding if she has to use them as pawns.

Kaysar asks her who will go up as a pawn if she wins. She says Maggie will do it for them.

"You swear on your life?" he asks.

"I swear on my life."[20]

Millions of people who had just voted Kaysar back into the house were all collectively screaming at their televisions.

Don't do it, Kaysar!

He lets go of his button. After fourteen hours, Jennifer wins HOH.

It didn't take long for him to realize she might not be quite as willing to put up her own people as pawns as he hoped. "I've been out for a week. I've gotten a little rusty. I wanted to come back and really outdo myself. If I was back obviously America had chosen me, and I didn't want to let them down. But I'm out of the loop. I think I made a bad decision by stepping down and allowing Jennifer to take the HOH."[21]

Jennifer did not adhere to the deal, nominating Kaysar's alliance instead of her own, but she continued to claim that the ultimate target would be James. The deal was fractured but not broken. She just needed to use a different method. Kaysar was worried, but the power was out of his hands at that point.

The reality was, Maggie had tricked Kaysar's alliance into making an awful move the week before by going after James instead of the Friendship. For Jennifer to target James and leave Kaysar and the rest of his allies intact with no more third party to distract them from targeting the Friendship would have been an equally awful strategic move.

Still, the week played on, and James thought he was cooked. He had no hope of staying. When Jennifer stood to announce her final nomination, he began to stand up and make his way to the nomination chair, only stopping when he was finally able to process what she'd actually said.

"Everybody in this house does not trust James. Kaysar single-handedly brought a group together with him as the leader. And he would admit it himself that his group fell apart without him last week. So I've thought about this a lot, and I nominate... Kaysar."

James sat back down with a look of pure shock on his face as Kaysar shook his head and stood up instead. Forlornly, in the diary room he tells us, "Forget integrity. Forget honor. Forget the deal. They wanted me out. They've just proven themselves to be...cowards."[22]

The house *exploded*. Blowout arguments were happening left and right. Online, things weren't much better. I can tell you what it felt like to a thirteen-year-old boy who idolized Kaysar: I hated Jennifer. How *dare* she do this to him? And she seemed so smug about it, too, not an ounce of guilt. After everything Kaysar had gone through, to go out again like *this*? It was too much. I felt so hurt by it. Kaysar's success felt so personal to me, to everyone who had voted him back in. It felt like I had been stabbed in the back myself.

In his final eviction speech he said, "I'd like to begin by thanking America for so graciously voting me back into this house, and on that same note I would like to apologize to them for what has transpired this week. It's been a rough week for all of us, but I handed over the HOH and in turn, now I'm being voted out. And for that I'm truly sorry."[23] He was unanimously evicted and walked out of the game for the second time in as many weeks. This time it was on his birthday.

This was the "Red Wedding" for *Big Brother* fans, years before *Game of Thrones* became the biggest show on television.

I was too hurt to continue to follow the rest of the season as closely as I had those few weeks, drifting temporarily back to the safer and more emotionally distant world of just watching the episodes, though I couldn't help but occasionally check back in to my newfound addiction.

It was an experience that left a lasting impact on me, watching Kaysar's rise and fall. In the years since changing schools, I'd all but given up on so much of the world around me. A growing apathy had developed in me as I sought after any escape I could find. Just as Kaysar did with the outcasts he'd gathered to his cause, he'd inspired me to fight on in the face of what felt like overwhelming opposition. Kaysar's rallying call had reached beyond that studio lot in LA all the way to a young boy in Maine still trying to discover who he was.

I did watch the rest of the season's episodes. I cheered on as Kaysar's closest ally, Janelle, won the following HOH and took revenge upon Jennifer, sending her out the very next week. But then I had to watch as the Friendship sent out the rest of the Sovereign Six one by one until Maggie herself took home the crown.

Big Brother doesn't always have happy endings. In fact, happy endings are pretty rare for the show. But isn't that kind of the point? With some hindsight and maturity, it's easy to see that Maggie was actually the star player of that season. She skillfully surrounded herself with loyal soldiers who both took shots for her and took hits for her. All the while she whispered poison into the ears of the Sovereign Six—rudderless without their leader, Kaysar—and tricked them into attacking their own, leaving the Friendship on top. It's as admirable as it is terrible.

I couldn't stand what Maggie and her allies did to Kaysar, but I couldn't help but respect the gameplay that she, Jennifer, and the others pulled off. They were just better.

Big Brother fans will tell you that disappointment is their constant companion. It's true. But it also makes those special times when things do work out all the sweeter.

"No. I sealed your partner's fate."

It still gives me chills.

For others, though, it's harder to let go. TeamKaysar.com, the self-proclaimed "Number one fan site," dedicated itself to raising two million dollars to give to Kaysar and his allies as a way of correcting history.[24]

"Team Kaysar plays the game with some integrity, honesty, and are just good genuine hearted folks." The site creator wrote. "And I know the rest of America feels the same way… I am looking to accomplish the impossible. To mount a grand prize equivalent or greater than that of what 'Big Brother' offers the winner—$500,000… Can you imagine the look on Jen's, Maggie's, Ivette's, April's, and Beau's faces when they find this out!!"[25]

Needless to say, the site fell a bit short of its goal. One update confirmed that Kaysar and three of his allies were able to receive $500 each. Which, hey, I guess is something.

On the other side of things were sites like JenVasquezSucks.com, a forum with thousands of posts dedicated to hating Jennifer with other subjects such as the "Friendsheep a.k.a. Nerd Herd" board, described as "Your board to post about the rest of the Friendsheep. We do not feel as strongly about the rest of those nerds to give them each their own board. Maggie, Beau, and Ivette have to share."[26]

The main attraction, though, was the "Jen Vasquez Sucks!" board, where users celebrated that she lost her job after anonymous letters were sent to her employer detailing what a horrible person she was and claiming she shouldn't be around kids—along with posts about how ugly they found her, scrutinizing every part of her body. One was called "Jen IS NOT WELCOME BACK IN TEXAS,"[27] and another suggests, "Someone (or more than one) should sleep with her boyfriend. Oh! And maybe take pics and send them to her??" believing themselves to be justified because "I'm not wishing death on her as some have here, but a good old-fashioned smack down is not beneath me."[28]

For my own sanity and yours, I'll stop there. But rest assured, there's plenty more where that came from.

Twenty years later, Jennifer took part in a reunion of sorts focused on the return of the Pressure Cooker competition in season 25. She explained that even just the show bringing this competition back after twenty years elicited up a new wave of hate for her on the internet. *Twenty years later.*[29]

"My favorite quote that I saw online was 'If I could bomb her twice and it be effective, I would do it,'" she told her former castmates.[30]

Hearing about this, James said, "I wore a shirt to *House Calls* that said 'America hates you April' and production made me take it off because we just thought it was a joke. A fan had made it for us because they heard us talking about it and gave it to me at the wrap party. And it was just one of those things where you didn't realize it because we were normal people put into this Orwellian experiment. From the bottom of my heart, I'm sorry you had to go through that."[31]

That's the story of Kaysar and Jennifer on *Big Brother 6*. It's a story of heroes and villains, one that's emblematic of how the *Big Brother* community functioned in the early days of the show. It was a fractured juggernaut, full of infighting, tribalism, obsessiveness, and cruelty but also genuine connection, discovery, analysis, and above all extreme passion.

Many years later, social media would come to infiltrate every corner of internet discourse and forever change the nature of community interaction with both the show and the players. It's a change that has allowed many former players to create careers for themselves after the show while making others truly regret ever stepping foot in the *Big Brother* house.

5

Twisted

"Before I went in the house, the last interview I had with the psychologist, they said to me that my exams came back and that I was like, a very manipulative person. To me that wasn't a huge surprise."

Jun Song, winner of *Big Brother 4*[1]

The *Big Brother* format is simple: a group of strangers from different backgrounds live together in a house while voting each other out one by one until only the winner remains. There's a sense of freedom that the game provides. For the contestants, *Big Brother* is an opportunity for you to reinvent yourself. It might not matter who you are or where you came from, because the second you enter that house, the game is the only reality any of you know.

With this in mind, self-described manipulator Jun Song entered the house prepared for anything the show could throw at her. She was ready to lie, cheat, steal, and manipulate her way to the top. Anyone she encountered along the way was just a waiting victim for her schemes. Nothing could throw her off her game.

That's when her ex-boyfriend Jee walked through the door of the *Big Brother* house and the reality of her life back home irrevocably collided with her plans for the game.

Just like that, the very nature of the show changed forever as four more ex-boyfriends and girlfriends entered the game in what was being promised as the most dramatic season of the show yet.

Longtime *Big Brother* fans will tell you that there's a golden era of the show that starts with season 2 and culminates in the first *All-Star* season, *Big Brother 7*. These are the seasons with Arnold Shapiro at the helm, and they tell the story of a show that is trying to discover its own identity.

After Shapiro righted the ship that was *Big Brother* by injecting the second season with American competitiveness, the next task was to figure out how to keep people around for the long run.

Who Wants to Be a Millionaire's meteoric success was a major inspiration for the rush to acquire all of these foreign-import reality shows back in 2000. However, by the year's end, ratings for *Millionaire* were dropping rapidly.[2] By 2002, ABC had canceled the show outright. *Survivor* had actually managed to increase its viewership going into season 2[3] only to also see a big dip in ratings for its third season in 2002.[4]

It seemed like there was a formula to these shows: they debut to massive numbers as everyone checks out this new, controversial, attention-grabbing concept, only for the audience to quickly lose interest after seeing it play out a few times. It's a formula that still exists. Twenty-five years later, reality TV concepts are popping up almost every week trying to get their own flash-in-the-pan moment before fizzling out. Only the truly strong and repeatable concepts are able to survive and develop long-lasting franchises.

Back in 2002, you couldn't point to *Survivor* or *Big Brother* as a success story yet. They were both trying to do the impossible and create something that truly lasted.

Shapiro's approach for season 3 was to clean up the image of the show while leaning on its intriguing social dynamics and strong characters. But it seemed as though they didn't have confidence those things would be enough to retain the audience they'd built in season 2. Additionally, they'd learned some things from their first foray into the world of game design.

With that in mind, Shapiro added some wrinkles to the format. The most prominent was the introduction of the "veto."

To help explain the veto, I need to explain another iconic moment in the show's history.

> "I wouldn't have had this go any other way."
>
> Marcellas Reynolds[5]

Marcellas Reynolds was destined to be the first boot of *Big Brother 3*. He was nominated in the first week by HOH Lisa, and most of the house planned to vote him out. He had trouble fitting in initially, and despite the fact that he absolutely *slayed* in the diary room, that charisma was not translating to his fellow Houseguests.

The veto was the first of many "twists" introduced to the show's format over the years and is easily the most successful. It's become a mainstay of the format and a key component to making compelling television decades later.

Here's how it works. After a player becomes Head of Household (or HOH) by beating everyone else in the HOH competition, they have the power to nominate two other players for eviction. We know that part. In season 2, everyone but the nominees themselves and the HOH would then vote one of those two players out, and then everyone except the outgoing HOH would compete to become the new HOH.

What the veto did was introduce another competition into the mix. After the HOH nominated two players for eviction, there would be an opportunity for the winner of the "veto competition" to veto one of the choices for nomination, forcing the HOH to choose another player instead.

This new veto competition was played weekly, and the winner of the competition could choose whether they wanted to use the veto and save one of the nominees or keep things the same.

This is how Jennifer blindsided Kaysar in that ill-fated week. She hadn't initially nominated him, instead choosing to nominate two of his allies. Then the plan was supposed to be that they'd use the veto to take one of the initial nominees down and replace them with the mutually agreed-upon target, James.

Kaysar's ally Rachel won the veto and planned to use it to save herself, which meant Jennifer was free to nominate James as her replacement. However, at the veto ceremony, Jennifer pulled a fast one on Kaysar and nominated him instead.

Back to Marcellas, though. In season 3, he was nominated in the first week, and without the veto, that would have been it for Marcellas—a footnote in the history of *Big Brother*. But in the very first veto competition, a man named Gerry won the veto and bravely decided to use it on Marcellas in defiance of the house, removing him from the chopping block and forcing HOH Lisa to name someone else as a replacement.

So Marcellas became the first person in the history of the show to be saved by the veto. But that's not the end of his storied history with this clever twist.

The veto is genius for a few reasons. First, the show runs three times a week, so having a full episode dedicated to what happens with the veto gives them more content to work with. After the veto was introduced, the weekly formula became one episode for the HOH competition and initial nominations, one episode for the veto competition and decision to either leave things the same or force a replacement, and then one final episode for the nominees to campaign and ultimately be voted out.

Additionally, the veto adds many more layers of strategy into the game. The drawback to being HOH is that you have to nominate (and therefore upset) *two* players, and only one of them can go home at a time, leaving one player in the game who's likely not feeling very good about you. The veto makes it so that if one of your initial nominees is vetoed off the block, you now have to nominate a *third* player, potentially leaving in two newly made enemies for the next week when you can't even compete in the next HOH competition (as the outgoing HOH cannot compete in the next competition, preventing someone from being HOH two weeks in a row).

The veto also gives hope to players being targeted by the HOH. They may be down, but they're not necessarily out. They still have the opportunity to win safety for themselves or be saved by an ally. This also meant that weeks that should have been a forgone conclusion all of a sudden have layers of intrigue to them as plans have to change and shift to different circumstances surrounding the veto.

For most of season 3, the rule was that you couldn't actually use the veto on yourself, only on someone else. In that first week, Marcellas wasn't able to save himself with the veto; he needed someone else to win it and use it on him. Luckily, Gerry did just that, and Marcellas survived the week.

Marcellas then went on to win the week 2 HOH, going from the very bottom to the very top in classic *Big Brother* fashion. He used the week to solidify his position in the house and eventually went on to outlast Gerry, who had saved him, making it all the way to the Final Five in an impressive underdog run.

When the players got down to the Final Five, the rules for the veto changed as the producers introduced the "Golden Power of Veto." This allowed the winner of the veto to save *themselves* from the nomination block.

And wouldn't you know it, Marcellas's time had finally come. Despite his impressive run, he was slated to be evicted at the Final Five—until he miraculously pulled out a clutch win in the veto competition, becoming the very first winner of the Golden Power of Veto.

This was a problem for the HOH at the time, Jason. He and his partner in crime Danielle had been running the show thus far and really wanted Marcellas out that round. He was too big a threat and too well liked to be allowed to get any closer to the end. But he won the veto and could save himself; what could they really do about it?

Turns out, a lot.

Convinced that he wasn't the real target, Marcellas was willing to entertain the idea of *not* using the veto on himself, intentionally leaving himself up on the block for the vote with the assumption that his allies Danielle and Jason would vote to keep him. He felt that the only reason he was on the block in the first place was the lack of options with only five players left in the game. Additionally, the player he thought was the real target was his good friend Amy, and staying on the block meant he wouldn't have to be a vote for her to go.

Using these things as leverage, Danielle and Jason pressed Marcellas for days to not use the veto on himself, culminating in an infamous decision made live on television.

"I played this game looking out for other people…" Marcellas declares. "Gerry used the veto once for me and it was the most amazing thing that ever happened to me within this game. My sisters, my brothers, my momma, they're sitting at home and they're like, 'use the veto fool!'… I'm not going to use it."[6]

As soon as he makes his decision, you can see both Danielle and Jason visibly react, almost in horror at what they've done. The players are then called into the diary room to cast their votes. Danielle votes out Marcellas; Lisa votes to keep him. With the vote being a 1–1 tie, Jason the HOH has to stand up and break the tie in front of everyone.

Jason looks shaken, struggling to even look at Marcellas, and says, "This is a game, and there can only be one winner… As harsh and as terrible as it is, you should have used the veto. I'm sorry, but I vote to evict you, Marcellas."

Marcellas stands up in a daze, quickly walking to his bed to grab his things. He'd been so confident that he hadn't even packed his bags.

They all hug him before he silently exits the house, not having said a word.

He walks out the door to a stunned Julie Chen, and he embraces her in tears.

After they sit and get ready for the interview, Julie says, "First of all, Marcellas, I need to do this to you," and smacks the back of his head with her cue cards. "What were you thinking!?"

Marcellas Reynolds, the first person to have the veto used on him, the first holder of the Golden Power of Veto, the first person to ever *not* use the veto on himself. Another *Big Brother* gravestone echoing through the halls of legend screaming out its lesson: Always save yourself with the veto.

Big Brother 3 also introduced the concept of evicted players returning to the game. In this variation, the players themselves voted someone back in. This twist has been less successful for the show overall, with Kaysar's brief return likely being the most celebrated outcome of it despite the fact that he was promptly evicted right after returning.

Season 3 performed well, improving on the success of season 2. Of course, this didn't guarantee that the audience wouldn't move on as they had been doing with other big shows at the time.

Strategically, the game was more interesting than ever, with some players far surpassing anything that the players in season 2 had thought of, maneuvering around the house with expert precision and setting records of success that are still gold standards in today's game. We'll examine these strategic innovations in a future chapter. For now it's just important to know that the season was a hit with the core audience, but its controversial ending created a huge problem that production was forced to solve as they headed into season 4.

A key component of the show is that contestants will go into the diary room to give their unfiltered private thoughts about each other.

The diary room is what made Dr. Will a star in season 2. He'd be clowning on people in the diary room talking about what idiots they were for believing any of his lies, and then we'd cut straight to him telling those lies to someone in the house, then cut to the player who was lied to saying they believed what Will was selling to them. It's a compelling method of portraying a narrative, and Dr. Will was an expert at developing a relationship with the viewers. He made us feel like we were in on the joke and everyone else in the house just didn't get it. Four years later, Jim Halpert would win the hearts of many viewers using his own (fictionalized) version of this in *The Office*.

How it works is that players will individually be called to the diary room over the loudspeaker and then enter the soundproof room, where they are free to share their thoughts without fear of other Houseguests hearing them—though there have been rare audio glitches from time to time, where small snippets of diary room sessions have accidentally been broadcast to the house.

Inside the diary room (or DR for short), players look at a blank wall in front of them with just a hole for the camera to look through. They don't see anyone; they just hear the voice of a producer, asking them questions, sometimes laughing at their jokes. It's meant to be a safe space.

In *Big Brother 3*, there were some fantastic diary room characters. You had the dramatic and charismatic Marcellas, the raw and unfiltered Josh, and the devious cutthroat Danielle Reyes. Danielle used the diary room as her outlet to say all the things she couldn't say while playing a game based on social relationships. She let us in and described in detail how she was manipulating those around her to advance herself in the game. She'd do things like call her adversary

Roddy "the Devil," and after every eviction she'd run her countdown. "Three down, seven to go."

Needless to say, when these contestants got out of the house and saw the edited version of the show complete with Danielle's confessionals, they weren't pleased. When it came time for the finale, after masterfully navigating her way through the game, the evicted players chastised her for the things she had said in the diary room and refused to vote for her to win despite most of them feeling that she had easily played the best and most deserving game.

So the season ended with disappointment. But the problem ran deeper than that, and it's something that the producers picked up on pretty quickly.

There was a severe flaw in how they ran the game.

Disappointing results are par for the course in reality shows; the "better player" not winning the game in an upset jury vote is almost a common occurrence. That wasn't the issue. The issue was that if the audience perceives that things you say in the diary room can come back to haunt you and cost you the win, what message does that send to future players?

After watching the ending of season 3, what future *Big Brother* player of sound mind would ever go into the diary room and give their honest thoughts? They wouldn't, of course. They'd approach diary room sessions with care, making sure to avoid saying anything that would alienate a future juror deciding if they were going to win the game. That is, be as bland and inoffensive as possible.

This is reality TV kryptonite.

So Shapiro had two problems to solve heading into *Big Brother 4*. First, he had to get ahead of the audience's losing interest in the show's format. With ratings falling everywhere, he couldn't know whether *Big Brother*'s fan base would stick around for the same old thing every season. Second, he had to find a way to convince future contestants to remain unfiltered in the diary room.

The solution? *Big Brother 4: The X-Factor.*

> "I was told explicitly that what happened with Danielle... They told me don't worry, we're not going to do that this season. They told me over and over again. It was like they really wanted everyone to know that we were not going to have our diary room sessions shown to our fellow Houseguests."
>
> Jun Song[7]

The problem of diary rooms wasn't an issue on *Survivor*, which had a similar game mechanic of using the eliminated players to act as the jury and vote for the winner. *Survivor* was all prerecorded and only aired the edited episodes with confessionals long after the final votes were cast. *Big Brother* airs live, so they had to come up with a more creative way of keeping the jurors from seeing diary room sessions.

So yeah, they just locked them up.

"Shapiro further said that only seven would vote for the winner—like the *Survivor* jury—and those seven would be sequestered after being evicted from the house. In fact, they will be put into a second house where they will still be taped, and some of that footage will be added to the show," wrote David Bloomberg of *Reality News Online*. "However, they will only be allowed to see selected portions of the show, and nothing from the diary room, so they cannot change their minds based on what they see there. This decision was made because of what happened last year, where many of the Houseguests were apparently angered by what they saw Danielle saying, which caused a lopsided vote."[8]

Basically, the last seven people to be evicted from the game don't go home. Instead they go to the "Jury House," where they continue to be filmed, cut off from the world, and are only given clips to watch of the game still being played as each new evicted player joins them.

While perhaps not the most elegant solution, it certainly worked. The Jury House is now a staple of the show and has even created some unforeseen (but not unwelcome) consequences. Not only does the Jury House solve the diary room problem, but it also gives the show more compelling footage as evicted players still may hold grudges against each other from their time in the game.

We must also talk about the other big twist on the format for season 4: the "X-Factor."

"*Big Brother* will reunite broken-up boyfriends, girlfriends, and spouses. In fact, the producers are calling it *Big Brother 4: The X-Factor*," wrote Bloomberg. "When I first heard this news, I thought somebody had fabricated a parody press release. It sounds more like something Fox would do for a one-time show. But I have checked with several sources and it is indeed true. *Big Brother* this year will not just feature people who don't know each other being locked in together, but rather it will feature that situation with people who know each other and decided at one point that they don't *like* each other!"[9]

This was the first big departure from the original premise of the show, and it reeked of desperation. You could feel the fear that the producers had for the longevity of the show. It was one thing to introduce interesting game wrinkles but an entirely different thing to turn the show into a relationship drama factory. It's interesting to look back at this choice seeing that *Big Brother* was so clearly trying to emulate the hot new reality shows of 2003, knowing that they all eventually failed and only *Big Brother* managed to live on.

Fans of the show weren't particularly pleased by the concept at the time. Discussing the new exes twist, O'Sean Aieghlans of *Reality News Online* wrote of Shapiro and his coproducer Allison Grodner, "Their own personal vision of hell, which they seem so eager to share with America, has shaped this show until it has turned into a kind of perverted version of what life must be like in Los Angeles… Is this supposed to be fun?"[10]

It certainly wasn't fun for contestant Alison Irwin, who had tears in her eyes the moment it was announced her ex would be entering the game. "I want to go home!" she declared to the house. In the diary room she explained further, "I know that my current boyfriend is not going to have any of this."[11]

This twist seemed to want to push the show into the realm of *Temptation Island*, which premiered in 2001 with the premise of casting couples and tempting them with hot singles to entice them into having an affair. The premiere drew big numbers for Fox, but after its third season (which aired alongside *Big Brother 4* in the summer of 2003), the audience lost interest, and it was canceled. Maybe not the best formula to emulate at the time.

Still, *Big Brother* is a game at heart, and that component shined through quickly. There were eight original contestants and five exes brought in after. In the short time the original eight had before the exes came in, they quickly agreed to a pact: every ex would be targeted and evicted one by one until they were all gone. To make this happen, they formed the biggest alliance the show had ever seen, the "Elite Eight."

After getting over the initial "disappointment and disgust" of knowing her ex would likely be entering the game, contestant and future winner of the season Jun Song managed to see opportunity where others saw misfortune.

"I realized, OK, this is Jee. I was with him for six years, and I know him probably better than he knows himself. And at the core, he is a *good* person, so I was like all right, I'm going to use him and I'm going to manipulate him!"[12]

I've come to know Jun primarily through my numerous interviews with her. I remember the first time I spoke to her on the phone. It was an odd hour for her, as she now lives in Belgium, her voice soft and gentle as she tried to be quiet for her sleeping child. I found her to be a sweet and caring conversationalist, something that contrasted heavily with her performance on *Big Brother 4*. Which isn't to say that she doesn't still have that edge to her all these years later.

Jun applied to be on the show after seeing a commercial for it on TV. "I saw the commercial for it and it said, do you think you have what it takes to manipulate and backstab your way to $500,000? I was like, yeah!" she said.[13]

Back in 2003, the only way to apply was to send your application in through the mail with two Polaroids and a three-minute video tape. "It was literally like, I don't know eighty questions, so it was like forty pages or something. It was very long." Jun explained to me that in order to get cast, she felt like she was performing even in her written answers to the questions in the application. To her, she was already playing the game.

"Back then in 2003 nobody was really making videos of themselves. The whole camcorder thing was still a new thing... So that took me a while as well," she told me. "It's kind of like when you go into the *Big Brother* house; if you have this fake facade, that can only last so long, because eventually you do have to just let go and be yourself. I think that's where it all came together. At the time I said the reason they needed me was that they'd never had an Asian woman on the show. What the hell are you guys doing?"

Jun received a callback from casting within a few days of sending in her application. This only served to bolster her confidence for getting on the show. They met with her in a large, fancy suite at a hotel in Times Square.

"I told myself, do not hold back. Do not be shy. Do not be coy... So it was very easy for me to just let loose. Zero filter. And I could tell they were loving it."

She met with them again in New York before receiving another phone call telling her they wanted her to come to LA for the casting semifinals.

Still confident they'd pick her, she made the journey across the country. At semifinals there were all kinds of small office spaces with people running in and out. Phones were ringing, and there was lots of paperwork. "At that point it felt like, OK, this is a real TV show."

Jun had strict rules to follow. She'd go from one thing to another. Go here to get your headshots, then here for an interview, then a psych exam over here (where she'd later be told that she was very manipulative). Then more exams, back to the hotel room, more talks with the psychologist, and then the big one, a talk with the executive producers.

"You couldn't even see their faces because they were all the way in the back where it was dark," Jun said, but she took it in stride and maintained her confidence. "For me, it didn't matter. I didn't care... I knew that what they wanted from me was entertainment—to be raw, to be the antithesis of the typical passive, sweet, docile Asian woman. So I gave it to them full force, and they seemed to eat it up."

The way Jun saw it, the only thing that could go wrong was if she got in trouble for breaking one of the many rules put in place for them. There were other applicants at semifinals, but she wasn't supposed to interact with any of them. However, she did once make eye contact and shared a smile with future castmate Dana during one of their meals. "I thought, did somebody see us do that? Am I going to get in trouble? But I also observed the other people that were there."[14]

Of course, the producers went through a lot of trouble to prevent applicants from knowing that their exes were also going through the casting process. This didn't, however, prevent some things from slipping through the cracks.

Contestant Scott Weintraub and his ex Amanda Craig had mostly managed to figure out the twist ahead of time. Both were big fans of the show, and despite the fact it was against the rules, Scott called Amanda to tell her he felt he was going to be on season 4. Amanda, who was deep in the process herself, didn't admit to it. They were both a bit suspicious of the whole scenario and weren't at all surprised to see each other in the house.

Scott was later ejected from the game on day 8, before the first eviction, following an outburst where he was yelling and throwing chairs, making some of his fellow Houseguests feel unsafe. Amanda became the first person to be officially evicted that season and also holds the distinction of being one of the first two people to have sex in the American *Big Brother* house, along with Houseguest David Lane.

Yeah, it was a bit of a wild season.

Despite some things slipping through the cracks, others didn't. The producers did take their rules seriously. Jun explained to me that one day while sequestered in her hotel room in the days leading up to entering the house, she noticed a random piece of tape near her door. She wasn't sure what it was for until later, when she learned that they had taped the outside of the doors to each room so that they would know whether the applicant had attempted to leave at any point.

These kinds of security measures were enough to catch one potential Houseguest in the act. Brandon Showalter was all set to enter the house in the week leading up to the show's start. His photo and bio were released as part of the official cast promo, and fans and outlets alike were dissecting his character, trying to determine how he'd do in the game. That is, until his photo was quickly pulled from CBS.com. Just like that, there was no more Brandon.

CBS later released a statement that Brandon had attempted to contact someone while he was supposed to be sequestered and was pulled from the cast at the last minute. Rumor has it, he had attempted to call his girlfriend before entering the house.[15]

So Jun followed the rules, stayed confident, and prepared herself for the journey to come. She later found out that the production crew liked to take bets on who they thought would win. Executive producer Don Wollman (also known to *Big Brother* fans as the voice of *Big Brother*, as it's his prerecorded messages that often come over the loudspeaker to give commands to the Houseguests) had bet on her to win.

The producers are known for having their favorites. Some former players have leveled accusations of favoritism at the show, and I've personally heard stories of players hearing cheers from inside the walls when certain players won a competition.

Jun was known for her cooking on the show. She'd plant herself in the kitchen, which was in the middle of the house, and cook for everyone. After the show, she had crew members coming up to her asking about certain sauces and techniques that she used.

It's difficult to shake the feeling of being watched while you're in the house. Despite outward appearances, it is just a studio dressed up as a house, specially designed to allow for camera tracks in the wall. The studio lights are abnormally bright for the "house" setting, and you need to have your microphone on you wherever you go. The aforementioned voice of *Big Brother* is always looming, ready to chastise you if you accidentally start singing (not allowed on the live feeds for copyright issues) or to call you to the diary room. In this modern panopticon you can't escape the feeling of being monitored no matter where you are. Behind every mirror is a camera pointing right at you.

"Sometimes you could see their shadows behind the mirrors if the sun or lighting hit it right. You knew there were people behind the walls... It never quite felt like home. But because that's all you had, you had to mentally make peace with the fact that this *is* home," Jun told me. "Even though you knew you were on the show and that there were cameras and the producers were watching you...you forgot about it. You *had* to forget about it. Otherwise you would probably have a breakdown because you were always on edge... That's why if and when a voice ever came on over the loudspeaker it was always like, oh my gosh, is something wrong? What's going on? In that sense, you knew that someone was always watching or listening. And because it was mostly Don Wollman's voice in the recordings, he kind of became like God. It always felt paternal... So even though I felt like I was in power over the other players in the house, I never felt like I was in power over the show. There was always an authoritarian figure above me."[16]

Don Wollman was right to place his bet on Jun Song. She went on to win *Big Brother 4*, abandoning the idea of a house divided between originals and exes, deciding instead to manipulate and use her ex to get in with both sides and maneuver herself to the end, trailblazing an entirely new kind of *Big Brother* strategy.

At the end of the season, the producers made good on their word, not showing the jurors any diary room sessions until after they cast their votes. Once they *did* see the diary rooms, all hell broke loose. One by one, they slowly revealed that nearly all of them had voted for Jun to win the game, but none of them were happy about it after seeing the way she tore them apart in her diary room sessions.

The jurors were so furious with Jun that in future seasons the producers decided to avoid showing the jury any diary room sessions at all until after the finale had finished airing and the show had ended. Sure, the diary rooms didn't impact their jury vote, but seeing someone get roasted for their diary room sessions in the finale would still have discouraged many from being open in them in the future.

Regardless, the season ended on a high note. The ratings had again improved on the previous season, and it was beginning to look like *Big Brother* might just weather the storm. But what lessons should they take away from the success of *Big Brother 4*? There was a vocal component of the audience that felt the show didn't need these flashy and trashy twist concepts because the format itself was the true strength of the show.

"The Shapiro team has a strange—if very American—way of never being satisfied with the *Big Brother* formula, as if they are hoping beyond hope that this little twist or that will make the show a blockbuster. Get real, Shapiro, it is not going to happen. While gold coins may be falling into your lap, no one is going to be carrying you around on anybody's shoulders so stop the tinkering: too much tinkering has broken many a toy," wrote O'Sean Aieghlans of *Reality News Online*.[17]

Arnold Shapiro, however, disagreed. He wasn't done tinkering, and that message became very clear when *Big Brother 5* was announced with the most ridiculous twist the show has *still* ever seen. Its name?

Project DNA.

6

Do Not Assume

"You fucked Cowboy's mother's life up, you've fucked my mother's life up, you've fucked my sister's life up. Everything we thought was normal you fucked up! Huge internet ratings. I hope you loved this! I hope you like this for your fucking reality TV show because this is fucking real... *Big Brother* I hope you got that you fucking sadistic assholes!"

Jennifer "Nakomis" Dedmon, *Big Brother 5*[1]

Project DNA: Do Not Assume. Shapiro's latest move to spice up the *Big Brother* formula came with a warning. In a video promo for the season, host Julie Chen said the new twist would make "the X-Factor from last season look enjoyable."[2] I can't say she was wrong.

Back in season 3, a twenty-one-year-old man named Michael Ellis had applied to be on the show. In going through the casting process he told producers the story of how he had been raised without a father and had spent a long time fruitlessly trying to find him. Michael did not make the final cut for season 3, but he didn't give up hope that one day he'd make it onto the show.

Michael's story was compelling. A man looking for his father, going onto a nationally broadcast show. Surely there was a story there. It made enough of an impact that the producers decided to do some sleuthing. What if, instead of waiting for Michael's appearance on TV to do it, they tracked down the man's father themselves? The possibilities were endless.

Michael knew his father's first and last name but had still never found him. As it turns out, *Big Brother* is a bit better at finding people. They eventually discovered that the issue Michael was having was that he had an incorrect spelling of his father's last name.

Guy Dedmon was contacted by *Big Brother* casting in the lead-up to season 5. Ignorant of how and why they'd found him, Guy was under the impression that they were trying to recruit him for the show. He had that impression because that's exactly what they were trying to do. Instead of telling Guy about his son, or informing Michael about the situation, they decided that this opportunity was too good to pass up. They wanted Guy to show up on *Big Brother 5* and have no idea that his son was standing just feet away from him.

Turns out Guy didn't even know he had a son. He had dated Michael's mother decades prior, moved on, and had a family of his own without ever knowing Michael existed. The situation couldn't have been more perfect for what Shapiro and the producers were looking for. Imagine the drama as the father Michael has been searching for his whole life ends up in the same house as him. Will Michael tell him right away who he is? What will their interactions be like? How will it all impact the strategy of the game?

There was just one problem. Guy said no. He was a Vietnam vet; he wasn't interested in being on this reality game show.

So what now? They could tell him about his son, but even if that was enough to convince him to be on the show, it would ruin the big surprise moment on TV. They could scrap the idea entirely, but there just seemed to be so much promise in it. But then, there was another option. Guy had started a family of his own. They asked if he had any children over the age of twenty-one who might be interested in being on the show.

Wouldn't you know it? His daughter Jennifer was living in San Antonio and had just turned twenty-one.

Plan B then. Casting reached out to Jennifer. "I thought that they were creeps trying to get me to go to some weird audition for something nefarious," she said on *The Wayne Holtz Podcast*.[3]

After some convincing, they did manage to get her through the casting process and onto the show. Just like that, the twist was in place: Project DNA. Michael "Cowboy" Ellis and his half sister Jennifer "Nakomis" Dedmon were slated to play the game of *Big Brother* together. Well, *together* might not be quite the word.

Big Brother is a game of both skill and luck. The best players recognize this and use all of their skill to position themselves as favorably as possible—regardless of how any particular scenario plays out. It doesn't always work out, but in a game where a bad competition outcome or unlucky twist can blow up your plans, putting as many pieces in place as possible can be the key to success.

So like any good *Big Brother* player, Shapiro had multiple plates spinning in the air for season 5. Getting Nakomis (Jennifer's preferred name) on the season with Cowboy (Michael's nickname in the house) was just one example. With a season subtitled Project

DNA, what would happen if that delicate house of cards crumbled at the ten-yard line?

Easy: come up with another absurd family twist.

When the players were introducing themselves on the first night of the season, contestant Drew Daniel was shocked to discover that fellow Houseguset Diane had a twin sister at home. "I couldn't believe it when she said she had a twin sister. It was so weird that we were sitting right next to each other!"[4]

Drew was also a twin. This experience would be the longest time the two of them had ever spent apart. It was something Diane could relate to. She and Drew grew very close over the course of the season, eventually getting into what Dr. Will would call a showmance.

But this wasn't just a coincidence on a season called Project DNA. There was actually a third player in the game who had a twin as well. Only this player had some incentive to keep that a secret.

Adria Klein introduced herself as "Adria from Alabama." She said she was totally lost being here, so far from her home. This is a role she'd often play in the house, but it wasn't because she was from Alabama.

A few days later when talking to Cowboy, Adria strangely hadn't remembered a conversation they'd had the day before. Cowboy didn't think much of it, but Adria was terrified—because she wasn't actually Adria, and she'd never actually had that conversation with Cowboy.

Part 2 of Project DNA was the famous "Twin Twist." Adria and her twin sister, Natalie, were *both* playing the game under one identity. For a few days at a time, one sister would be sequestered away from the house while the other played the game as "Adria." At some point, "Adria" would be called to the diary room, where she would find her sister waiting inside. She'd have just a few minutes to try to give her sister as much of a download on all the things that had happened in those few days as possible as they swapped clothes. Then the sister would enter the house, and the previous "Adria" would be sent off to be sequestered.

From the perspective of the players in the house, Adria was called to the diary room and then walked back out. But in reality, sometimes when Adria went into the diary room, it was Natalie who walked back out.

The goal was to see how long the twins could go without being detected by the other players. They were identical apart from a few small differences that they often agonized over, so the biggest hurdle was making sure they weren't caught with any glaring knowledge gaps. Thus, "Adria" was sometimes just a little "lost."

"When we only have fifteen minutes to do the switch and transfer information, you pretty much got to kind of narrow it down to what's your top five situations and then transfer that over briefly, clearly, to the other person," Natalie tells us in the diary room. "The emotional side of it is hard for me. I want to wear my wedding ring… It's tough to look at A's face on the wall when I keep trying to be her and people call me 'A' all day. It's hard."[5]

If they could make it five weeks without being detected, Natalie would officially enter the game as her own player, and the twist would be revealed to the remaining Houseguests.

It was brilliant. It added a layer of intrigue to every conversation "Adria" had in the house. The live feeders loved tracking when they thought she was switching out with her sister and trying to figure out what she knew or what she might have missed from her time sequestered away.

There were so many ways this twist could interact with the game as well. One sister might have different feelings about her relationships with the others in the house and might have an opposing opinion on where to cast a vote, which group to side with, etc. Not to mention the great TV it would make when the grand reveal happened.

It all did come to a head in week 4, when Natalie-as-Adria made a promise to vote one way, but Adria herself felt they needed to vote another way. This understandably caused some tension in the house as other players felt she was needlessly lying to them. Lucky (or unlucky) for Adria and Natalie, the end of week 4 was when their secret was to be revealed to the house and they would both enter as individuals. And boy, did it make for good TV.

"How many total Houseguests have been playing the *Big Brother* game?" Julie asks Diane in front of the entire house.[6]

"Thir—thirteen."

"You are incorrect. Actually Diane, fourteen Houseguests have lived in the house and have played the game since week one."

"Fourteen?"

"One of your housemates has been playing this game with an identical twin."

Diane immediately looks to her right, where her showmance, Drew, is sitting next to her. They are the only two people in the house with known twins. Drew shakes his head. It's not him.

"It's Holly! It's Holly!" proclaims Cowboy with utmost confidence. Holly had been voted out the week prior.

Julie goes on to explain how the twist worked and that the twins did in fact manage to achieve their goal and will now be entering the game together.

"It's one of us…"

It's a true "the call is coming from inside the house" moment for the show. Watching these people's world just shift around them is fascinating.

Then in walks Natalie, dressed exactly the same as Adria, like a clone walking through the door. The house erupts.

Reality TV loves these kinds of reactions. Filming for these moments is full of artificiality. The host will read a line and pause for thirty seconds or more before reading the next line to give as much time to film reactions as possible. If they don't get what they need, they might do another read of the line. "Can you guys give a little more energy?" For frequent reality TV viewers, it's exhausting to watch contestants overreact to every minor announcement and twist.

But this? This was real. This was genuine. It's the stuff reality TV dreams are made of. And it all happened on live television. Five weeks of buildup. Drew looked like he was having trouble accepting the reality in front of him.

"So I did not make a promise to Scott—I'm sorry!"

"I thought you were the biggest liar ever for doing that!"

"What is your name!?"[7]

It's one of the most well-received "social experiment" twists the show has ever done—right alongside one of the worst-received twists, with Cowboy and Nakomis. Over a decade later, *Big Brother 17* would run the twist-back, casting a new set of twins in an attempt to fool the house. Future star Da'Vonne Rogers quickly clocked them, however, so the impact wasn't quite the same, though strategically there's still quite a story to tell there later on.

In *Big Brother 5*, the impact of the Twin Twist was actually pretty interesting. As "Adria," the twins were forced to play a deliberate and careful game, trying to stay good with everyone and remain protected from as many angles as possible. For some, that might be paralyzing, but for these twins it was perfect. After they both entered the house and felt free to play the way that was more natural for them, we learned what that was: all out.

They quickly turned on their allies, and the house felt that they'd become arrogant after the reveal, thinking themselves untouchable. It was like they were entirely different people.

Just two weeks after Natalie entered the game, she found herself on the block and sent to the jury with Adria following behind her the following week. As individuals they flamed out, but as twins they made a long-lasting impact on the game.

There was one more twist to *Big Brother 5* worth talking about, which is another attempt at tinkering with how the veto worked. After the Marcellas moment in season 3, producers decided to make *every* veto a Golden Power of Veto, so that there was always an opportunity to save yourself with it. Once again though, there was a problem.

Throughout *Big Brother 4*, no nominee managed to win the veto for themselves until the Final Five. What's the point in the rule change if the nominees aren't winning? The producers were trying to find a way to increase the likelihood of the veto being won by a nominee to shake up the week and make things more interesting. Their solution? A new veto selection process.

The issue was that too many people were competing for the veto, decreasing the chances of a nominee winning. So they decided to limit the number of people who were allowed to compete each week to just six players. Those players would be the HOH, the two nominees, and three others each chosen by one of the first three. So for example, the HOH would choose one person to compete, and each of the two nominees would do the same, making six total.

This worked brilliantly. Throughout *Big Brother 5*, a nominee was able to win the veto and save themselves four times, leading to more drama and intrigue in the game. Once again, though, there was an oversight.

Let's say you're the HOH in a house of ten people. You and the majority of the house all have a single target you're looking to take out this week. The Golden Power of Veto was basically designed to help give this player a fighting chance to stay. And now with only six players in the competition, their odds of winning are even higher. So ideally, you'd love to prevent them from having any shot at saving themselves.

What do you do?

Really, if you don't already know the story, feel free to try to solve the puzzle yourself. If you manage it, you'll have seen something the producers were unable to anticipate themselves even though multiple players in the house managed to figure it out within the first week of playing the game.

Mike "The Don" Lubinski, Marvin Latimer, and Nakomis herself are all somewhat credited for having seen this loophole, but only Nakomis was able to actually execute on it in what she called the "six-finger plan."

Here's how it happened. Jase was a rambunctious and aggressive player, young and fit and wildly abrasive to the rest of the house. Despite attempts to get him out in the past, Jase was able to win the veto to save himself. So when Nakomis won the HOH in week 5, she didn't want to leave anything to chance.

Instead of nominating Jase right away, which would have given him a guaranteed ticket to play in the veto, she instead nominated two allies who both had the common goal of helping take Jase out of the game. The rest was simple. She and the two nominees all chose players for the veto who weren't Jase and who were all willing to use the veto if they won, allowing Nakomis to replace the saved player with Jase, at which point Jase would have no way to save himself.

It's called the six-finger plan because it requires six people to all be working in concert to achieve one goal.

Jase was incensed. How unfair for the house to be allowed to conspire against him so wholly as to deny him the opportunity to even have a chance at saving himself. Unfortunately for him, there really was nothing he could do in the face of a house united against him, and he was sent home.

It was this six-finger strategy that was supposed to be used to take out James in season 6. James had been crowned the "Veto King" that season, winning four veto competitions. However, Jennifer betrayed Kaysar, choosing to nominate him instead of following through on the plan to nominate James.

It wasn't until season 7 that producers came up with a solution to this loophole. The reason it existed was that the HOH and nominees were allowed to choose which other three players got to join them in the veto competition. So instead of allowing them to choose, it was changed to a random draw, making it more difficult to prevent a specific person from playing.

This solution worked and was the final change of the veto's journey in *Big Brother*. From then to now, the HOH and the two nominees draw names out of a bag to determine which three other players join them in the competition. Though there are some chips that say "Houseguest Choice," allowing them to choose who will play, most are just the names of other players.

Still, the six-finger plan's legacy lives on. Just because there's a *chance* your target can still be picked to play in the veto competition doesn't mean they *will*. The act of nominating two pawns in the hope of nominating your real target after the veto is played (with the hope that the target doesn't get picked to play and never has a chance to win) is now referred to as "backdooring" someone, the idea being that you're getting them on the block via the backdoor—not coming at them directly.

As for Nakomis and Cowboy, they had quite the journey on *Big Brother 5*. It was one that made some people question whether it was morally excusable to even be watching the show.

Cowboy was quickly able to figure out who Nakomis was. He knew his father's name was Guy Dedmon, even though he didn't have the spelling right.

Sitting around the pool, the players had been telling each other their last names when Nakomis said hers was Dedmon. Cowboy's mouth drops as his head begins to spin with possibilities. He starts asking her more questions. She was born in Houston like he was. Her dad had served in Vietnam and lost half of his foot to a land mine. Those were some of the only facts Cowboy knew about his father.

"*Really?* OK," he says to her, clearly in shock. "What's your dad's name?"

"Guy."

Cowboy puts his hands over his mouth. "Guy?"

"Yeah."

In the diary room, he tells us, "My emotion right there was

another, I mean, wind that pushed me back a little bit. I mean, gasping for air just a little bit as everything was piecing together… I did realize I had a sister in the house."[8]

But, he tells us, he came into the game to win it, and he worries that revealing this information could hurt him strategically. So he stays quiet about it and continues to ask Nakomis questions about her father. What was he like? Was he built? How tall was he?

"What would you rather have? Another brother or sister?" he asks.

"I'd probably rather have an older brother."

Not knowing what to do for his game, Cowboy approaches his allies Jase and Scott. The three of them along with Drew made up what they would call the "Four Horsemen" alliance, the first of a long history of "bro" alliances that would develop on *Big Brother*.

"Jennifer… She's my sister. I just found out today. We have the same father. I never knew my real father," Cowboy tells them.

Jase and Scott were extremely confused. "Are you serious?" Jase asks as Nakomis walks by them.

"She doesn't know," Cowboy replies.

Something becomes immediately clear. They don't believe him.

"I'm like, this guy lost his damn mind day one!" Jase tells us in the diary room.

"It's the twist!" Cowboy says.

"Like, for you personally?" Jase asks incredulously.

They grab Drew and explain the situation to him. Then Jase beckons in Marvin, and Scott gets serious. "Do not lie to us, man," he says.

Jase is particularly suspicious because he had just recently become the first HOH and had been planning to nominate Nakomis for eviction.

"If she goes up, though, you've got to... I mean...," he tells Cowboy.

"Right! Right. OK, the world might hate me a little bit, but it's a game... I just met this person," Cowboy proclaims as things get a little heated.

Jase says he wants to grab Nakomis and clear this all up, so they pull her into the room.

"I've got something to tell you," Cowboy says. "I'm not making this up... We have the same father."

Her eyes narrow at him. In the diary room she tells us. "I did think he was messing with me. I thought him and the guys were pulling my leg."

In real time, she's less outwardly skeptical. "Listen, I don't have any reason to doubt you, man. You haven't given me any reason to doubt you. And if that's so, then that is a trip!"

Marvin grabs a Bible and has Cowboy swear on it.

Jase starts thinking about what this could mean. "I wonder who I'm related to in this house, man! Oh my God." In the diary room he tells us, "Homeboy and homegirl... They got the same daddy. And all I've got to say is, thank God they weren't making out on the first night because, hey, if she would have showed up with a cowboy hat on, it might have been *on*."

They have everyone gather up in the living room, and Cowboy explains it all to them. Contestant Will calls it *Jerry Springer*-ish news.

Cowboy and Nakomis are then called into the diary room, where they're each given letters from Guy Dedmon. He'd been told the real reason he'd been contacted by casting just a few days before the season started.

"When I went to get my letter I almost had a heart attack. I was like, OK, either I'm going to have a brother or this is going to be like, you've been tricked by *Big Brother*," says a shocked Nakomis.[9]

Natalie-as-Adria starts sobbing as Nakomis and Cowboy each read their letters aloud to the house. A few days later, she was forced to briefly explain it all to her sister during one of their diary room swaps.

"Michael and Nik found out that they are brother and sister. They've got the same dad," she explained, then continued. "You and Michael played Hacky Sack—"

"Wait, Michael—"

"Shut up. Don't get shocked."[10]

For Guy's part, he seemed to be grateful to *Big Brother*. "I want to tell *Big Brother* thank you. I have always wanted a son, and up until now I didn't realize I had one. And now I do."[11]

I must admit this was also compelling television. It was even a bit heartwarming. That didn't last though.

You might have been able to guess by the fact that Cowboy told Jase and Scott before approaching Nakomis herself that the two of them didn't naturally click. In fact, they found themselves on opposing sides for most of the game.

Eventually it became clear that there were two major forces in the house. One was Nakomis and her ally Karen, the last remnants of the crew that dismantled the Four Horsemen and ran most of the game. On the other side was the showmance Drew and Diane. Bonded from both being twins, the two of them came together from different sides of the house and forged their own path.

And then there was Cowboy. He spent most of the game being led around first by the Four Horsemen and then just Drew after Jase and Scott were evicted.

At the Final Five, Cowboy, Drew, and Diane colluded in the veto competition to usurp Nakomis's HOH and force her to put her own ally Karen on the block, where they subsequently sent her home, leaving Nakomis vulnerable at the Final Four.

With Drew as the HOH at the Final Four, Cowboy won the veto, which meant that he would cast the sole vote to evict either Drew's showmance Diane or his own sister Nakomis.

After having a new brother sprung on her and spending seventy days in this pressure-cooker environment unable to contact her sister or mother about the situation, Nakomis was now about to be evicted by this new brother of hers when she had come so close to the end. It was too much, and the ever calm and collected Nakomis finally broke down on the live feeds.

"I don't know where I'm going, and I don't know what's happening! I don't know what's happening, and I'm going fucking nuts! I'm not being myself!" she screamed at the cameras. "I'm sorry, but I'm just a normal person! I'm only in this game because I have a brother I never knew I had! I made him that fucking promise… I got you to the end, Cowboy, and that's all I care about anymore. Fucking send me home on Thursday!"[12]

The rant managed to have an impact on some viewers. Hamsterwatch herself wrote, "Nik did good tonight: she broke through that one-way glass between 'us' out here and 'them' in there, and she made many of us feel a little guilty for watching something that was private and none of our business… Best of all, she called out in a big way the show producers and CBS for the biggest sleazy deal going: springing a surprise brother on her on national TV, in front of her game opponents, and in front of us—without even having the opportunity to ask her dad what the hell is this about?"

It was almost enough to make Hamsterwatch reconsider the very idea of covering these events. "At the time she said that, I considered shutting down and not reporting this at all...'cause it's true—we do wait for stuff like this to happen, and that's kinda sick. But it's all part of the story: we've come this far, and we have to see it through to the end, even through the scary and uncomfortable parts."[13]

She wrote to me that all these years later it still stands out to her. "Nakomis's breakdown ran complete on feeds for more than an hour, and she spent much of that time bashing production for springing a surprise half brother on her, and how that had affected her game and was the reason she was about to be evicted. (I forget the details now, but she'd promised Cowboy she wouldn't put him up or vote him out or whatever, and he used that all season to emotionally blackmail her.) That stunt casting was *the* most despicable thing this show's ever done imo. She'd gone seventy-plus days having learned her father had another family before hers, and she hadn't been able to talk to her mom or anyone about it all that time. They did put some of her meltdown on the show but made it seem like normal late-season stress/block fever if I recall, but it was raw and intense and very finger-pointy about the sleazy trick the show had pulled on her, and so, so emotional."[14]

The season's emotional punches weren't quite over yet, as after Cowboy evicted his own sister, Nakomis, Drew followed up by evicting his own showmance, Diane, taking Cowboy to the Final Two, where he won the game in a 4–3 jury vote.

All in all, the season was a success, seeing only a small drop in the ratings from season 4. However, just as with season 2, many were starting to feel as though the show had gone too far and it was time to take a step back.

Besides, the real question at hand was *why* these seasons were seeing such success. Was it these absurd and borderline trashy concepts? Other reality shows at the time seemed to prove that false, as they all started dropping like flies. Maybe all this excess wasn't necessary, and it was the strategic tinkering to concepts like the veto alongside the core format of the show that was continuing to draw in audiences.

I knew where I fell on that scale, watching at home as a twelve-year-old boy. I was there for the *game*. And luckily seasons 6 and 7 delivered that in spades.

For season 6, Shapiro did dial things back instead of trying to escalate them further. The twist of the season was that the cast was made up of secret partnerships. Kaysar's line about "Sealing your partner's fate," to Maggie? That was because Cappy was literally Maggie's secret partner in the game, since they'd known each other for years before entering the house.

It was a cute concept, with each pair initially thinking they were the only ones who had an outside connection. The players quickly figured it out, however, and it didn't make too big of an impact in the overall direction of the season.

The other notable change for *Big Brother 6* was that they built a whole new "house" for it. The show had been renewed for a few years in advance, and it was time to invest in a new set for the show. The new house was bigger, with more cameras, more microphones, and more bedrooms. This is the house you'll still see used today.

In season 7, the show focused even more on gameplay over twists. This time it was their very first *All-Stars* season. They were bringing back some of the biggest and best players from all six previous seasons of the show to compete in one house and crown a winner. They brought back the wild Jase from season 5 alongside his bitter enemy, Diane, still reeling from being betrayed by her showmance at the Final Three, which had cost her the win. Kaysar made his triumphant return just a year after being evicted twice in a row following Jennifer's betrayal. Veto man Marcellas was back for a second shot, vowing never to make the mistake of not using the veto on himself again. And of course Dr. Will himself came back with his buddy Mike Boogie to reinstate Chilltown as the dominant force on *Big Brother*.

The season was another smashing success as well as a major evolution for the strategy of how the game was played, and the fan base had never been happier. It felt like the show was firing on all cylinders. It had finally figured out what it was and what it should be. *Big Brother* had now survived over half a decade on television with a minimal loss of viewers and was already beginning to look like one of the most successful reality shows of all time. The community was full of hope for what was to come next.

Arnold Shapiro apparently felt his job was done. When CBS announced *Big Brother*'s renewal for season 8, Shapiro also announced that he'd be stepping down as executive producer for the show. He'd be leaving it in the hands of coproducer Allison Grodner, who had come with him from his show *Rescue 911* back in season 2 of *Big Brother*, when they'd taken the Dutch format and turned it into what it is today.

"I'm gratified that Allison and I were able to successfully 'reinvent' *Big Brother 2* and turn the series into an annual summer hit," Shapiro told *Variety* as he announced he would be leaving the show.[15]

Grodner added, "We consider *All-Stars* sort of the end of an era, and now we're getting a chance to start once again with a fresh cast and new twists."[16]

It truly was the end of an era for the show. Many old-school fans look back at the Shapiro days as a golden age, before Grodner took over and screwed everything up. I'm not quite sure that's the truth of it, but there *was* a distinct shift that took place when Grodner took over.

If the Shapiro era taught us anything, it was that even with the wackiest, most out there, *Jerry Springer*–ish twists, the core of the show has, and always will be, the game. The X-Factor twist wasn't interesting because of the arguments that exes had with each other; it was interesting because of the ways the players maneuvered when there were exes in the house. The Twin Twist couldn't work in the same way on any other show. Even Cowboy and Nakomis are a fairly run-of-the-mill story on most other reality shows that will run on daytime TV. *Big Brother* the game elevated these things. But with that in mind, did we ever really need them at all?

I honestly don't know the answer to that. Maybe those twists *were* the boost *Big Brother* needed to get over the initial danger phase of the show, before people got hooked on its core premise. Like with many what-ifs in *Big Brother*, I don't think we'll ever really know what the show could have looked like without them.

One thing I do know is that Shapiro took his job very seriously. He was an accredited and respected documentarian who brought some respectability to the show while simultaneously being behind some of its most heinous twists.

In his last season working on the show, he expressed his views of this role. "While I don't consider myself the most talented producer in Hollywood or the most creative producer in Hollywood," he said, "I do consider myself one of the most ethical and honest. And somebody that places a great deal of importance upon integrity. I have a long career of doing important documentaries and of trying to improve society... When we make a decision that you don't like, believe me, it is not done in haste and it is not done half-heartedly. We do it very carefully. We're consulting with CBS attorneys... So have your opinions."[17]

Shapiro's departure ushered in a big change in the tone of the show. The way it was edited and presented became a bit wackier. Nowadays contestants are dressing up in pig suits, watching videos where *Big Brother* has inserted fake farts into footage of them, and having to rotate a mechanism that has a shoe kick them in the butt every time they want to leave a specific room. And that was all from just one season.

The show also started drifting a little further away from the truth in its editing. Certain players were protected a little more, controversial topics more often shied away from. I think when people yearn for the Shapiro era, this is largely what they miss. Shapiro led the show down some treacherous paths, but his era did seem to have a level of transparency and accountability that later seasons have lacked.

In the early years of the show, the live feeds showed considerably more of the behind-the-scenes elements of how production worked, from eviction episodes to show segments. To start blocking these things from feeds, they eventually started showing an image of the front door instead of what was happening in the house. The fans called this FOTH (for "front of the house"). It was a cool idea except when they occasionally messed up and accidentally showed the evicted Houseguest leaving through that door. After a while they realized they should just show a static image of the door rather than an actual live feed.

Someone eventually had the idea to mimic the early days of live streaming and show footage of the fish tank on the feeds during blockages. This also had an unintended consequence, however, as live feeders were able to see *through* the fish tank to the meeting taking place. As Hamsterwatch tells it, "I remember however many of us were on whatever message board just busting up laughing about that, because the view was all distorted and bubbly and we could only tell who it was by what they were wearing or where they'd been sitting, BUT WE KNEW. hilarious."[18]

Still, things were much more laissez-faire back then. Shapiro seemed to believe in having an element of true transparency in the show.

The rant Nakomis gave to the cameras on the live feeds is not something that would ever have been permitted to go on uncut on a modern season. Nowadays on *Big Brother*, a producer's job security might depend on their ability to successfully hide controversies from the audience.

Fitting, though, isn't it? For a show called *Big Brother*? Maybe they just needed some time to grow into the name.

The Evolution of Strategy

Back in the Netherlands, John de Mol was struggling with his own version of *Big Brother*.

After the colossal success of its first season in the Netherlands, they started bleeding viewers with each subsequent season. By 2002, they were airing the show's fourth and final season of its initial run, with the show being canceled after its poor performance.

Meanwhile in America, 2002 was a great year for the show, and it *gained* viewership going into the following year. Despite all of John de Mol's success, he was being outperformed on his home turf. It must have been incredibly validating to Les Moonves, Arnold Shapiro, and everyone at CBS to see that the changes they had pushed for in season 2 were succeeding in creating a lasting hit.

De Mol attempted to bring *Big Brother* back to the Netherlands in 2005, but after a short-lived two-season run, it was again canceled in 2006, the same year that Arnold Shapiro was able to leave on a high note. And this wasn't an isolated incident.

The globe was becoming littered with *Big Brother* gravestones. At least twenty variations of the show around the world were created and canceled during Shapiro's reign. With only a few notable exceptions, it seemed like *Big Brother* was dying.

The thing that Shapiro had that these other formats didn't was the *game*. De Mol was using the very same tricks Shapiro was in the Netherlands: secret partners, wrinkles designed to cause drama among players—none of it worked.

So what is it that makes the U.S. version so special?

I made my career analyzing the strategy of *Big Brother*. From the moment I saw Dr. Will in season 2, I've spent my life being fascinated by the show. It clicked with American audiences because it was a reflection of us. It *stuck* with American audiences because it also *evolves* with us.

In the Shapiro era of *Big Brother*, players were exploring a new frontier of gameplay and strategy, wading their way through uncharted pathways and ideas. By the time Shapiro departed, strategy for the game had evolved tremendously in some interesting and unexpected ways.

Here's how a typical game of *Big Brother* goes: As people develop relationships, they start forming groups; those groups typically become alliances. The biggest alliances become the majority in the house; the smaller ones and the people left over make up the minority in the house.

Big Brother is fundamentally a game about power. If you have power, you need to choose how to wield it in a way that gives you the best odds of winning. If you don't have power, you need to find a way to get some lest you find yourself completely at the whims of a fate someone else has crafted for you.

There are no guarantees on *Big Brother*, and it's not always black-and-white. For instance, some players are so bad at wielding power that they're paradoxically better off just doing nothing and hoping to get lucky. It happens. But for the most part, if you're looking to actively play the game and try to tip the scales in your favor, the goal is to control where the power is.

That brings us back to the majority and the minority. The majority always holds the most power. They're more likely to win an HOH, allowing them to directly control who goes up on the block, and they control which of the people on the block get voted out through their numerical advantage in the eviction vote. If this were a sport, it would be like if two teams were playing football and one team had twice as many players on the field as the other. If nothing else changes, the team with fewer players is going to find it incredibly difficult to win.

That's where social strategy comes in. *Big Brother* is not a team game; only one player can win. The majority structure thus becomes tenuous. The longer alliance members stick together, the further they'll go as a group, but the dynamics within that group aren't going to be favorable for all of them, giving each one an incentive to defect before fully eradicating the opposition.

That's the basics of how alliances work in the game. On *Survivor*, that game loop is their bread and butter. Where are the numbers? When do those numbers shift? In *Big Brother*, things get even more complicated.

While having a majority allows you to control the power in the game, in *Big Brother* only one person can wield it at a time: the Head of Household. Additionally, the outsiders aren't as toothless on *Big Brother* as they are on *Survivor*. The outsiders may be less likely to win an HOH, but it doesn't mean they won't. If they do, and nominate two from the majority, nothing can stop the majority from just having to eat a loss. So who takes that bullet? The majority group is forced to choose which of their two members to turn their back on. That tension can crack the game wide open. These are the tools the outsiders must use to usurp the power of the majority.

The point is, in a nutshell, the majority is trying to maintain their power and use it to advance themselves in the game while the outsiders are trying to disrupt the power of the majority and take it for themselves so that they can use it to advance themselves in the game. Or put even simpler, the game is harder if you find yourself on the outs, and only the best players are able to climb their way from the bottom to the top.

Dr. Will was the first player to weasel his way to a win from a relatively powerless position. His win came in a time before the veto existed, before anybody really understood many of the basic mechanics of the game. He proved that *Big Brother* is not just a game of numbers and loyalty; it's a game of social strategy and deception.

But the first real pioneers in the evolution of *Big Brother* strategy came the next season, on *Big Brother 3*.

Season 3 began exactly how I've described a typical season. A group of mostly young, attractive members of the cast quickly bonded and formed a majority six-person alliance.

Big Brother 3 contestant Jason Guy explains, "What happened initially—and it does happen in a lot of seasons—you've got these bros and they're tight, and they start hanging out with a couple of girls, so there's some showmance things in the works. Now there's this alliance of four really strong, really beautiful people. And I feel like there are others who will gravitate to this group, so I was like OK, where do I find myself?"[1]

An alliance of six can still be considered a majority alliance despite it being a cast of twelve when the other six players do not have a proper counteralliance of their own. This is usually how things go, as it's much easier to gather six people of your choosing into a solid alliance when you have twelve to choose from. When those six are now already committed and you're outside of it, you're stuck with a ragtag group of people who may or may not even get along, let alone be willing to come together as a team to counter an existing group. Additionally, if you *do* attempt to form a counteralliance, you're almost certainly going to shoot up to the top of the target list of the original majority alliance.

So already we're seeing parallels to some things you might see in American society. For one, how a unified front can subjugate a group of people that is of equal size or sometimes even bigger by wielding its power in such a way as to scare off any individuals looking to organize opposition.

In season 3, that majority of six held power in the first week. Alliance member Lisa Donahue won the first HOH competition. You might recall that the week 1 target that season was the veto guy himself, Marcellas. Marcellas was a gay Black man and had a little bit of a harder time fitting in than the rest of the cast. He made for an easy target.

The first veto winner, Gerry, was originally part of this alliance and was in on the talks that led to Marcellas being targeted. However, over the course of the week, he got to know Marcellas better and started to feel that something was wrong about what had gone down.

At the veto ceremony, fellow nominee Lori expressed her feelings about the alliance being based on "first impressions."

Gerry then stood up in front of the entire house and used the veto on Marcellas, saying, "Let he who is without sin cast the first stone. And I have to cast a stone at myself. I have to look deep into my soul and realize that I allowed myself to pick on Marcellas because he was Black and because he was gay... I should have known better, but that is the racism we must confront. That is the demon we must face every day. I allowed those factors to color my judgment, and that is sinful, and my soul is not for sale."[2]

Marcellas came off the block, and the alliance of six were livid with Gerry. They kicked him out and replaced him with a different player, who was more than happy to join the majority alliance.

"Gerry is on the chopping block next... He's not going to last," said HOH Lisa.[3]

Through all of this week 1 drama, though, two players were quietly concocting a plan that would change *Big Brother* strategy forever.

> "We don't get upset with people when they play poker and they don't tell us the cards they have."
>
> Jason Guy[4]

Danielle Reyes and Jason Guy were one of those unlikely duos that pop on reality TV. Danielle was a thirty-year-old Black woman, a married mother of two from Fairfield, California. When asked how she was going to win the game, in her preseason bio she wrote: "As innocent as a dove and sly as a snake. People will underestimate me. I will be fake as my implants. As soon as I step foot in the house, the game is on! Everyone there is my enemy."[5]

Jason Guy was a twenty-five-year-old virgin from Mobile, Alabama. He described himself as "too nice. I might get attached to someone and not want to vote them out."[6] This wasn't an exaggeration. Jason Guy is pretty widely considered to be one of the nicest people to ever play the game. Which is saying something, considering his role in one of the most cutthroat moves the game has ever seen. He's soft-spoken, what some might call a "gentle soul." But he was secretly ready to play it harder than anyone could have expected.

Jason was a big fan of the show, almost certainly one of the first players to have ever been a live-feed watcher before entering the house. Unlike most players in their preseason bio, Jason admits he's probably just an average competitor.[7]

"Watching season 2, I saw the players have to readjust their strategy, and Dr. Will did that masterfully. I didn't think going in I was going to be this Dr. Will and be able to control everybody and run the house. I was young, and I didn't know what I didn't know. So I didn't go in there thinking that I knew everything, and I think that was very helpful."[8]

Talking to Jason is like having a conversation with a beam of light. He's incredibly humble but engagingly passionate about any topic you put in front of him, especially strategy. The shy young man from season 3 is now a successful news anchor in Orlando, but he remains involved in the *Big Brother* community to this day.

Jason had talked over different game plans with his dad prior to entering the game. "I knew I needed somebody who's got some eyes and ears for me and will watch this house when I couldn't," he tells me. "Inevitably I'm going to be out in the backyard and there's a conversation happening in the house or I'm going to be in the shower and there's a conversation in the kitchen. So you need somebody else with eyes and ears."

Jason was very close to his mother, so his dad suggested he try to find a mom in the house to work with.

Danielle was perfect for Jason. They both were not initially invited to the cool kid club that made up the alliance of six. Not a great start to their *Big Brother* journey. But after getting to know each other, they formed a quick bond. Their mutual love for strategy had them discussing all kinds of ideas for how to play the game and get ahead despite finding themselves as outsiders in the house.

Here's a big problem for people outside of the majority: the more power you try to accumulate by gathering allies, the more of a threat you become to the majority. They'll then do their best to use their power to shut you out, ostracize you, and get you evicted. It happens at the beginning of nearly every season. In fact, one of the reasons the alliance of six really wanted Marcellas out in week 1 was that after being nominated, he was doing a fantastic job of winning people over and gathering allies.

Danielle and Jason had a very simple solution to this problem. Something that Jason had actually discussed with his dad before going on the show. Something that quickly became a core tenet of *Big Brother* strategy: keep the alliance a secret.

"I think if you keep it a secret, it's going to benefit you," Jason recalled his dad saying.

In the house, Jason quickly realized that there was an alliance that didn't include him. "I said, Dani, I feel like there's an alliance and I'm not in it, so I need to get in one! And she was saying the same thing. And like, let's keep it, you know, very quiet. Let's stay secret so that no one, *no one* has a clue what we're doing in here. So I can find out information for you and you can find out information for me. It worked very well because it didn't seem like this young kid from Alabama was going to connect up with a mom from California. We seem like an unlikely duo."[9]

Of course this had been thought of before. Danielle and Jason aren't pioneers because they vaguely knew that keeping things on the down-low would probably be better for them. What they did was actually plan and *execute* on the idea of a secret alliance. It's a lot harder than you might think.

The *Big Brother* house is, despite the name, not very big. It's almost impossible to avoid people noticing who you hang out with the most, who you talk to the most, and ultimately where your loyalties lie. At this time most alliances were basically just names attached to friend groups.

Facing down a majority alliance, Danielle and Jason were forced to be very careful to avoid detection. "We tried not to hang out a lot. That was a really smart thing that Danielle came up with… We would just play a card game every day. We never really played cards; we just put cards down and act like, oh you got it!"[10]

Every night they'd play their fictitious card game and do their best to quickly fill each other in and discuss plans for the following day. "We did a lot of thinking and strategizing on our own. We didn't have long for a meeting," Jason explained to me.

The "secret alliance" unlocked all kinds of new ways to play the game, the most important of which I often refer to as the "divide and conquer strategy." Because nobody knew the true extent of Danielle and Jason's relationship, they were able to separate (or divide) in the house and work on different people from different angles. In practice, this meant that Danielle developed a really good relationship with the first HOH, Lisa, while also pulling in some outsiders like Marcellas and his friend Amy. Jason, meanwhile, worked on buddying up to another key figure in the majority, Roddy, and portrayed himself as an extra number for their alliance.

These connections with the power structure helped keep them safe. Roddy was looking out for his buddy Jason, and Lisa felt it was important to keep Danielle around for her own game. It also allowed Danielle and Jason to gain a bit of power for themselves through the influence they had over these players. Danielle would constantly be in Lisa's ear about playing her own game, not allowing the others in her alliance to be dictating what she did. Jason would often be disarming Roddy, who was suspicious of Danielle with her influence over Lisa and connections to Marcellas and Amy.

Before long, Danielle and Jason had amassed a secret army of their own, a powerful group of people that wasn't quite an alliance but more a web of influence with a bunch of players who didn't even realize that Danielle and Jason were at the center of it.

"The secret alliance gave me an opportunity to seemingly pick a side and work with them and be protected by them but also figure out ways to dismantle them. I'm the Trojan horse, the spy telling all their secrets to Dani. And she was a spy in her camp. We were pulling apart one alliance at a time."[11]

The majority alliance began to quickly crumble from Danielle and Jason's machinations, basically shattering by the time Gerry won an HOH and took a shot right at the heart of the alliance, nominating Lisa and her showmance, Eric. These moments are critical for the survival of an alliance. You have to choose between two of your own, and if you're not careful, that can spark a civil war within your group that you can't recover from.

Danielle and Jason saw their opportunity. Roddy wanted to keep his buddy Eric and pushed the alliance to fall in line. Meanwhile, Danielle was in Lisa's ear telling her that her alliance was turning on her but that she'd have her back. Lisa looked up to Danielle as a mentor in the game.

In order to ensure they struck a death blow to this alliance, Danielle and Jason helped orchestrate a tie vote, where Roddy and his allies in the majority voted Lisa out thinking they'd have the votes, but everyone else voted to keep Lisa.

Secrecy was their superpower, but it had its drawbacks. Trying to coordinate a vote like that is tricky to begin with, but to do so secretly is another level of difficulty.

"We were back and forth on how it was going to go down. And Dani was like, I'm going to tell you if we flip. But then the wires got crossed and I wasn't sure what she'd said. So I got in the diary room to vote and I was like, hey guys, I need to leave to go ask Dani again because she told me something as I was walking in here and I don't know what it was. They were like, nope you're in, this is your vote. I came out after voting and I was like, Dani, I may have messed this all up."[12]

Jason didn't mess it up. The vote tied, Gerry as the HOH broke the tie, and Lisa stayed, now knowing with certainty that she was low on the priority list for her supposed alliance members.

The chaos of that failed vote destroyed the alliance as they tried to pull Lisa back into the fold. At this point, Lisa was following Danielle's mantra, "Keep your mouth shut, and your eyes open." The alliance turned on each other the following week, leaving just a few scattered remnants, while Danielle and Jason now held a secret majority.

The rest is history. They proceeded to eliminate the rest of their opposition one by one. Charismatic Marcellas again proved difficult to evict in the endgame, forcing them to get more creative as they convinced him not to use the veto on himself.

Danielle and Jason were truly masters of their craft. They both made it all the way to the Final Three without ever once being nominated for eviction. Their strategic innovation has left a legacy that runs deep in the world of *Big Brother*. Almost every season has a player enter the game describing a desire to replicate Danielle and Jason's strategy in the house. Secrecy is *the* main tenet of *Big Brother* strategy, and nobody did it better than the OG secret alliance.

Danielle and Jason ended up in the Final Three with Lisa, who beat the both of them in the final HOH in a heartbreaking result, then went on to beat Danielle in the Final Two with the jury berating Danielle for her cutthroat gameplay and unfiltered diary room sessions.

It's always important to remember that nobody can guarantee victory for themselves in *Big Brother*. It doesn't care how well you played; fate can always find a way to a different outcome. The best you can do is give yourself the best odds possible.

To that end, *Big Brother* strategy still had a lot of room to grow.

"It's not easy. It takes a lot of discipline, planning, willpower, and consistency... We have to float in our everyday lives. Like, if you have a job or if you're in a social circle, we're all floating to some degree. Some people are just doing it better than others."

Jun Song[13]

Just a year later Jun Song introduced the world to an entirely new way to play the game, trailblazing a path to her victory in season 4.

Season 4 was the X-Factor season. The original eight players in the house made a pact to eliminate all five exes before turning on one another. It was the first of many oversized majority alliances throughout *Big Brother*'s history. What set the Elite Eight apart was that their opposition had an identity of their own; they were the exes. It bonded them and helped launch an open resistance to the rule of the majority.

The result of this is the first true example of what we call a "split house." This is what happens when there are two opposing alliances in the game that battle back and forth for an extended period of time. It's rarer than you might assume. Without well-executed secrecy, it's hard to build a resistance to the majority, and even if you do manage it, one side often crumbles quickly in a two-sided fight.

In season 4, the exes had no option but to work together and fight hard for survival. On top of that, despite being low on numbers, they were pretty good at competitions and weren't without some charm. They won the week 2 HOH, and by week 3, the Elite Eight was falling apart. As it turns out, an alliance of eight is tough to manage, especially when the alliance came together by default rather than being handpicked.

The exes managed to flip Dana, a member of the eight, to their cause and had her fire directly at her own people when she won HOH in week 3, which evened out the numbers a bit.

Split houses create all kinds of unique dynamics in *Big Brother*. Things become tribal as the two sides take shots back and forth. If you flip to the other side, you're labeled a traitor. The drama is often right out in the open.

But remember, soon after seeing her ex walk into the house, Jun realized it presented an opportunity she couldn't pass up. She helped encourage the two sides to publicly go at it while secretly utilizing her relationship with her ex, Jee, to make inroads on the other side.

Jun recognized that she was a low priority for members of the original eight and that if she went to the end with them she'd be outnumbered and outgunned. Similarly, though, she couldn't just flip to the exes' side like Dana did. She'd be labeled a traitor. Plus the three guys over there were extremely tight, and even Jee would choose his bros over her at the end of the day. Jun realized that her position was best while both sides were busy fighting each other, getting weaker and weaker.

So with no shame, she just floated back and forth between the sides depending on who had power that week. She was only able to do this because of the relationships she had developed with the exes via her in with Jee, and it was super effective. When the exes won HOH, she'd be in the HOH room with them, celebrating and discussing best steps for moving forward. Then the following week when the original eight won, she'd be right back with them, cheering them on.

"I had to… I decided I'm going to go over to where the power is," she told me. All the while she'd be telling the eight she was still with them. "My thing was, I'm still with you guys, I'm just keeping an eye on Dana."[14]

This wasn't a secret. How could it be? The key to its success was that even though both sides eventually caught on to her doing this, what could they really do about it? If you have the choice between targeting a known enemy, someone you're *sure* is coming after you, or targeting the person who's all on their own, floating back and forth between the sides, you're almost forced to take a shot at your more pressing threat.

Of course it's not *quite* as simple as that. Jun had to do a lot of work to make sure the two sides remained at war, making sure to fan the flames and keep tensions high while also making sure one side didn't get too much of an advantage and completely demolish the others. Additionally, when others saw what Jun was doing, the obvious thought was, why can't I be doing that? Turns out, someone else *was* doing that.

Alison Irwin also had an ex in the house. She was nearly in tears when she found out he'd be entering the game. This left an impression of her that the players and audience alike were shocked to discover was wildly off base.

"Me and Dana both fell for Alison's girl-next-door sweetheart kind of act," Jun explained to me. "Especially that first day when she was crying about Justin coming in… We thought it must be a domestic abuse case or something and she was scared of him. But then we discovered no, Justin's pretty normal and a stand-up guy and *she's* the psycho! She totally fooled us those first few days. We totally fell for it."[15]

Alison quickly got her head in the game and, like Jun, realized she could use her ex Justin to her benefit. She eventually became known for being a bit of a seductress in the house, flirting with her ex and famously convincing Nathan, a guy who became smitten with her, to ruin his game by saving her with the veto.

Alison was an extremely savvy player and won the respect of many fans for her strategic prowess. When she saw what Jun was doing by floating back and forth between the two sides, she realized that she'd need to follow suit if she wanted to succeed in the game.

So Jun and Alison ended up warring throughout most of *Big Brother 4*. They were vying for the same spot and tried to sabotage each other's positions constantly.

"Me and Ali were playing pretty similar games at that point and I think we realized that we were our biggest threat," Jun said.

Week after week, they both survived. And toward the end of the game, they came to a realization. Almost as if they were taking inspiration from Joop van den Ende and John de Mol when they created Endemol, the two women realized that they would be stronger if they combined forces rather than competing, creating a new secret alliance.

"I was racking my brain for how I was going to get rid of this girl and then eventually I realized, I'm not going to be able to do it!" Jun continued to explain. "So I was like, that's ok because everyone really dislikes her so this is the perfect girl to take to the end with me."

Together, they dominated the endgame and made it all the way to the Final Two, forcing an extremely frustrated jury to choose between the two of them—the two least loyal, slimy, spineless players in the game. Jun had always been the better social player between them and won the game with six of the seven jury votes.

Jun's win ushered a new strategy term into the *Big Brother* lexicon, one that is often misunderstood in the modern era. Jun's strategy of flocking to whoever held power in any given week became known as "floating." These players float along in the game, drifting across the house from one player to another just following the power around while everyone else is stuck in place on whatever side they've chosen.

Jun is considered the queen of floaters. It's a strategy that's more effective for survival than actually converting a win, but Jun paved the way, and many would try to replicate her success moving forward.

> "This is truly an *All-Star* season because I'm astonished by your gameplay here... Season 2, the season I won, there were a lot of people I hated, and it was easy for me to motivate and find individuals that I disliked. And it gave me power. It gave me a reason to want to play. It gave me a reason to want to fight. It gave me a reason to want to remove people from the game. Then I thought, so why haven't I had that motivation? And I thought it was because I really liked everyone here. But then I realized it was the *opposite* of that. I can't find an individual to hate because I hate *you all*!"
>
> Dr. Will Kirby[16]

As the Shapiro era came to a close, one season stood above the rest both in terms of its entertainment and in the way it pushed the metastrategy of *Big Brother* forward. It's a season that gathered players from each of these strategically unique prior seasons and forced them to all play together, mixing and evolving existing strategic concepts to find new formulas for how the game could be played. It's a season that is widely considered to be one of the best the show has ever produced.

It's *Big Brother 7: All-Stars*.

First, we have to talk about pregaming. Over the years, former players got to know each other outside the game, and when casting started making calls to them for *All-Stars*, it was inevitable that they'd talk among themselves and create alliances with each other before even entering the house.

Dr. Will himself has a reputation for being the most infamous and prolific pregamer, with rumors claiming he called many of the players he suspected would be cast and made secret deals with them. It's also alleged that he told production the only way he'd agree to play was if they cast his number one ally from *Big Brother 2*, Mike Boogie, with him.

Compare this to players like Nakomis and Alison, who followed the rules more closely and weren't as active in the former player community. The two of them came back to play a second time only to find themselves the first two boots of the *All-Star* season, targeted for their reputations and lack of connections.

The next two to go were Jase and Diane from season 5, who had made a pregame secret alliance with each other that they called the "Mr. and Mrs. Smith" alliance, believing nobody would think the former enemies would ever work together. It didn't matter. The rest of the house was playing a larger game, and it left many of those without a pregame network out in the cold.

Pregaming is a very controversial topic in the *Big Brother* community. It can be frustrating to a viewership that's used to being able to see *so much* to feel like they've been left out of very important context to the game playing out in front of them. Additionally, many feel it's unfair and not in the spirit of the game for some players to be iced out simply because they don't have the same kind of nongame relationships that others do. Regardless, it's an inevitable consequence of *All-Star* seasons.

In the game, things were still interesting. Coming right off the heels of the immensely popular season 6, Kaysar had returned to *All-Stars* with his closest allies, Janelle and Howie. With them also came the free agent from their season, James, who was promising this time around that he was loyal to the cause. Four people with a built-in alliance was a lot to contend with. No other prior-season alliance had that many players. On top of that, they were dominating the competitions, winning the first four HOHs in a row. The season was theirs to lose.

Unfortunately for them, some players in the game were experts at dismantling powerful majorities. Secret alliance pioneer, Danielle Reyes, was scheming Dr. Will "I'm lying to you right now" Kirby and his network of pregame relationships were treacherous, and free agent James was up to his old tricks again.

Here's what was happening behind the scenes in those four weeks while the Season 6 alliance was in power. Dr. Will had reinstated the Chilltown alliance from season 2 with Mike Boogie. Will called out the Season 6 alliance to their face and encouraged the house to resist their rule, while secretly he was making deals with them behind everyone's back.

Will did his best to act like he was above the game throughout the season, saying he didn't care if they evicted him and acting offended each time he wasn't targeted. Despite being met with eye rolls and disbelief, he did find himself avoiding eviction week after week.

"I have made the target on my back so giant that it's become invisible," he said in the diary room.[17]

Bless his heart, but Kaysar was susceptible to Dr. Will's manipulation. He'd warn Kaysar of the bigger threats in the game, like those pesky players from season 5, Nakomis, Jase, and Diane, who were all coming for the season 6ers. And hey, even though Will was calling out season 6ers in public, he knew it was better to work with them than against them. After all, who else did he have in the game?

James saw right through Will and tried to warn Kaysar, Janelle, and Howie not to trust the mischievous doctor, but they wouldn't listen. Frustrated, James started looking elsewhere for allies. One of the people he'd bonded with the most was Danielle, who was looking for a replacement for her original partner, Jason—who hadn't accepted his own invitation to play in *All-Stars*. So James and Danielle created a new secret alliance.

This time, though, Danielle knew no amount of scheming was going to pry the remainder of the Season 6 alliance apart. They were extremely loyal to each other and had a strong relationship from outside the game. She was going to need more allies. She was going to need to make a deal with the devil.

Enter: the "Legion of Doom," a *Big Brother* supergroup. James, Danielle, Dr. Will, and Mike Boogie formed a secret *four-person* alliance—the largest of its kind to that point. Just like the original secret alliance had done, successfully hiding an alliance of four opened up even more avenues of gameplay that had previously been impossible.

James continued to play up his loyalty to the Season 6 alliance, while Danielle worked on regaining the trust of Marcellas, who had come back to play again after his infamous veto disaster. Since Danielle was the one who had caused that disaster, it was a tall task. Danielle also worked on Erika from season 4, a relatively straightforward player who had loyally stayed true to the original eight alliance in season 4 while Jun played both sides.

Dr. Will and Mike Boogie, meanwhile, worked on their own relationships in what they called "Operation: Double Date." Will flirted with Kaysar's fellow season 6 ally Janelle while Mike Boogie romanced Erika.

Four people with hidden allegiances meant their influence could reach every corner of the house, allowing them to almost use the floater strategy as a group, all while remaining undetected. It was truly the culmination of every strategic innovation the game had seen thus far.

But it didn't last long.

Will was far too conscious of the danger Danielle posed to him long term. She was far too savvy for him to manipulate, and they both understood that the only reason they were working together was out of necessity.

After the Season 6 alliance finally lost an HOH to Danielle herself, she evicted Kaysar. This was the third time he'd been evicted in the span of a year, which broke my young heart all over again. The guy just couldn't catch a break. Next on the hit list was supposed to be Kaysar's closest ally, Janelle. The problem was that she just kept winning competitions.

Janelle won the following HOH and struck back at Danielle and her allies, ultimately missing her shot and taking out Marcellas when Danielle won the veto.

With Kaysar gone, Will had a lot more influence over Janelle. They were basically in a showmance at this point, and even though he was supposed to be helping the Legion of Doom take her out, he was secretly working to help her win competitions so she would stay as a thorn in Danielle's side.

Meanwhile, Mike Boogie was in a full-blown showmance with Erika and had won her loyalty over Danielle. Eventually the time came to strike. Mike Boogie won HOH and evicted James, betraying the Legion of Doom. The following week, Will convinced Erika to turn on her ally Danielle and send her home. Operation: Double Date had made it all the way to the Final Four.

But this is where Will and Boogie screwed up. Throughout the season, they were bragging in the diary room about how easy it was to manipulate everyone and that they were playing these women for fools. Using that influence, they approached both Janelle and Erika with the same pitch: To Janelle they said, it'll be the three of us against Erika. Boogie is willing to send her home. To Erika they said, it'll be the three of us against Janelle. Will is willing to send her home.

To Chilltown's credit, both women believed them initially. However, when Janelle won the veto at the Final Four and had the power to choose who to evict, things got messy. Erika had been told that Janelle was her only enemy in the house, so as soon as Janelle won, Erika knew she was screwed. What did she have to lose? She approached Janelle and spilled everything the boys had told her. Janelle realized the two guys had been trying to play them for fools and, when it came time to vote, turned the tables on the Evil Doctor, evicting him from the game after an impressive 147-day run of avoiding eviction across his two seasons of play.

After everything, Dr. Will seemed to have forgotten the lesson he should have learned from Danielle: secrecy is everything. If he and Boogie had kept their allegiance to each other a secret from the women, framing the Final Four as a battle between two couples, it's a near certainty that Janelle would have evicted Erika, who wouldn't have had any dirt to spill on Will.

Despite having turned the tables on Chilltown at the Final Four, Mike Boogie managed to beat both women in the final HOH, cutting fan-favorite Janelle, and easily beat Erika in the jury vote to win the game. The *All-Stars* jury was focused on giving the win to the most active player regardless of their feelings.

With both members of Chilltown now having *Big Brother* wins to their name, they took their rightful spot at the top of *Big Brother* legend.

Patterns emerge as you look through the evolution of *Big Brother* strategy. It's a game that's just as much about *not* having power as it is about wielding it. It's a game that makes heroes of the powerless as they scrap for agency while the powerful try to deny it to them.

It becomes easier to see why a young boy may idolize a player like Dr. Will or cheer on Danielle and Jason. It wasn't the lies and manipulation; those were just the tools available to them. The reason we love these players is their ability to overthrow a structure of power larger than themselves. It's a variation on the hero's journey made real in a studio that resembles a house with a set of rules for a game.

It also explains the community's fascination with underdogs. Not that it's unique to *Big Brother*, but the underdog effect is remarkably strong with this audience. It makes sense: if you start the game with power and stay in power for an extended period of time, it won't matter how nice and likable you are; you're still the Empire that the Jedi and scrappy Rebel alliance are trying to take down. It's hard to compete with that.

I was entering high school at the tail end of *Big Brother: All-Stars*. Freshly motivated by Kaysar's heart, Dr. Will's wit, and Danielle's savvy, I had hope for the first time that I could find a new beginning and determine the strategy that would allow me to move forward in my own life. To that end, I still had some big challenges ahead.

As did the show.

If the Shapiro era of *Big Brother* was all about developing strategies to take down the majority, then the second half of the show's run could be called *The Empire Strikes Back*, as powerful majority players started developing strategies to more effectively consolidate power and subdue any opposition.

I don't think it's a coincidence that the first strategic innovations came almost exclusively from players who had been pushed to the side and forced to come up with alternative methods to succeed, even as many of these methods would eventually be co-opted by powerful, majority-ruling players in the future.

For now, this closes the chapter on Shapiro's era of *Big Brother*. He left the show in the hands of Allison Grodner and her new coexecutive producer, Rich Meehan.

From here, things got weird.

8

Controversy

"You couldn't write this shit if you tried. And when you do try, it isn't nearly as entertaining, and it's thoroughly unbelievable."

Eric Stein[1]

On November 5, 2007, the Writers Guild of America launched a strike that would last until February of 2008. This dealt a big blow to the entertainment industry, but there was one genre that was poised to profit from everyone else's misfortune: unscripted reality.

Allison Grodner had just taken over *Big Brother*, and in her first year on the job she ended up being tapped to shoot an extra season of the show within months of the usual one airing to fill space in the broadcast schedule. This was the first (and last) time this would ever happen for regular seasons of the show.

Thus, seasons 8 and 9 were born, and they were two of the most wildly out-of-control experiences the show has ever produced.

Season 8's casting twist felt like a rehash of what had come before. There were three sets of "enemies" in the house—people who knew each other prior to going on the show and had reason to dislike each other. The nature of these relationships varied sharply in severity. There were high school rivals, a pair of ex-boyfriends, and an estranged father and daughter. As with the X-Factor twist, they were not aware that they'd be playing the game together.

The twist almost entirely flopped right away with the high school rivals and ex-boyfriends quickly being split up in the first two evictions. This left just the estranged father and daughter, Dick and Daniele Donato.

"There's my daughter that hasn't talked to me in two years," Dick said when he learned she was in the house. "I couldn't give a fuck." He proceeded to cheer when she lost the first Head of Household competition.[2]

Needless to say, she wasn't pleased to discover that her father, a man who calls himself "Evel Dick," was going to be spending the summer with her in the game. "My dad's never really been a dad... He's been more of a friend, and he's a mean friend."[3]

Evel Dick caused quite a stir that summer. He was openly antagonistic to his fellow contestants and extremely abrasive. It wasn't long before he became the most controversial player the show had ever seen, prompting many media outlets and organizations to call for his expulsion.

"CBS has reached new lows this season in promoting misogynistic tirades in the *Big Brother* house," wrote Marcy Brown of *Indybay.com*.[4] "The Houseguest Evil [sic] Dick on CBS's *Big Brother* reality show has spent the past few weeks verbally abusing a young woman, Jen Johnson, with threats of rape, insults focused on her sexuality, and hopes for her death. His abuse has been so severe that she has asked to drop out of the competition. This weekend Evil Dick… added homophobia to his repertoire."[5]

The National Organization for Women called for the show to remove Dick from the house, writing that he "has repeatedly verbally attacked 23-year-old Jen, calling her crude names, telling her he'd like to sodomize her until she bleeds to death and that if he wasn't in the house (and at risk of being expelled) he would like to kill her. In a recent episode, he dumped a glass of tea over Jen's head, laughed about it, and said he wished it had been 'piss.'"[6]

This is where *Big Brother* is like no other reality show, because almost none of what was described above was in the edited episodes and was only available to see on the live feeds. In the episodes, Dick was portrayed as abrasive, yes. They showed him dumping tea on Jen's head, and they even showed a later altercation where, after he intentionally blew cigarette smoke in her face, Jen attempted to grab the cigarette from his hand.

He warned her, "You're going to get burned, I promise."

"You're burning me on purpose!" she declared.

"Fuck off! Get the fuck out of here… Get out of here, you crybaby little bitch! Go home, you psycho bitch."[7]

Despite scenes like this playing out on the show, would it surprise you to know that Evel Dick was far and away the audience favorite that season? He was, at least for the audience who only watched the edited TV show. The nastiest things were kept out of the edit.

"The producers are operating essentially two different realities," Andy Dehnart told the *Orange County Register*. "One is for the feed watchers… The other is on TV. They've condensed things that aren't really representative of reality… We can show Dick is a horrible person without including the words he's using. But the producers choose not to."[8]

This was the first time the show had seen such a dramatic rift between its two audiences. I was fifteen then, having spent almost half my life watching the show. I was spending more time on sites like JokersUdates.com, craving more and more discourse about the show as I fell deeper and deeper into the rabbit hole through seasons 6 and 7. I was appalled at some of the things Dick was doing and saying. Though admittedly I didn't have the perspective to understand just how bad things were, I just felt that he was mean, and I didn't like him because of it.

Still, when I'd watch the episodes, I couldn't help but feel for him. Here's this forty-four-year-old guy with red spiky hair, tattoos, piercings, the whole thing. He's bold and speaks his mind, but he's also in the diary room in tears because he just wants to make things right with his daughter. At one point, the two of them were on the block together, so he decided to try to piss off everyone in the house as much as possible, banging pots and pans in their faces and screaming at them, all in an attempt to make sure he was the one they evicted instead of his daughter. This is how the show often tried to portray Evel Dick. His "abrasiveness" was all part of his strategy.

I found myself being pulled in two completely different directions. I hated seeing what he was doing on the feeds, but when I watched him on the show I felt so much empathy. His story was compelling.

I remember thinking about how one person can seem like two entirely different entities at once. How the edit can take real and genuine aspects of a person and get you to empathize with them through that lens, even when they could just have easily taken the worst parts of that person to make you hate them. It says something about both how a reality show is edited and how we view people in general. Any view of someone is often shaped through the lens of what you decide is important about them, despite the fact they contain qualities of all kinds. To this day, Dick has many fans in the community.

The producers also seemed to be fans. His edit is considered to be one of the most slanted in the history of the show, and I'm the first one to admit that it made for phenomenally compelling television. But gone were the days of Shapiro's dedication to honesty and transparency in the eyes of the fans. The Grodner era had begun.

"Daniele revealed that the diary room producer called Jen a 'cunt.' She told Dick and Nick, 'What I told you about yesterday, about in there, the name that was used.' Nick guesses 'Transamerica?' And Dick says, 'Cunt.' Daniele confirms that, in the diary room, 'somebody called her that, and it wasn't me,'" wrote Dehnart.[9]

After eventually being evicted from the game, Jen said, "I definitely think he should've been kicked out, but obviously he was definitely entertainment for the show, so that's why he wasn't."[10]

You might wonder why the other "enemies" were quickly evicted while Dick and Daniele remained in the game together. The reason for that largely comes down to the other big twist of the season.

> "Two or three days before moving in, all of the executive producers came to my room and they said, 'Hey, we want you to read through this and tell us what you think.' And as they were leaving my hotel room, one of them turned back around and said, 'Actually, we don't care what you think. Just read it and sign it or you're going home.'"
>
> Eric Stein[11]

Eric Stein had applied for *Big Brother 2* when he was twenty-one but was out of the country when he got the call from casting. By the time he came home and found their message on his answering machine, it was too late. They had moved on.

Eric was a huge fan of these competitive reality shows. His brush with almost making it on *Big Brother 2* didn't deter him at all from continuing to watch every season he could get his hands on. Fed up with his bragging about how he almost got on the show, Eric's friends drunkenly told him he needed to put up or shut up and apply again. So he did.

They quickly called him back, and before he knew it, he was cast for *Big Brother 8*. "The night before I leave for the show, I basically blow up my hard drive at work," he said. "I delete all of my emails, all of my files, like everything. And then the next morning as the handler is coming to take me away, I sent a one-sentence email like, 'I will not be coming in for a while because I have received another opportunity. I'm sorry.' I did not even say what it was. And all my boss wrote back, which I didn't see until three plus months later was, 'You've got to be fucking kidding me.'"[12]

Unlike Jason Guy, who was also a big fan of the show when he was cast, Eric had six seasons' worth of knowledge and strategic evolution to study before he went on the show. In many ways, Eric Stein was the precursor for a casting archetype that would soon become a staple of the show. They didn't refer to him this way at the time, but Eric was the first "superfan" player.

He knew the game in and out. He'd learned from watching Danielle and Jason, Jun, Dr. Will, and the other pillars of *Big Brother* strategy. He'd also learned from watching the mistakes of many others. When a good portion of the cast has never seen the show at all before playing the game, this is a massive advantage. In just a few short years, fans of the show would start to absolutely dominate the game, culminating in an uninterrupted decade-long run of winners that had been big fans prior to being on the show.

Back in season 8, though, this was still a bit of a rarity. Eric's charm, strategic mind, and knowledge made him poised to go on a legendary run. Which is *exactly* why he was cast for this particular season.

Right before entering the house, the producers ambushed him with a proposition they knew he couldn't refuse. They explained the secret twist of the season to him and told him that if he didn't agree to participate, he would be sent home and would not be allowed to play the game.

Julie explains the twist in the first episode of the season: "Do you ever find yourself shouting at your favorite Houseguests on the TV screen because you *know* they're about to make a fatal mistake? If so, we have a twist just for you. Because for the first time in *Big Brother* history, *you*, America, will be in the house. One of our Houseguests is called 'America's Player.' This person will follow your instructions throughout the game. Everything from who to get out of the house to who to make out with in the house."[13]

It was explained to Eric that he would be "America's Player," which meant that every strategic action he could make in the game would be controlled by the audience. They would vote for who he'd try to get nominated, they'd decide who he'd try to get voted out, they straight up would control his eviction votes. If he won HOH or veto, they'd even control his nominations and the decision he made with the veto. In short? He wasn't allowed to play his own game *at all*.

"I was too big of a fan to let it pass by me or to decline it," he told me. "It was honestly hell for me. It really was… Here I am.

I'm on the show. I'm doing pretty well. I'm living my dream. I'm having so much fun. Everything's rolling my way. And yet, I can't *play* the game. Look how much people struggle in this game as is. And then I had to do thirty things that were directly detrimental, and not minorly so, *very* detrimental to my game. And all of the problems I had in the game were directly as a result of it."[14]

Eric tried looking for loopholes immediately. How hard did he *really* have to try if the audience directed him to save an enemy from being evicted? Couldn't he just make a token effort or just outright decline a directive? He quickly found out that the answer to that question was an emphatic no.

"I was jumping through hoops to accommodate these things and work my way through them," he explained. "And I felt like the show did a really poor job of representing the actual rules and the actual impact of the twist on my season. I felt like they glossed over the whole thing. It was not clear that I was contractually obligated to do these things. These were not by choice… I was begging them to not have to do all of these things."

He couldn't get away with not giving his full effort because he was always being watched. *Big Brother* truly became a reality for Eric as he was literally not allowed to have a will of his own. The producers knew he could get his way in the house if he wanted, so if he wasn't succeeding, it was because he wasn't giving it his all. He was forced to give it his all, and *boy*, did he succeed.

"I think at one point eight consecutive people that America had me nominate or go after went home in succession. I really resent when people say the outcome of the season was really affected by America and the America's Player twist. I'm sorry. The America's Player twist was not in the house getting all of these things done.

I was. America was not there implementing these asinine strategies and maneuvers that were sinking the game of all of my allies as I'm doing them and making me look batshit crazy."[15]

What does all of this have to do with Evel Dick Donato? You might have put the pieces together already. While there was a big rift in the fan base about his actions, he was the hero of the TV show, and Eric was forced to make many moves that helped Evel Dick and his daughter, Daniele, stay in the game, including a week where he directly was forced to flip the vote to save his enemy Dick and evict his ally Dustin.

To call this a mess would be an understatement. While debate raged about Evel Dick and whether he should be expelled from the game, America was forcing Eric to work against his own interests to help Dick succeed. This only compounded the issue of the edit smoothing over the roughest edges of Dick's actions, as it was that very edit that seemed to be leading the general audience (who wasn't aware of many of his actions) to vote for things in his favor.

On top of all of this, another contestant, Amber Siyavus, made anti-Semitic remarks in the house that caused a huge backlash. After she was evicted, *Big Brother* producers refused to allow journalists to ask her about the remarks, causing the Associated Press to refuse to conduct the interviews at all.[16]

But if *Big Brother 8* was messy, *Big Brother 9* was an infestation the likes of which the show couldn't have imagined possible.

"They do search you with bomb dogs and drug dogs if we go on there... I dug a hole in the clay of my pomade. You know the hair stuff? That's how I got past the dogs."

Adam Jasinski[17]

Big Brother 9 is the black sheep of the Big Brother family. It's known as the "winter season" because of its unique airing time. Many might simply call it a fever dream. You might have heard it referred to as the season where they had an orgy on the live feeds. Many are satisfied to simply say it's the trashiest and most controversial season of the show.

But the thing Big Brother 9 is most known for trumps all of that. And it all comes down to one contestant.

Adam Jasinski was an addict and a drug dealer. It'd been that way since he was a kid. "Yeah, thirteen, fourteen, fifteen, sixteen, every year until I got locked up. That's how it went down… I learned how to sell drugs and do drugs for free," he told season 21 contestant Kat Dunn on her Conspire Away, B*tches! podcast.[18]

He ended up spending a couple of months in a French prison after getting caught with "a big brick of hash"[19] on a plane. Afterward, he continued dealing, experimenting with different drugs, and eventually ended up being cast for the special winter edition of a reality show that was airing to fill space due to the writers' strike. It was Big Brother 9.

Adam talks a mile a minute. His personality leaves little room for anyone else. His brother described him as "intelligent and manipulative, a salesman and a hustler."[20] In other words, a great person to cast on reality TV. You know, besides the drug dealing. He eventually met a casting director who tried to get him onto a reality show, but things didn't work out because "I was too crazy." But there was another show he apparently wasn't too crazy for.[21]

"I just got a phone call to show up to the casting… Robin's like, 'What are you doing sweetheart?' She was like, 'You want to be famous?' I said, 'Where do you need me?' She said, 'Get to Tampa by next week.'"[22]

He did. And he was cast for the show. The twist for the season was that the contestants would play in pairs. Win as pairs, be evicted as pairs. And you'll have never guessed it, but secretly two of the Houseguests knew each other from outside the house because they were dating! They called it *Big Brother: 'Til Death Do You Part*. But nobody calls it that.

Thing was, Adam was addicted to pills. He was cast for a show that would cut him off from the rest of the world for three months. So obviously he decided that he needed to sneak pills into the house.

He hid them in his hair products and somehow managed to get through all the security checks, bringing them into the house. Once he was inside, however, it didn't take too long for production to catch him riffling through his hair product for pills. They quickly confiscated the pills and otherwise kept the whole thing quiet, with even live feeders unaware of what had happened.

With no pills, Adam started going through withdrawal in the house. He was able to mask it because he also happened to be a "have-not" at the time. Have-nots are a feature of the show where some players (oftentimes those who lose a competition) are forced to sleep in an uncomfortable room, take cold showers, and eat a disgusting concoction with oatmeal-like consistency they call "slop" for a week.

"It was slick as hell," he told Kat Dunn. "It was tough. I stayed in bed for a couple of days, you know, and I slept as much as I could... It was just two days where I felt like a severe discomfort. I just stayed in bed."[23]

Despite being unaware of Adam's drug predicament, the audience was already up in arms about him. Adam worked with autistic children for the United Autism Foundation, which in his mind gave him permission to refer to them as the r-word on the show. This promptly got him fired from his job.

"The *Big Brother* contestant who stirred up a controversy when he called autistic children '[the r-word],' has been fired from his job. But Adam Jasinski, who worked for the United Autism Foundation, doesn't know he's been canned. He's sequestered in the *Big Brother* house in LA, cut off from contact with the outside world, in keeping with the show's rules," a writer for the *New York Post* wrote. "At least one advertiser pulled out of the show following the public outcry over the crude remark, and several autism groups even called for CBS to cancel the reality series because producers chose to air the remark in an edited version of the program. Jasinski was heard on the program saying that he could call children with autism whatever he liked because he worked with them."[24]

The show was in crisis. What did it want to be? This is the closest the U.S. version ever came to imitating the formula of the original formats still being broadcast around the world. With the audience basically voting to control the action in season 8 and the continued focus on controversial characters into season 9, it was beginning to look like *Big Brother U.S.* was on the path back to its origin.

> "The television set, once so idealistically thought of as our window on the world, has become a dime-store mirror instead. Who needs images of the world's rich otherness, when you can watch these half-familiar avatars of yourself—these half-attractive half-persons—enacting ordinary life under weird conditions?"
>
> Salman Rushdie[25]

Around the world, *Big Brother* operated on controversy. Controversy sold the show even as it caused people to try to stop it from being made, perhaps even *because* people were trying to stop it from being made.

Back in 2000, John de Mol was forced to bring Bart, the winner of the very first *Big Brother* season in the Netherlands, with him to Germany so that Bart could explain the show was perfectly safe for the participants and that, in fact, he'd love to do it again if he had the opportunity.[26]

Eight years later, Bart seemed less convinced. "If it's true that I helped create that mindless monster, I'm not too proud of it," he told *The Times*.

In order to appease German regulators, they eventually agreed to turn the cameras off in the bedrooms for an hour a day to preserve the privacy and dignity of the contestants. In response, the contestants avoided the bedrooms during that hour.[27]

In Spain, a literal clown named Leo Bassi protested the show, saying it "cheapens democracy... What faith can we have in a population that is so easily manipulated." Attempting to shut the show down, he leased the land next to the *Big Brother* house and spent six days reading the entirety of George Orwell's *1984* via megaphone. By the end of the six days, the ratings had gone *up* from all the publicity.[28]

Even the participants in Spain felt that nominating each other was unfair and immoral, so they made a pact to tie up the vote between all of them so that everyone was up for the audience to vote out. It was a noble idea in protest of the nature of the show and the furthest thing from the U.S. version.[29]

By the second set of nominations, the pact had fallen apart.[30]

In Italy, they had to deal with a cardinal of the Catholic Church. "He also wrote several newspaper articles arguing that recording people for twenty-four hours was like stealing their souls," wrote Peter Bazalgette in his book *Billion Dollar Game*. "Even the Pope weighed in to condemn *Big Brother*."[31]

The cardinal also had an issue with the diary room sessions being called "confessionals." Eventually it was agreed that they would change that terminology.[32]

The Church was also critical in the UK, saying that the show was obsessed "with the imperfect personal integrity failing to disguise the underlying collective lynch mob morality of the whole experiment."[33]

Bill Clinton himself was a critic of the privacy-invading concept, telling ABC News, "Privacy should be protected… Privacy shouldn't be auctioned off to the highest bidder. These people are prostituting themselves to media conglomerates. It's very troubling."[34]

The Malawian parliament went as far as to order *Big Brother Africa* to be pulled from the air over seventy days into its third season before the ban was eventually overturned and the show came back.

All around the world, the show's very format was met with controversy and, thus, interest. As we've established, though, that interest waned and ratings fell as opponents to the show became quieter. The fact was, the *Big Brother* concept alone quickly became outdated. Other reality shows were being developed that could push the genre a lot further than a bunch of strangers living in a house being voted out by the audience could.

But *Big Brother* did still have a few advantages. Most notably, it had the live feeds, which not only provided a steady stream of controversy but remained a wholly unique offering to a hungry, voyeuristic audience. In the U.S., the strategic game element pushed the show over the top and kept a loyal fan base coming back. Elsewhere in the world, they found a different draw. German writer Ansbert Kneip labeled them "trash heroes" in an article for *Der Spiegel* during the first season of *Big Brother Germany* in 2000.

"Around 5,000 people, hardly any of them older than 25, came to celebrate a Swabian-Macedonian industrial mechanic who, within five weeks, went from simply stupid August to an idiot with cult status: Zlatko, nicknamed 'the Brain.' Like no one else at the moment, Zlatko stands for the exaggeration of the world, for the—more or less ironic—fun in the simple mind. Zlatko struggles with grammar and pronunciation ('I greet everyone who knows me'), cuts his chest hair with paper scissors (three stab wounds) and even knows the video of Shakespeare's 'Romeo and Juliet' ('Fool's Talk'). In short: a trash hero in sweatpants, a talking chain-link fence."[35]

In *Billion Dollar Game*, Bazalgette wrote, "Zlatko was ill-educated, prejudiced and he didn't mind who knew it. Early on a remark of his became nationally celebrated. 'Who was William Shakespeare? If you were to ask me what he did—words, films or documentaries—I'd have no idea…' He was not sure precisely what 'homosexual' or 'heterosexual' meant, but he knew what he liked: 'Adam and Eve. Man and woman. He didn't write Adam and Adam. I don't care what men shove up their arses but leave me out of it.'" He went on to write, "That someone could honestly admit to crushing ignorance on television had its appeal—such people had not really been seen before on their own terms. And with his crude, politically incorrect opinions German viewers also found his honesty refreshing. Zlatko was saying publicly what they themselves sometimes thought but felt constrained from expressing."[36]

Zlatko became a superstar overnight. He got his own show, he started a music career and released multiple number one singles, and he starred in a movie, all within a year of leaving the house. Zlatko's story wasn't unique either; it was happening all over the world.

Jade Goody became the biggest star of *Big Brother UK* when she became known as the "most hated woman in Britain." "She was large, she had a snub nose and a strong Cockney accent. She thought chickpeas came from a chicken, that Cambridge was in London... Britain's tabloid news-papers dubbed Jade 'Miss Piggy,'" wrote Bazalgette.[37]

"She was relentlessly cheery and cheerily ignorant... A national debate ensued about a failing education system. She got drunk. She was vulnerable. She was silly, and at one point naked. The public were encouraged to despise her by a fit of fake respectability from the tabloids whose symbiotic relationship to reality TV was in full swing. This chatty girl was soon an object of scorn... It was fine to call her a pig... it was fine for Graham Norton to dress up in a fat suit to imitate her, or for Jonathan Ross to say men would be wanting to 'shag her brains in,'"[38] Suzanne Moore of the *Guardian* wrote.

Through all this attention came fascination, and sentiment began to turn just as it had with Zlatko. Goody became a celebrity overnight. She got her own TV show, created her own successful fragrance, and began calling herself "the most 25th inferlential [*sic*] person in the world," according to the *Independent*.[39]

Goody eventually returned to *Big Brother UK* for a celebrity edition, where she was removed by producers after Bollywood star Shilpa Shetty accused her of racism, having been told to "go back to the slums" among other remarks.[40]

"When Gordon Brown, then chancellor of the exchequer, flew to India to discuss trade, he was met by more than twenty news crews asking him about a program he had clearly never seen. In India, effigies of Goody were burned," wrote Moore.[41]

Big Brother variations around the world were able to take advantage of characters like this to generate controversy and buzz around their version of the show.

In the first season of *Big Brother UK*, a contestant named Nick Bateman was accused of cheating by his fellow contestants for attempting to coordinate nominations so that they'd fall on a specific person. They all confronted him in a scene that drew so much attention it nearly collapsed the website that hosted the live feeds. The producers removed Nick for his attempts at strategy, and he forever became known as "Nasty Nick" to the British public.

Other prospective reality show producers saw what was happening on *Big Brother* with hunger in their eyes. What if you could find these trash heroes and make shows dedicated to them? Eventually you could outpace *Big Brother* at its own game. As reality TV boomed in the early 2000s, massive hits started popping up under this new genre. Turns out, there were all kinds of personalities that could fit under this umbrella. Eventually juggernauts like *The Osbournes, The Simple Life, Duck Dynasty, Here Comes Honey Boo Boo, Keeping Up with the Kardashians,* and *Jersey Shore* started making headlines.

The format lived and died on the controversy and attention it could generate. Mark Lawson wrote in the *Guardian*, "*Big Brother*'s success was encouraged, from early on, by unusual levels of publicity. Much of the popular press…were willing to give headline coverage to the housemates and their departures, both from the show and the rules… Conventional stars also became less willing to cooperate with the tabloids… In this context, the housemates were a Red Cross food parcel dropped onto the battlefield of Wapping. They willingly behaved badly in the public domain, their actions were recorded quite legally and consensually on tape, and they were unlikely to have lawyers or PR companies trying to spin their stories in a kindlier light. Their names and faces were also immediately recognizable to readers... In fact, curiously, the combined readership of the papers reporting on *Big Brother* generally exceeded the size of the Channel 4 audience, so that some people clearly knew these fresh celebrities purely from the news coverage of them."[42]

The easy controversy fed into celebrity, which fed into more controversy—a serpent eating its own tail. But it just wasn't sustainable. Controversy can only remain controversial for so long. Lawson wrote, "The first series of *Big Brother* and the debut of its celebrity sister were brave and innovative programs, achieving a height of naturalistic interaction and depth of psychological insight that have rarely been equaled on TV. But, like a young child invited to perform an encore of a cute song, the show rapidly became too knowing and desperate to be noticed."[43]

And honestly, the other shows that the trash hero inspired were doing it better and getting more attention. *Big Brother* couldn't keep up.

Around the time that seasons 8 and 9 of *Big Brother U.S.* aired, *Big Brother UK* was seeing its lowest ratings yet and was soon canceled. Tabloids had started to move on to other topics, and there just wasn't as much buzz as there had been in the past. The show had still been performing admirably, but it seemed the metaphorical and literal writing was on the wall.

Another network decided it was worth picking up the show but didn't want the hassle of live feeds to accompany it. "Following speculation surrounding the live feed, we can confirm there will not be a 24-hour live feed from the house available online or on air," they said in a statement released to the press. "This year, we have decided to focus on the nightly highlights show and on directly engaging with the show's viewers through social media platforms... The aim is to reflect the habits of our audience today, and we believe that prioritizing social media is the way to get people involved in the show."[44]

This was an extremely unpopular decision. Live feeds had been so ubiquitous in the UK that TV remotes had a dedicated button to turn to the dedicated channel for the feeds. Ratings for the show nosedived and continued to bleed over the next seven years that they tried to keep it running. Online engagement was also at an all-time low.

This was despite a hefty amount of controversy that the series continued to generate. Russell Brand made his name doing a sideshow for *Big Brother* and was later accused of an alarming amount of sexual misconduct, some of which happened while he was working for the show.

Andrew Tate, a prolific misogynist content creator who has since been indicted on charges of rape, human trafficking, and the formation of an organized crime group to sexually exploit women, also made his name as a contestant on *Big Brother UK* back in 2016.[45]

Also in 2016, Stephen Bear won *Celebrity Big Brother UK* and was later found guilty of sex-tape offenses.[46] In 2015, former *Baywatch* actor Jeremy Jackson was kicked off the show after pulling open another contestant's dressing gown.[47]

> "Participants who seemed to have been chosen to be disliked were then edited to be detested while taking part in stunts which, for the first time in the format, appeared calculated only to humiliate."
>
> Mark Lawson[48]

This almost seems like an inevitable consequence of chasing controversy, of actively promoting behavior designed to incite outrage to grab attention. These are the times I question the existence of this show the most. This is when I was, at fifteen, watching as Evel Dick went on to win *Big Brother 8*. America had chosen for America's Player Eric Stein to attempt to make sure the man won out over his estranged daughter in the Final Two.

It's also where I was when Adam Jasinski went on to win *Big Brother 9* and within the year would be arrested for using the prize money he won on *Big Brother* to "kickstart a drug operation and bragged about selling thousands of pills to East Coast customers,"[49] alongside his fellow *Big Brother 9* contestant Matt McDonald. Adam had flown to Boston with two thousand oxycodone pills stuffed into a sock that he had hidden in his pants and attempted to sell them to a man cooperating with DEA agents.

"I'm sick. I won $500,000 and I blew it all," he reportedly told the judge.[50]

Adam was later sentenced to four years in federal prison. "Being on a reality show made it worse, just magnified his problems. It was crazy. But the casting director wants that person, the person (like Adam) that makes the show crazier," Adam's mother said to Kevin C. Shelly of *PhillyVoice*.[51]

Luckily, Adam was able to get sober after his arrest and has since written a book aimed at helping parents with children who are addicts, and he volunteers at a drug addiction treatment center.[52]

But where does that leave *Big Brother U.S.*? This felt like a turning point in the series, and the fact that these seasons had been aired so quickly in succession made the turn feel overwhelming. There are some who enjoyed the mess of *Big Brother 9*, even more who applauded Evel Dick's antics on *Big Brother 8*. But for me, it was too much. I felt as though I had lost something special. The new era of *Big Brother* had lost its identity. The game was gone; the strategy was gone. It felt like it was on the same path as *Big Brother UK*, destined to gnaw away at itself until it became a shell of what it once was.

In the spring of 2008, I turned sixteen and decided I was no longer going to watch *Big Brother*. I had outgrown it. I'd spent exactly half my life watching this show, and it was time for me to move on and spend my summer on more productive pursuits. One of my favorite directors, Danny Boyle, had recently released *Slumdog Millionaire*, and I was about to make everyone think I was a movie genius by recommending my friends see it, long before it eventually picked up Oscar buzz. So yeah, by *productive* I meant I was still obsessed with television and film. But now I was going to be intellectual about it. No more of this show that was too trashy for me to ever publicly admit I watched it.

It wasn't an idle threat either. I really had no intention of watching *Big Brother* anymore. It was part distaste for where the show had gone and part apathy for where the show might go. Gone were the days when Kaysar's success could bring a spring to my step. It had been two seasons and nearly two calendar years since I had loved *Big Brother*, basically an entire lifetime in the eyes of a sixteen-year-old. The *Big Brother 10* premiere came and went, and I didn't even know it had happened.

Having spent so long meticulously tracking the colossal web of interactions that make up this game, what's become abundantly clear to me is how often a single moment or decision can avalanche out into a whole new world of possibilities—all of it hinging, perhaps, on one fleeting moment of chance.

One player on *Big Brother Canada* was the first real target of the season, put on the block and set to go out before he ever really had a chance to play. That was until, while going to the bathroom, he happened to overhear a conversation among other players trying to form an alliance. They had forgotten to check if anyone was in there. Sharing this information changed the target that week, and player Kevin Martin ended up making a deep run in the game, got into a showmance, and became one of the stars of the season. Because of that, they brought him back a second time, and he went on to win the game. He eventually married the woman he got into a showmance with, and his story has continued from there.

I think a lot about how different his life would be if he hadn't needed to go to the bathroom at that exact time.

I think a lot about how different my life would be if I hadn't watched *Big Brother 10*.

My mom wanted me to watch. She tried to convince me after the premiere. It wasn't exactly something we shared; she didn't even know I was into the live feeds. But it was a common point of interest in a sea of distance. If anything, that made me more interested in avoiding the show altogether. She told me it was a "back-to-basics" season, with no major twists. It was true; for the first time since *Big Brother 3*, the show had a cast of all strangers, and they were willing to let the game play out instead of interfering with the formula. I didn't care. I was interested in running away from who I was and where I was. I was as lost as *Big Brother* seemed to be.

I was on an upward trajectory in high school, focusing on bettering myself and discovering who I wanted to be. But the places and people that had previously left me scarred were ever present in every area of my life. I'd found myself retreating again, just trying to keep my head down until I could escape to college.

I couldn't wait to leave home and surround myself with strangers, becoming a new person and finding my own voice. I didn't see it at the time, but I wanted *Big Brother*. The game. The experience. The allure of the fantasy the show provided. I wanted that feeling I got when I watched Dr. Will dig himself out of a hole and come out on top.

That's when my mom said something that changed the course of my life.

"I really think you'll like this season. There's a guy on it... He's like the next Dr. Will."

9

The Renaissance

"Not since the days of Dr. Will have *Big Brother* fans seen a truly ambitious mastermind pulling strings in the house."

Adam Bryant, tvguide.com[1]

The next Dr. Will.

Fans had been searching for the next Dr. Will since, well, Dr. Will. Forums lit up before season 3, wondering if there'd be "another Will" on the cast. There were certainly glimpses here and there, other players who had made their own mark in their own unique ways. Danielle Reyes crushing season 3, Jun maneuvering through season 4, Dr. Will himself running it back in season 7. But nobody seemed to scratch that same itch of lighthearted diabolical genius better than the Evil Doctor.

That is, until *Big Brother 10*.

The premiere introduced us to a player who was good-looking, full of charisma, and more diabolically strategic than anyone we'd seen in a while. He quickly started making allies and formulating a plan to secretly run the house. It was part Danielle and Jason, part Chilltown, and all kinds of exciting for the fan base.

His name was Brian Hart.

Brian was a twenty-seven-year-old telecommunication manager from San Francisco. He'd served in the air force for six years before entering the *Big Brother* house. It's this background that he used to bond with Jerry MacDonald, a seventy-five-year-old marine vet who became the first HOH of the season.

Jerry was (and still is) the oldest person ever to play *Big Brother*, and he was a huge fan of the show, having watched every season plus live feeds. Brian, on the other hand, had seen only one season, *All-Stars*. He'd seen Dr. Will and Boogie get together early and plot out their game, playing hard from the start.

Brian also found an early ally in the quiet schoolteacher and assistant football coach Dan Gheesling. Polite and courteous, the twenty-four-year-old Dan promised us that people wouldn't see him coming. Maybe not the Mike Boogie, maybe more the Jason Guy to Brian's Danielle Reyes.

The two of them teamed up with Ollie, a preacher's son who didn't drink and told them that his word was everything. The plan was simple: use Brian's connection to the HOH Jerry to influence his nominations, take out a threat, and use the week to gather strength and allies.

Jerry had been thinking about nominating Dan right away as a pawn against another player named Memphis Garrett. Memphis was a mixologist. "It's not a bartender, it's um… I'm a creator of cocktails. I'm a chef for alcoholics."[2] Memphis had won a car on the first night of the season and looked like he was going to be a big threat in the game. Quiet Dan seemed like a good pawn to put next to him.

But the plan worked perfectly: Brian used his connection to Jerry to convince him he shouldn't put Dan on the block. "My impressions of Brian were that he had been in the service," Jerry told us in the diary room, "and I looked at that as a sense of maturity and also as a sense of trust."[3]

Jerry told Brian he'd been planning to play this game for a long time and that if they wanted to play together, they'd have to be committed. Brian agreed. In the diary room he told us, "I'll keep Jerry around, but when the ship starts to sink, the rats are the first to bail."[4]

Under Brian's guidance, Jerry nominated two players who had already been involved in some drama, bodybuilder Jessie and the bold and brazen Renny, a beauty salon owner from New Orleans. The two went on the block, and none was the wiser to the fact that Brian had been behind it all. He, Dan, and Ollie laughed about it together and raised their glasses to their success. "I can't say I have control of the house, but are things moving along the direction I would like them to? Yeah, they are."[5]

This was what the show had been missing in the last couple of seasons. Brian Hart was here to play.

Brian Hart was the next Dr. Will.

Brian Hart was going to save *Big Brother*.

Brian Hart was the first person evicted from *Big Brother 10*.

> "I have enough votes to where I can do whatever the fuck I want. And nobody's going to have the balls to take me down."
>
> Brian Hart[6]

It was almost Shakespearean. Bodybuilder Jessie won the veto and planned to remove himself from the block. Brian decided the backup plan should be pulling the trigger on Memphis the mixologist after all. He talked with Jerry, and the plan was in place for Memphis to be the replacement nominee.

As the next Dr. Will, Brian Hart had all the arrogance that came with it. He started walking around the house as if he owned it, unaware of how he was coming off to a cast of strategically savvy players.

One of these players was Libra Thompson—dubbed a "stanch Obama supporter" in her bio,[7] she had graduated magna cum laude from Rice University[8] and was not there to sit back and let others have free rein of the game.

With Jessie coming off the block, Libra and her allies were concerned about what the plan for his replacement would be. They asked Brian what he thought was going to happen that week, and he confidently told them, "This week, Memphis is going home. You guys need to be ready for that. It's just the way it's going to have to be. Then next week…Renny will be gone. That will be my promise to you."

"Did you see him?" Libra asked the other women in the room after Brian left. "I felt like he was trying to be a Dr. Will flashback… He's doing that whole mind control bullshit! They want to take out the stronger boys. So, if we do their dirty work for them? That's like birthday cake!"[9]

This sentiment spread like wildfire around the house. Brian Hart was trying to be the next Dr. Will! The hammer really fell when Ollie, the preacher's son who said his word was everything, spilled Brian's entire plan to the rest of the house. Ollie had fallen for another player, named April, and like the rats Brian described, decided to bail on Brian's sinking ship to join his future showmance.

In an act of mob justice the likes of which had never been seen before on *Big Brother*, Libra organized and led a plan to convince Jerry to turn on Brian. April slyly asked Jerry if she could use his bathroom up in the HOH room and led him away from Brian and Dan upstairs, where the rest of the house was waiting for him in ambush. They pulled him into the HOH room and told him he needed to put Brian on the block instead of Memphis. Though he was initially reluctant, they collectively were able to convince Jerry that Brian was just using him and trying to play the whole house.

At the veto ceremony, Jerry spoke before making his replacement nomination. "This is a rather difficult chore for me to undertake," he said. "I formed an alliance and I wanted this alliance to be loyal to the end, but I found out that this person that I went with had other alliances. It got all over the house what was going on. Everybody got together…and I was informed of this. They have chosen who they want to see put up for nomination and leave the house. And I'm going to honor that. I'm going to nominate…you, Brian."

He later told us in the diary room, "If I had not nominated Brian, I would have paid the price. So I made my mind up that I would sacrifice him to save myself."[10]

Just like that, Brian was toast. The next Dr. Will shut down before making it through a single week. *Big Brother 10* did not play around.

That first week was indicative of the level of gameplay that season 10 brought to the table. This wasn't a cast that would be easily manipulated. They were savvy and hungry for the win. To top it off, there was nothing getting in the way of playing hard, no twists, no secret partners, just pure *Big Brother* strategy. A CBS 2 headline read, "*Big Brother 10* Back with Less Twist, More Scheme."[11]

Big Brother 10 is famous for a few things, but its biggest claim to fame is that it's widely considered to be the best season the show ever produced. It fires on all cylinders: the gameplay, the drama, the cast—it just doesn't miss and has something for everyone.

Here I was, sixteen and giving the show a shot because I'd heard it had the next Dr. Will. Before I knew it, he was gone. I was impressed by the cast, but I couldn't help but wonder what could have been. What potential did Brian Hart's exit leave on the table?

Brian did try to dial it back before he left. He focused on his charm and charisma, organizing puppet shows and winning people back over. Before long, he had some allies back and almost had the votes to turn things around for himself. But by the end of the week, it became clear that all hope was lost and those allies jumped ship again, not willing to stand out from the pack and put a target on their own backs by voting for Brian to stay.

The votes came in one by one. Brian, Brian, Brian, Brian.

It looked to be unanimous. But one player went against the crowd. Brian's quiet ally Dan, the schoolteacher, cast the sole dissenting vote to keep Brian.

Big mistake.

In a game that's all about being in the majority, voting in the minority sets you apart from the rest of the house and puts a target on your back. Dan was choosing to be loyal to Brian against his own interests. Ollie, Jerry, and all of Brian's other former allies did the smart thing: they played for themselves and cut ties when it became clear Brian would sink them all. But Dan foolishly stuck his neck out for him in a spot where his sole vote wouldn't have mattered anyway.

After Brian walked out the door, he told Julie in his exit interview, "I don't know if [Dan's] conscience will allow him to do what he needs to do to win."[12]

Inside the house, Dan looked to be near tears. "I've still got a lot of fight in me, but I'm going to have to get very creative," he said.[13]

After Jessie the bodybuilder won the week 2 HOH, Dan had to explain why he'd gone against the grain: "I gave Brian my word, and even though I was exposed and hung out to dry, I still gave my word. So that's why I voted [the way I did]."[14]

"Dan...yeah, he was on the other side, but he straight came up to me and said, 'I'll give you that same loyalty,'" Jessie described in the diary room. "I can take that into consideration to further myself in the game. I mean, that's huge... I have no reason to not have Dan in my alliance. He will stick by it, literally, all the way until the end."[15]

Somehow, sticking by Brian until the end seemed to be working in Dan's favor. His steadfast loyalty was a valuable asset in the game, and crucially, he was able to use it as a bargaining chip with the other players—which was *exactly* what he had intended from the start.

Dan was playing possum. He intentionally set himself apart from everyone else, claiming he now had nobody because he was *too* loyal.

"I'm not down and out by any means," Dan said. "I'm about to start chipping away at the other Houseguests piece by piece."[16]

While the Houseguests and the audience alike watched the rise and fall of Brian Hart, "The Next Dr. Will," we all missed the quiet schoolteacher standing right behind him. And when you go back to watch those first few episodes, it's clear to see:

Dan Gheesling was the one who pulled in Brian, not the other way around.

Dan Gheesling sent Brian to talk to Jerry.

Dan Gheesling was the one pulling *Brian's* strings the whole time.

And when Brian let the power get to his head, Dan was the only one clever enough to realize that if the rats are the first to bail when the ship starts to sink, maybe the best way to separate himself from Brian's Dr. Will label was, counterintuitively, to go down with the ship.

Dan hadn't just survived Brian's eviction, he'd *weaponized* it.

This was America's introduction to the man who would eventually become known as the best *Big Brother* player of all time.

He told us we wouldn't see him coming.

This was Dan Gheesling.

> "*Big Brother* is a lot like poker. As long as you just have one chip, you have a chance to win the whole thing."
>
> Dan Gheesling[17]

Dan's first *Big Brother* con was on the producers themselves. In the first episode of season 10, Dan's intro package includes him packing an American flag into his bag, saying, "We wouldn't even have a flag to wave in the air if liberals were in power in this time of war." Smash cut against Libra's intro package saying, "I am an Obama supporter in Bush land. It seems like I'm the only one that knows what's going on around here!"[18]

The intention couldn't be more clear. Dan the conservative Catholic schoolteacher was meant to clash with liberals like Libra. In his casting interviews, Dan told them that if Hillary Clinton became president, he'd move out of the country. He was loud and abrasive, and he clashed with producers and CBS executives alike throughout his casting process. He was going to make a splash on the show. He was going to be controversial. In many ways, Dan was meant to be the *Big Brother U.S.* version of a trash hero.

While promoting the season, Allison Grodner said, "It's going to be interesting to see people that come from such opposite worlds living together… We really do have our most diverse group ever."[19]

Except, the second he walked into the house, they saw an entirely different Dan. He was quiet and reserved, never spoke about politics, and quickly made a friendship with Stephen—a gay man on the cast. They tried to turn that friendship into a segment for the show, but this was no Kent and Bunky—Dan was just not who they thought he was. There's a reason for that.

The story begins all the way back in 2001, when a seventeen-year-old Dan had just finished watching Dr. Will win *Big Brother 2*. "Here's this dude who just won half a million dollars, not being faster, stronger, or tougher than anyone. He just understood people and how to move chess pieces around… That was a huge inspiration."[20]

As Dan describes it, he was particularly susceptible to influences at that time, really looking for something outside of his family core to identify with. "And for whatever reason, right, wrong, or different, I identified with how Will played the game and really looked at him as like, this dude is doing things in a completely different way… I deployed some of that stuff in high school."[21]

Like Eric Stein, Dan was a big fan of the show. But where Eric had studied the game, Dan *embodied* it. He was the vanguard for a new generation of players, people who had grown up with the show, who'd had it impact their very personalities during a formative period of their lives. *Big Brother* was no longer just a mirror to society, reflecting back what it saw; it was shaping the reality it reflected.

Of course it was. It always had been. You can't look into a mirror without being impacted by what you see. Do you like what you see? Can you improve on it? Are you ashamed of it? In the time since *Big Brother* started airing, reality TV had blossomed into an entire genre that was now a staple in cultures around the world, with many of the shows in the genre having direct inspiration from the characters, concepts, and themes of *Big Brother*.

As the show started casting players who'd grown up watching the show, its impact became more distilled. Dan Gheesling was a product of *Big Brother* and would go on to define what the show meant for a whole new generation after him.

Back in 2001, Dan had watched Dr. Will win season 2 and vowed that he would someday win this game that had so inspired him. With four years before he could apply as a twenty-one-year-old, Dan didn't wait idly by; he dedicated his time to preparing for *Big Brother*.

"I spent the next four years trying to position myself in the best possible way to pull the trigger on the application the minute I turned twenty-one. From the age of seventeen to twenty, I would spend time every week thinking about how I could get on the show. I cannot recall a time when getting on *Big Brother* was not important to me," Dan wrote in his book *How to Get on Reality TV*. "I would read through interviews online, scour the internet forums for casting experiences, and do whatever I could to uncover any information about the casting process."[22]

After four years of waiting, Dan finally was able to make an audition video and apply for *Big Brother 6*. Through his research, he knew what kind of video to make and how to spin it. He needed an angle, so he played up the fact that he was working for a football team in college. In the video he was loud and confident in a way that wasn't quite accurate to his everyday personality. "I'm inherently a shy person," he told me. "Growing up I was very shy… At a party, I'm at the edges, maybe talking to one or two people."[23]

But the video worked. He was brought to casting semifinals and quickly advanced to the finals for season 6.

There were two problems, though. One was that for some weird reason, they kept asking him about his friends and what kinds of personalities they had, asking for names and photos. Of course, season 6 was the season of secret partners, so it may not have been the fit for Dan regardless. However, the other issue was the timing. Dan had gotten on a scholarship trip to Italy, something he could never have afforded otherwise, and the trip was exactly the same time as casting finals. Bolstered with the confidence of having made it so far on his first try, Dan decided to decline the offer to go to finals that year, planning instead to go for it the following year.

The following year was *All-Stars*, which meant no new players were cast. Then in season 8, they never even responded to his application. No rejection, just nothing. He feared he had made the biggest mistake of his life in turning down the opportunity for season 6.

Then came the writers' strike and the surprise winter season for *Big Brother 9*. With less time to work, casting rummaged through their contacts and gave Dan a call, inviting him to submit an application. After submitting, though, he was rejected, only to then get another call a month later from a desperate casting producer. Season 9's twist was that there would be a secret couple playing the game, and the couple had dropped out. Dan had a girlfriend at the time, and they wanted him and his girlfriend to fly to LA to take part in finals. Dan's girlfriend had no interest in being on the show, so despite initially agreeing, she turned it down. Dan desperately tried to get casting to take him solo, but they rejected him again.

It had now been nearly eight years since Dan vowed to be on the show and three years of casting trials. Three years of tough decisions, close calls, and a process that treated you like a star while you were in favor and then would ghost you the second they decided they didn't want you anymore. Dan was tired of it.

"The Season 9 fiasco was an emotionally tough one for me. What it did allow me to do was sit back and analyze what the heck went on with the casting process. There was no rhyme or reason to the process nor did there seem to be any loyalty," Dan wrote in his book. "This was the first time I realized that I was a puppet in the casting process game, and the Casting Producers could pull whatever strings they wanted at any time, and they didn't owe me a thing… No longer did I see a straightforward interview process. The casting process was now a game; it just took me three years to finally figure it out. At last, I was ready to play the casting game by my rules."[24]

For season 10, Dan went full *Big Brother*. Instead of just sending in an application video, he reached out to some of the staff he'd met through the casting process, buttering them up and asking for advice on how to proceed. "Let me know since you RUN the casting biz," he'd write.[25] The strategy worked: he had an in for semifinals. From there, he ramped up his cocky persona from a seven to a ten.

He also tried to read what the interviewers were looking for. After years of going through the process, he saw that casting was trying to fill specific spots, sometimes for twists or themes and sometimes just for archetypes or to manufacture conflict between the players. It wasn't long before Dan recognized what they were trying to get from him in his semifinal interview. The man interviewing him was asking about the upcoming election. Who would he vote for? What were his thoughts on Hillary Clinton?

"Against my normal everyday judgment, I let my exaggerated

personality take over. 'If she was elected, I would move out of the country!' I yelled. [The casting producer] must have laughed for two minutes straight as I ranted about how the country was going to be worn away by liberals," Dan wrote in *How to Get on Reality TV*. "To say I believed everything I said would be a complete and utter lie, but I did not care, because right then and there, I found a trigger point and slant on my personality that he liked."[26]

It worked. He finally made it to finals in LA, where he was brought before a panel of CBS executives who grilled him about his political views, trying to get him to break character, wanting to make sure he'd really be this aggressive and confrontational in the house. He never broke.

Just like that Dan had finally made it onto the show, where his aggressive, political persona evaporated into thin air, instead becoming the quiet, reserved, loyal-to-a-fault player his fellow contestants came to know him as—at least at first.

> "My alliance is totally imploded. If we were a city, the only thing that would be standing would be myself, the former mayor of the town. And right now I'm searching through the rubble."
>
> Dan Gheesling[27]

Following Brian's eviction, Dan made a number of counterintuitive moves that set him up for success moving forward in the game. First was his vote to keep Brian as a show of "loyalty" in a house full of people who were looking to target anyone associated with him. Second was his willingness to be a pawn on the block for the bodybuilder Jessie's week 2 HOH.

These broke the first two laws of *Big Brother* strategy.

The first lesson *Big Brother* taught its players was that pawns go home. Dan wasn't worried.

The second big lesson the show taught was to always use the veto on yourself. Dan intentionally threw the veto competition while he was on the block, refusing the opportunity to save himself with the power. "A lot of people think it would be insane to throw your only chance, but you know what? It's so insane that it just might work."[28]

Dan *wanted* to be on the block. He hoped to cultivate the perception of a lost, loyal guy who wasn't even good at competitions. It was a massive gamble, one that Dan would never willingly take again in his time playing the game. But after a disastrous first week, it was exactly what was required for him to get his foot back in the door.

The strategy paid off. He stayed unanimously in week 2 while Stephen, a former Brian ally, was sent home. In week 3, Dan had garnered enough favor around the house to avoid touching the block entirely as the last of Brian's former allies was taken out of the game. Ollie, Jerry, and Dan were the only three players left to have any remaining association with the former "Next Dr. Will."

Dan hadn't just been sitting back through these weeks, though; by the fourth week he had successfully infiltrated the majority—the people who had forced Brian on the block and subsequently sent out the allies who tried to distance themselves from him in the following weeks. It was a cast of gamers, and the large group had been splintering from the start. By positioning himself as a valuable (and loyal) ally to pick up in the game, Dan was able to court both sides of what was becoming a split house, all while whispering poison in the ears of key players on both sides to keep them at each other's throats. It was Jun's game all over again, except nobody was able to see what Dan was doing.

There were now two factions both vying for Dan's single swing vote for the eviction. On the block was the bodybuilder Jessie, who had helped bring Dan into the fold, seeing him as a loyal, trustworthy player. The other nominee was Memphis, the big competition threat and target of Dan's alliance in the first week. Three votes were there to keep Jessie; three votes were locked in to keep Memphis.

Dan was promising both sides he would be voting with them, which meant that when the vote came in, one side was going to be very upset with him. Not typically a situation you want to put yourself in, but Dan had little choice in the matter. The producers had decided to bring back the America's Player twist for just a week, and Dan was chosen for the title role. He didn't actually control his vote that week—America did—and he needed to make sure he was well positioned on both sides depending on which way America forced him to go.

Luckily for Dan, he was popular with the audience, and when he talked to the cameras asking for America to allow him to vote out Jessie, they agreed. The vote was read, Jessie left the house, and the players all stood around in silence, with those Dan had betrayed seething with anger.

"When the vote came down four to three, everyone looked at me. I put myself in a very awkward position. No matter what I did, or what America did, someone was going to be mad at me. So I've been preparing for this," Dan said in the diary room. "In the kitchen there was so much tension, if you tried to cut it with a knife, the knife would break. I just tried to look at the floor and not make eye contact. I felt they could have killed me with their looks."[29]

Jessie spoke to Julie and told her, "I had a lot of faith in [Dan]... He just made probably about four different people upset in there... Kid doesn't even go to church on Sunday and he's Catholic."[30]

Jessie wasn't wrong about people being upset with Dan. Inside the house, Jessie's closest ally had just won the HOH and screamed, "Traitors! This is for you, Jessie! I'm going to get them, don't worry about it."[31] She later says to the cameras, "I'm going to get him, Jessie. I promise you."[32]

Dan had gambled again, and this time the cards were not in his favor. His carefully crafted image of a loyal nonplayer was gone. Dan had just reintroduced himself to the house as a traitor and a liar, and the people he had just betrayed were now in power. It looked like there was no way out for him this time.

"Put down that Bible, put down that cross. Because I don't even think he's a schoolteacher."

"He needs to be praying."

"He's a disgrace."

"He's probably burning right now."

"I won't ever talk to him again."

"Burn in hell."

"Dan deserves more than just being put on the block. In my house he will always be known as Judas."[33]

That last line came from Jerry, the seventy-five-year-old who had turned on Brian in the first week. Dan had gotten back into Jerry's good graces after the events of the first week. Dan had given Jerry his word that he'd vote to keep Jessie, and Jerry had taken that to the bank, reassuring his allies that he had Dan's word and therefore they were all set. After Dan's betrayal, nobody was more upset with Dan than Jerry.

But Dan *had* prepared for this. As the house exploded into chaos after Jessie's eviction, Dan ran to his bed and put his face into his pillow. He was determined to avoid getting into a fight with anyone and had a new persona he needed to craft in order to survive the next portion of the game.

"Why? Why'd you do it, Dan?" asked the new HOH Michelle, who was on the warpath and looking to avenge Jessie.[34]

Looking pitiful, and speaking with the voice of a little boy who knew he'd done something wrong, Dan replied, "I don't know. I don't have an answer for you. I'm embarrassed."

Most players respond to conflict by playing defense. They'll make attempts to justify their decision in order to win the argument. Everyone who was still out in the kitchen fighting was doing it that very moment. Dan had no interest in arguing at all. He admitted fault and took whatever heat the aggressor had for him. For Michelle, it was disarming.

"I just can't believe you would do that," she said. "For them? They're making you do all their dirty work… I don't know why you would go on that side, man. Jessie never did nothing for you but stick up for you."

"I mean, you know I'm not a good player in this game," he responded. "I haven't won anything. And I know that you liked me, and I know that I definitely jeopardized that."

"They're playing you like they're playing everyone else, Dan," she replied, "but not no more. You want to talk to me later? Talk to me, OK?"[35]

She walked out, leaving Dan still lying on his bed, his face buried in his arm. As soon as the door closed, he slowly picked his head up, looked right into the camera, smirked, and then lowered himself back down into his dejected position.

The audience was obsessed. "Tonight on *Big Brother*, it's all about Dan. Who likes him? Who hates him? Who suspects him of duplicity?" wrote William Hammon of *Reality News Online*.[36] Fans had already enjoyed Dan's unconventional tactics and antics in the house;

they loved watching him accomplish his America's Player task of having to hug Jessie for ten seconds. But they really seemed to fall in love with how he responded to the fallout of the Jessie vote. In some ways, there was almost a collective guilt. We the audience had forced him to vote Jessie out and had caused all the heat he was catching for it, being called Judas, people going after his religion, and he was just lying there and taking it. You can't help but feel for the guy.

Jerry told him in front of all the other players that he would always be known as Judas in his house, and Dan's response was simply "I understand."[37]

The side Dan picked with his vote seemed to echo that same sentiment America had at the time. Viewers felt bad that Dan was taking all this heat for *them*, when they were the ones who had (in their minds) convinced him to vote to keep Memphis.

It certainly must have been a tough thing for Dan to deal with emotionally. In the diary room, he told us, "You know, I don't know if things in this house can get any...can get any... *better* for me! This is incredible! This is the one thing that I could have asked for. Jerry has called me out in front of everyone...and it's created so much sympathy for me I can't even contain it!"[38]

This was around the time that the audience realized Dan didn't really experience the game in the same way that most other players did. He had grown up with the show; it was part of who he was. He had checked his emotions at the door and played the game as if it was, well, a game.

Despite being one of the most cutthroat players the show has ever seen, Dan never came at anyone personally. It's hard to explain how rare that is for reality TV if you're not an avid viewer. Dan held few grudges, he got in no fights, he never insulted anyone, and it's not like he was a saint or anything; it just was only ever about the game for him. Somehow this resonated with an audience usually thirsty for blood and drama as if they're the screaming attendees of the Colosseum that is modern-day reality television.

But it wasn't just sympathy that Dan was relying on to get through the week. As I mentioned, he had been preparing. The player Dan saved that week, Memphis, was his true secret weapon. Dan leveraged the fact that he had been the swing vote that saved Memphis to help develop a strong bond with him, one they kept hidden from the rest of the house. After Memphis stayed, he and Dan formalized their relationship into a secret alliance they called the "Renegades." Dan used the relationship Memphis still had with Michelle along with Dan's ploy of being a weak player manipulated into doing bad things to avoid the block that week. This was despite Michelle's initial vow of vengeance on the man who'd taken out Jessie.

Dan's work proved incredibly effective, and by the end of the week he found himself in the ludicrous position of being the swing vote for the second time in a row, this time saving his ally Keesha over Libra, the woman who had clocked Brian way back in week 1.

Dan and Memphis then branched out and started secretly accumulating allies. Like Danielle and Jason's hidden alliance before them, their secrecy gave them ample room to maneuver around the other players without their realizing they were being repositioned to suit the Renegades.

> "I had enough of the game being me sitting back. It's time to score some points."
>
> Dan Gheesling[39]

The story of Dan's time on *Big Brother* could be described as "How many times can the worst-case scenario happen?" particularly when it comes to competition outcomes. He always did want to play a game that didn't rely on competitions, and he often threw them, but his luck regarding who *did* win them was consistently terrible.

What do you do if you can't win competitions on your own merit? As Dan himself said, you just have to understand people and how to move chess pieces around. In week 7, he found himself competing against his nemesis Ollie for an HOH that could make or break the game for himself and Memphis.

Ollie and Dan were both hanging in an endurance competition. All the other players had exhausted themselves, dropping out of the comp. Dan found himself in a predicament. His entire game revolved around the perception that he was a weak player. Winning HOH would not only break part of that perception but also reveal where his true loyalties lay. At the same time, he couldn't afford to let Ollie win and continue to lose his allies.

Ollie was determined to win. "There's no way I'm dropping to the ground. This is life and death for me. If I lose I go home, and I'm not going to get this close and quit," he said.[40]

After nearly four hours of hanging with water pouring down on their heads, Dan was starting to fade. So he got creative.

"The first deal I offered him was telling him, hey man, you're safe… That didn't work. He needed something else. And that's when the gears in my head started spinning," Dan told us in the diary room. "I'm thinking to myself, is there a way I can still seem weak *and* win HOH? Yes, of course. What I need to do is give almost all the HOH power to Ollie so the blood this week will be on his hands."

After some negotiation, Dan offered Ollie a two-for-one deal.

If Ollie dropped from the competition and gave Dan the win, he could keep himself and one other person safe, choose one of the two nominees, and choose the replacement nominee if the veto was used.

"So the deal simply comes down to this: Dan gets to pick one nominee. The rest of the responsibilities belong to me. I call all the shots after that one nomination Dan picks. So, you be the judge. Who gets the better end of the deal?" Ollie asks us before he drops from the competition. "Ladies and gentlemen, you're currently looking at the week seven HOH. It's me, Ollie. I just don't have the title...but right now I'm calling the shots."

Dan's explanation? "I don't think there's any doubt I made one of the worst deals in *Big Brother* history, and I couldn't be more excited about it. I feel very confident that it's going to all work out for me in the end; otherwise I wouldn't have done it!"[41]

Ollie's stipulations were that he wanted Dan to protect Michelle and nominate Memphis. At this point the house was divided. On one side were Ollie, Jerry, and Michelle, while on the other were Dan, Keesha, Renny, and Memphis. However, Dan and Memphis were able to hide both their connection to each other and the depth of their connection to Keesha and Renny. And it was Dan's weak, easily manipulated persona that allowed Ollie to think that he could walk all over him on his HOH week with this awful deal.

At this point, you've read the story of Kaysar and Jennifer and you've heard me talk about Dan's ruthless game savvy, so it's probably not difficult to guess what happened next for Ollie and his "deal" when he tried to get Dan to put his closest (secret) ally on the block.

Dan honored the deal. He put Memphis on the block.

Once again Dan had broken another fundamental rule of *Big*

Brother. With Memphis on the block, Dan risked the absolutely disastrous outcome of having his closest ally be voted out on his own HOH, leaving Dan completely exposed the following week.

"These nominations are a calculated risk," Dan explained to us in the diary room. "My goals were to transfer some of the power to Ollie and hide the tracks of the hidden Renegade alliance, because who in their right mind would nominate one of their alliance members? But with any risk, there's a chance of it blowing up in my face."[42]

Memphis was not pleased and did not struggle to play up how pissed off he was at Dan for making this move, which really did do wonders to hide their alliance. Dan being Dan, he even went as far as to call Memphis a "Renegade" in his nomination speech as a wink to both Memphis and the audience.

If Ollie hadn't been convinced that Dan was going to honor the deal before, he was certain of it now. Why else would Dan follow through in nominating Memphis and pissing him off in the process? Ollie felt that he was running the show.

The trick to this for Dan was that with Keesha and Renny as locked-in votes, he was confident Memphis would stay regardless of what happened, but there was an even greater plan in place as well.

Memphis ended up winning the veto, which meant that Ollie expected Dan to replace Memphis with a player of his choice. Ollie wanted Dan's ally Keesha on the block.

"I made a deal with Ollie that's too good to be true. He thinks he's going to be able to pick the replacement nominee. In no way, Ollie, am I going to send home some of my own alliance to appease you. That's just not going to work."[43]

Dan was at yet another turning point in his game. First he played up the perception of a quiet, loyal player. After his betrayal of Jessie, he turned that into a weak, easily manipulated player. But now he was about to commit another massive backstab, and he wasn't going to be able to hold on to his weak persona any more.

"The whole 'weak' strategy at this point is a wash," he explained in the diary room. "No one's dumb enough to believe I'm a weak player in this game at this point. I've got to change gears and figure out what that gear is."[44]

What he eventually landed on was a throwback to the very first strategic winner of *Big Brother*. As was true with Dr. Will before him, it was time for Dan to lean into the role of being hated, a losing finalist who the jury would never vote for. This was important because he had just tested the limits of his alliances by putting Memphis on the block, so he had to make sure there was additional incentive for them to still want to bring him to the end. On top of that, he wanted to cause as much chaos and confusion as possible. This brings us to the veto ceremony.

"Everyone in here knows I like to have some fun," Dan said in his speech. "I have fun by playing games. So right now we're going to play a game. A very high-stakes game. And I like to call that 'Replacement Nominee Roulette.'"[45]

At the ceremony, Dan said he wanted to play a game where everyone names their target, and if they don't name their target, they go up on the block themselves. According to his plan, each of them named each other as targets, further dividing the house into two sides.

After this ridiculous display, Dan finished the ceremony with a flourish. "Now the thing about anytime when you gamble, you're taking a risk. And in this house someone has gambled with someone else's safety. Unfortunately, you better know who's making the bet for you. In this case, Ollie, you lost the bet. Michelle, go on the block."[46]

Then, I swear to you, he put on his shades, walked away, and gave a shrug to Ollie, who was still reeling from the betrayal.

With Michelle going home and his allies locked back in, Dan was set up well for the endgame. But before we get there, we need to talk about one more thing.

> "I swear to God. If I find out he's a fucking plant... Do you think I'm stupid? Does it have 'stupid' written on my head? I'm telling you. If you don't think that I know what's going on here, you've got another thing coming."
>
> Michelle Costa[47]

We've established by now that Dan was an unconventional player who broke all the rules of the game and made consistently counterintuitive maneuvers. This caused so much chaos and confusion for the other players that throughout the season a conspiracy theory began to gain traction.

Dan was a plant. He was not a real player.

After Dan orchestrated Replacement Nominee Roulette, Michelle and Ollie became entirely convinced that this theory was true. Dan was some kind of production plant put into the game to cause drama. There was no other explanation for his gameplay and behavior. None of it made sense.

"There are different things that leave me to believe he's a plant. He's definitely not a regular Houseguest," Ollie explained. "There's not a person in this world that would do half the things Dan has done and have a goal to win half a million dollars."[48]

To their credit, Dan *was* America's Player for a week, but suspicions had been sprouting up prior to that and solidified well after he had finished the role. I bring this up to show just how revolutionary and unique Dan was as a player. His fellow contestants literally couldn't believe he was even real.

Matt Richenthal of tvfanatic.com wrote, "Dan Gheesling has become the star of *Big Brother 10*. He is playing the game of *Big Brother* on a different level."[49]

After being evicted, Michele explained to Julie, "I think he [Dan] might be a plant in the house, personally. I think there's something more to Dan than meets the eye. One plus one does not equal two to Dan… What he did made himself look better in everybody's eyes and made everybody hate each other."

Julie then informed her that Dan was not a plant, just a regular player like everyone else.

"Oh my God… Then he's crazy!" was Michele's response.[50]

Dan was now, for the first time, in the majority and held all the power that a majority does. The strength of his position echoed that of Maggie back in *Big Brother 6*, with her central positioning in the Friendship alliance. The only thing left standing in Dan's way was seventy-five-year-old Jerry, who had called him Judas.

So of course Jerry won the next HOH.

Memphis had been genuinely pissed off about being nominated during the Replacement Nominee Roulette charade, which was great cover for their next scheme to survive the week: trick Jerry into thinking Memphis could be relied on to help take Dan out of the game.

With nobody else on his side, Jerry proposed a Final Two with Memphis and kept him off the block that week with a promise that Memphis would not use the veto on Dan if he won it. With Memphis off the block, he was now free to win the veto and save Dan, protecting the Renegades from this worst-case scenario.

And that's exactly what happened.

Dan and Memphis evicted Renny over Keesha and proceeded to the Final Four. This was where Dr. Will and Mike Boogie famously screwed up by approaching the other two players as a duo, a mistake Dan was not going to make. He decided to nominate Memphis *again* alongside Jerry, "proving" his loyalty to Keesha and allowing Memphis to get back into Jerry's good graces after he used the veto on Dan the previous week. Memphis was playing into the fact that Dan had once again betrayed him, which Jerry ate up, while Dan was playing up how he had to betray Memphis to keep his word to Keesha, who appreciated that Dan had always stuck by her.

This was important, because whoever wins the veto at the Final Four has the sole decision for who to evict. Will and Mike found themselves powerless when Janelle won the veto at the Final Four because Erika was able to expose that Chilltown was playing them both.

The Renegades were set up differently, as Dan explains: "Whoever comes up with the win in the veto competition will decide who goes home this week. The thing that's great for the Renegades is the fact that if Keesha or Jerry comes up with a veto win, I can influence Keesha…and Memphis can influence Jerry."[51]

In the Final Four veto competition, Dan crushed. He was miles ahead of Memphis, Keesha, and Jerry. It seemed as though all the setup was unnecessary because the competition was securely in Dan's hands. But Dan had one more gamble up his sleeve. As he stood at the top of the competition, at the precipice of victory, he looked over at how his competitors were doing and saw that Memphis had a small lead over Keesha.

So Dan waited. He intentionally got the final question wrong over and over while Memphis and Keesha battled it out to catch up. And for one last time, Dan threw a competition. This time it was to Memphis, who finally edged out Keesha, a much stronger competitor than Jerry, to win the Final Four veto.

By throwing the veto, Dan forced Memphis to be the ultimate decision-maker when they decided to stab Keesha in the back and bring Jerry to the Final Three with them instead. Dan knew Keesha well, and when she figured out that Memphis planned to evict her, she was predictably furious.

"I can tell, Memphis. I can tell by the look on your face… I didn't get this far in the game by *not* being able to read people," she told him. "Whoever sends me out of here better not think they're getting my vote. That's for damn sure. Better not think I'm not going to do everything in my world to change their minds in that Jury House too… After everything you're going to send me out of this house? And you're keeping *Jerry*?"[52]

Dan claimed to her that he didn't want her to go. It was all Memphis. Typically, this would be a risky maneuver. If Memphis caught Dan trying to court jury votes like that behind his back, that could be disastrous for Dan. Cleverly though, Dan convinced Memphis that it was a good idea for the both of them because it allowed Memphis to look like he was honoring his Final-Two deal with Jerry against Dan's wishes.

Dan milked this opportunity as much as he could. He was going to get Keesha's jury vote anyway, but with her this upset at Memphis and thinking that Dan was on her side, he was able to safely talk to her about how she could help him with other jury members once she was out of the house. The two of them agreed that Memphis would be the better person to sit in the end with, because Jerry was too well liked by the other side of the house. By the time she left, she was a full-fledged sleeper agent entering the jury to make sure Dan won the game.

"Guys, this wasn't an easy decision at all," Memphis said, standing in front of Keesha and Jerry before casting his sole vote. "I look at this game as a business plan, and I've chosen to evict Keesha."[53]

After another week of fake fighting while competing in the final three HOH, Dan came out on top, evicting Jerry and taking Memphis to the Final Two, where the two of them were to be questioned by the jury.

Season 10 was the final season to have a particular style of jury questioning. The jurors would come together to discuss the Final Two, then spend an hour questioning the two of them in a one-way video call. After the questions, the jurors would be individually sequestered for a few days before they cast their vote on finale night. Starting in season 11, much to the dismay of nearly every *Big Brother* fan, producers decided to change this format to have all of this happen live on the finale. The end result of this decision has been over fifteen years of bland jury Q&A segments, limited to mere minutes and tightly scripted for live television. I personally find it to be one of the worst formatting decisions the show has ever made, and it honestly baffles me that they continue making the mistake year after year. But that's beside the point.

In season 10, there was a lengthy Q&A filled with drama as the jurors interrogated Dan and Memphis about their various betrayals. They'd come to realize that they'd all been played by the two men. Keesha had done good work for Dan in the jury, and even those Keesha had had trouble reaching were at least impressed with his forethought to have sent her to the jury as his agent.

Most of the jury felt that Dan had played the better game and was the true "puppet master" of the season.[54] The sticking point for many of them was Replacement Nominee Roulette. It felt unnecessary and cruel, designed to make them look like fools. They were leaning in Dan's direction, but that stunt could jeopardize his win.

Dan knew he had to address this point, so he waited until his final speech to the jurors to drop his final scam of the season.

"As I stand here before you, I think back to where we were before this game even started. I walked through the door, and I saw a lot of big personalities," he said. "Some tough physical competitors, some athletes with strong wills, some intelligent people. And then I realized, you know, that I don't excel in any of those areas. So how am I going to win this game? I thought to myself, I'm going to have to be more creative. Try to outthink people if I can. Everything I did in this game I did for a reason. I aligned myself with Memphis. Memphis is not going to do anything that doesn't benefit him. What I tried to do with Replacement Nominee Roulette was upset Ollie and Michelle. I needed them to dislike me. Did it go overboard? Possibly. But I needed to get some dislike to me in the Jury House so Memphis would still take me should I get trapped in that position."[55]

"Unbelievable," Michelle declared with honest incredulity.

"Maybe you can set aside your emotions and vote...who you think played this game as a better player. I want to let you guys know that I enjoyed getting to know all of you personally. And thanks for a great summer."

"He's a good speaker," Libra commented.[56]

A good speaker indeed—especially because it was an outright lie. The real reason for Replacement Nominee Roulette *was* a little less noble. "You know, Replacement Nominee Roulette, that is probably the one time I took it a little over the edge... Let's just say it got a little out of hand in dedication to Brian," Dan told Oscar Dahl of *BuddyTV*. "I never forgot—I didn't want to make this about revenge, and it really wasn't. But you know Brian—Ollie took a shot at Brian and me, and I wanted to take care of that for Brian and I think I did that. However, if you look back at the jury speech, I addressed the Replacement Nominee Roulette. Although at the time it didn't have any strategy behind it, I just did try and pour some rhetoric over it and a little BS to make it seem like there was strategy... Yeah, it was a little lie. It was not true."[57]

Of course there were still some kernels of truth in there. Dan did actively play up how hated he was on the jury to keep his allies close; he just apparently came up with that particular plan *after* he put on the big show.

The lie was more than enough. As the votes started rolling in, even Jerry, who had famously called Dan "Judas" and spent most of the summer trying to get Dan back for his many betrayals, voted for Dan. When casting his vote, Jerry cryptically said, "This is for the person who always showed me kindness."[58] He later went on to explain, "Dan was the guy who said 'Goodnight, Jerry' to me every night in the house." Another juror agreed, "Dan would ask about my family, and ask me about me and my life."[59]

Despite everything, Dan always went out of his way to treat his fellow contestants with respect and kindness. That distinction became important when it was time for the jury to vote.

Dan won *Big Brother 10* with a unanimous jury vote, the first time that had ever happened in the history of the show. His game that season became known as the first "perfect game," having had zero eviction votes cast against him all season and then winning with every jury vote.

> "One of the things I'm proud of, especially now that I have two sons, is that I know I'm going to be OK with them watching the show. I'm not going to have to say, 'Hey look, Dad did this, but you can't do this...' I'm always proud of the fact that I never went after someone personally. I never made fun of someone... Yeah, I lied to them about the game, but I never got ugly. I'm super happy that I had the foresight to do that."
>
> Dan Gheesling[60]

Dan wasn't the next Dr. Will; he never was. That was always Brian's role. Dan was a whole new *institution* for *Big Brother*.

I was blown away at sixteen, about the same age Dan was when he'd watched Dr. Will on season 2. For me, after the stretch of seasons 8 and 9, nearly dropping the show from my life entirely, Dan was everything I came to the show for. He drew me back in so strongly that I never managed to get back out.

I wrote earlier that Dan embodied the game in a way no player before him had. As you track his game through season 10, the meaning behind that statement becomes clear. Dan hadn't just studied the game; he'd grown up with it. All of those strategic innovations that had been made throughout the Shapiro era weren't just things he'd mastered; they were second nature to him. Throughout the season he effortlessly transitioned from one of those staple strategies to the next depending on what the circumstances called for.

He threw comps and portrayed himself as a nonthreat like Will, created and utilized a secret alliance like Jason and Danielle, floated to power in the early game like Jun had, then combined it all with the secret alliance strategy like they did in *All-Stars*. By the end of his game, he had securely positioned himself at the center of his alliance like Maggie had and pulled off a maneuver that Will himself had been unable to accomplish. He played the game with little emotion or attachment to any one style or player, simply doing what needed to be done in the moment to advance himself in the game.

Like a true master of his craft, Dan was able to break every established rule of *Big Brother* strategy—from nominating his own allies to throwing veto competitions while being on the block to accomplish his goals. He was so paradoxically successful that his opponents literally could not believe he was a real player. He went on to inspire a whole new generation of future contestants, some of whom thought they too could break these rules and were severely punished for it in the game.

If *Big Brother* was a reflection of society, Dan was a reflection of *Big Brother*, molded by the show and what it has to teach us. He was someone who was able to almost entirely control his emotions and navigate the social and strategic landscape with ease. He was extremely cutthroat but also kind, never making things personal or going after anyone beyond the scope of the game.

Dan felt like the ultimate distillation of what the show had been crafting over the years. I can't blame anyone who might find that concerning after reading about all of the elaborate machinations he concocted. But I found it validating. I'd spent so much of my life diving deeper and deeper into this absurd voyeuristic reality game show, and as I reached a turning point in finding my own identity, Dan proved to me that there was value here. He changed the way I thought about the show and the game.

What I saw as Dan's commitment to kindness while dominating a game that did everything in its power to escalate conflict created this wave of relief that swept over me. It felt like a path I'd been searching for but feared didn't exist. When everything around *me* felt like it was forcing me into competition and conflict with others, I'd always felt like I was either rising to it and being someone I didn't like or, more often, rolling over and letting myself be taken advantage of.

Not Dan though. When the game required blood, Dan delivered. He knew that he couldn't change the game, so he sought to master it without losing himself to it. He compartmentalized "the game" and conducted himself with respect. I was determined to do the same in my own life.

It's funny to watch the season now, sixteen years later. I saw Dan in season 10 as this trailblazing adult, and now I'm eight years his senior. My current eyes see him as a plucky kid, forever frozen in time for that summer in 2008, continuing to inspire countless new fans as they discover their own love for the show through his antics, now over a decade old.

That summer in 2008, *Big Brother* looked into its own mirror and saw Dan Gheesling staring back at it.

10

Cancellation

As it turned out, my experience of nearly dropping the show after seasons 8 and 9 was not unique. Season 9 had been disastrous for the show; it not only saw an initial ratings drop as a winter season, it also lost viewers over the course of the season. To have fewer viewers on finale night than premiere night is a rarity in *Big Brother* and a surefire sign that the season did something wrong.

The premiere of *Big Brother 10* had the lowest ratings in the history of the show. If the audience had continued to abandon ship from there, *Big Brother* might have shared the fate of all the international versions that were being canceled at the time. Luckily Dan and the cast of season 10 carried that season's ratings to new heights over the course of the summer. To date, season 10 has the highest increase of viewership from premiere night to finale night outside of the initial growth in seasons 2 and 3.

The success didn't stop there. On the heels of season 10, the show started gaining viewers year over year for the next three years. It was again the biggest and most sustained growth spike since the first few seasons, and it was a massive win for the show's longevity. As everything else was falling, *Big Brother* was not only holding strong, it was climbing. The show started becoming a true cornerstone of the CBS summer schedule and could be relied on to have a solid performance while filling a lot of holes.

But there was still a problem. Dan Gheesling had been a mistake by production, a happy accident. They hadn't intended to cast him; they'd been aiming for someone who would aggressively clash with others politically to stir up controversy. Dan didn't give production what they wanted; he gave them what they *needed*. But they didn't seem to see it that way.

They dipped back into the well of controversy, and after season 10, incidents started ramping up again until they reached the fever pitch that was *Big Brother 15*, also known in the fandom as the "racist season."[1]

> "I feel like I was one of the very first, very widespread, publicly, like internationally canceled people."
>
> Aaryn Gries[2]

The summer of 2013 saw an explosion of mainstream news coverage for *Big Brother*. From CNN to *Today*, the *Hollywood Reporter*, the *Los Angeles Times*, the *New York Times*, and countless other outlets, headlines were flying off the presses all season.

They weren't good.

"*Big Brother* Already a Cesspool of Racist,
  Homophobic, and Misogynistic Comments"

"*Big Brother* Rocked by Big Controversy:
  Racism, Sexism, and Homophobia"

"*Big Brother 15*'s Controversial Houseguests
  Respond to Losing Their Jobs"

"*Big Brother 15*: Third Houseguest Criticized by
  Employer over Offensive Remarks"

"*Big Brother* Issues Disclaimer in Wake of Racial Controversy"[3]

The worst of what was said that season is well documented at this point, with targets abounding. Anti-Semitic, homophobic, misogynistic, and racist remarks and slurs were bandied about—almost as though they had a checklist.[4]

"Candice is already on the dark side because she's already dark."

"Be careful what you say in the dark—you
  might not be able to see the bitch."

"I get [n-word] insurance."

"Howard and Candice are going to be on the same team."

"Howard and Candice? Well yeah, because you know the two Blacks will stick together. They're like tokens."

"Freakin' Black Candice was in there."

"I did touch her vagina today. She didn't look like she was happy about it."

"Oh my God, I just said the n-word. So what?"[5]

The list goes on.

For the first time in over a decade, *Big Brother* was making a direct splash into mainstream culture, and the look was not flattering. The *New York Times* writer Brian Stelter grilled Allison Grodner about the decision to cast such vile contestants. She replied, saying that they don't actively "look for people who might say things like this" and suggested that *Big Brother* was simply mirroring real life, as ugly as it sometimes is.[6]

Big Brother certainly does tend to mirror real life, but who's holding that mirror? They seemed to be actively looking for cast members who might have extreme views and clash with one another. After over a decade of working on the show, were the incidents of season 15 really a surprise to them?

CBS issued a disclaimer in front of episodes and the live feeds that read, "BIG BROTHER is a reality show about a group of people who have no privacy 24/7. At times, the Houseguests may reveal prejudices and other beliefs that CBS does not condone. Views or opinions expressed by a Houseguest are those of the individuals speaking and do not represent the views or opinions of CBS. **Viewer discretion is advised.**"[7]

See, they had accidentally cast some racists on their show this time around, and they certainly don't condone the things those racists are saying. But really, what can be done about it? A few bad apples said a few bad things. It was a mistake! But they're being brave, addressing the problem head-on, and really, what are the odds it will happen again?

What were the odds that it had *already* happened?

Racism, homophobia, misogyny, and all kinds of other nasty things had been present in the show from the very start.[8] Sometimes the cuts would make the episodes, and sometimes they were relegated to just being on the live feeds. Going all the way back to the very first season of the show, *Big Brother* was infested with bigoted behaviors and remarks.

"Within the last week alone, Eddie has told racist 'jokes' about African Americans, Puerto Ricans and Asians; he has called a female houseguest a (misogynistic slur); and he has spoken approvingly about physical violence toward homosexuals," LA attorney Lisa Hoffman wrote in a letter of complaint to CBS.[9]

Eddie won *Big Brother 1* with America's vote. The issue had persisted from there.

It's important to know that this kind of behavior and language has been *extremely* present throughout the show's history. As Grodner said, it does mirror our society. Overt racism was and still is a persistently prevalent fixture in our culture. When you stick people with different backgrounds together into a pressure-cooker environment designed to provoke conflict and pull out your worst qualities, you're bound to run into some of the darkest parts of our society.

This just scratches the surface of the issue, but suffice it to say that these problems had been around for a while, and many international versions of the show had been torn apart trying to solve them. To this day, *Big Brother* is often associated with issues of race and other controversies, and *Big Brother U.S.* is no exception.

There's nothing that makes *Big Brother* more or less naturally racist or hateful than any other reality competition show. Through my work I've come to know many contestants from a wide variety of these shows all around the world, and controversies surrounding hate speech, bullying, and sometimes sexual misconduct can be found nearly everywhere you look. The difference with *Big Brother* comes back to the live feeds.

Through the feeds, *Big Brother* is forced to be more transparent than any other reality show in existence. For that matter, it's forced to be more transparent than any show period. More public footage exists of *Big Brother* than any other show in the world, and most of it is entirely raw and unedited. It's for these reasons that the show is so closely associated with this specific brand of controversy—because it reflects a society that is full of people who will say and do all kinds of heinous things. And here we are, our voyeuristic selves, watching the *real*, unedited America. Or at least, that's what Allison Grodner would have you believe.

In an attempt to justify the casting decisions for season 15, Grodner said, "Your neighbor is probably using racial slurs behind closed doors."[10]

There are many ways for the show to reflect the culture it exists in. The structure of the game we watch on *Big Brother* is a mirror image of our individualistic, zero-sum, capitalist culture in America. It reflects my own experience of existing in a society that constantly puts me in competition with others and encourages me to take all I can for myself and the people I care about, even if (or maybe *especially* if) it's at the expense of others. For better or worse, that is the game I enjoy watching as it's deconstructed in various ways by various players.

But the casting of this show and other shows like it—is reflective in a different way. The casting of these shows is more a reflection of the *people* casting the shows. The cast of a particular season of *Big Brother* can in no way fully represent America. What it represents is some amalgamation of a CBS executive's personal preferences; a *Big Brother* producer's idea for a twist, showmance, or conflict; a casting director's hunch; and maybe somewhere in there someone's idea of what a representative sample of America might be. There is still value there, and over the decades that *Big Brother* has been on the air, the makeup of the casts has followed societal norms to some degree. We'll discuss the biggest example of that later. But this connection is still reflective of active choices being made by production, not as a natural consequence of the show or the demographics of the country.

If you're in the *Big Brother* community, you may have heard the show described as a microcosm of society. This is true in that each season's cast creates its own miniature society, but I don't see the show itself as being a representative sample of our society and culture. Instead I see it as a funhouse of mirrors, reflecting back what's in front of it while also stretching, contorting, and exaggerating where it sees fit.

The live feeds put a microscope to all of this. They all but force you to consider every decision made by production as you watch the consequences of those choices echo through the game. The *Big Brother* producers are some of the most scrutinized people working in television, and boy, do they take a lot of heat.

But this all brings me back to an important question: If season 15 wasn't unique, if these kinds of incidents had been happening throughout the show's history, plain for everyone to see on the live feeds, what made it such a big deal for season 15?

To explain, I want to tell you about *Big Brother 11*. Just a year after season 10 blew everyone's expectations away, the show came back seemingly determined to correct their mistake of casting people who were there for the game and tried to find their group of "diverse people" coming from "opposite worlds" who they were shooting for the year prior.

This time they succeeded. In the first week alone, racist and homophobic slurs were being slung about in both quiet moments and during heated exchanges. Future fan-favorite contestant Jeff Schroeder was using the homophobic "f" slur liberally:

> "Way to show your true colors, f**."

> "Go upstairs and fucking jerk off, Jessie, you fucking homo."

> "Fuck you, you fucking homo f**."[11]

None of this made the edit.

The Jessie who Jeff was referring to was bodybuilder Jessie from season 10, back again the following year as a returning player among a sea of fresh faces. Without Dan to contend with, Jessie was cruising through the season until another America's vote got in his way. In one of the most overpowered twists the show has ever seen, America voted for their favorite guy Jeff to receive the "coup d'état" power, which allowed him to single-handedly overturn a rival's HOH and send Jessie home on eviction night. This twist completely changed the entire direction of the game, and Jeff's showmance Jordan went on to win the season.

Many were frustrated by the fact that Jeff's success in the game rested entirely upon the fact that America was backing him, and most of the audience had no idea what he was saying on the feeds. It was reminiscent of the Evel Dick situation, except this time the audience thought Jeff was a true stand-up guy with no hint at all of the darker parts of his personality.

Jeff was a superstar in the *Big Brother* world. He returned with his showmance Jordan for season 13, where he was again caught going off on a rant about gay people, this time when engaged in a conversation about Harry Potter's Dumbledore of all things.

"He was written to be gay? That'd be perverted," he said to a room full of people discussing the character. "He's in a school with little kids! You don't want to make that guy gay!"[12]

"What do you mean? Why? Gay men can't work with little kids?" fellow contestant Kalia responded.

"I don't think it's the right thing to have a little kids' book, and have the headmaster that they're locked away in a magical land with be gay. I don't think that's the right thing to do. I can see your PC view, but I don't think it's the right thing to do." He continued to get louder as the exchange went on. "You know exactly what I'm saying—don't make it seem like you're doing the right thing by saying it's not. You're going to let a storybook, where they go to fantasy camp, and it's all little kids without their parents and the guy is gay… Get the fuck out of here; don't start with that fucking shit. Don't tell me the right answer for fucking TV, when you don't think it's the right answer."[13]

Again, none of this made the air. Jeff continued to be both a fan favorite and a producer favorite. Later on *Big Brother 16*, they brought him on the show again in a guest spot, where he proposed to Jordan. The two of them went on *The Amazing Race* together, he took part in other CBS shows, and he conducted official CBS *Big Brother* interviews for years.

Jeff wasn't the only problem on *Big Brother 11*. Braden Bacha also drew heat for his racist slurs and comments in the house, which were also not put into the edited episodes.

As Andy Dehnart of Reality Blurred put it, "Besides ignoring Braden's racial slur, the editors excised Jeff's repeated use of the other f-word, which he uses to demean other men. In fact, the editing almost made him look sympathetic, like the victim of an attack. Not surprising, still disappointing."[14] He later wrote, "The rest of the episode was an exercise in the producers' cowardice and pathetic distortion of reality… The most despicable part of the episode was the producers' editing and manipulation of the backyard fight between Braden, Lydia, and Kevin, which skipped over all of Braden's racism and instead made it look like Kevin and Lydia were overreacting to Braden calling her a 'bitch' and a 'skank,' not that those words are okay. In subsequent footage included by the editors, Lydia repeated those terms, as if that's all she was really upset about."[15]

Dehnart finishes with a slammer: "The episode overall proved the producers have no respect for their audience or its intelligence, and after watching it, I grew ever-annoyed with wasting my time with the shit they want to force-feed me. It's just season after season of this nonsense, with a one-time reprieve last summer, and it's harder to sit through each time."[16]

Julie did grill Braden a bit about his behavior in the house in his exit interview, but only the extended cut version—not the one that aired in the episode. In a later interview conducted by *People* magazine, Braden was asked if he regretted throwing water on Kevin, the man he'd called a racial slur. Braden's response was "No. He's flamboyantly gay, and you can't punch a gay guy, let alone push him."[17]

Contestant Chima Simone, a thirty-two-year-old journalist, had a pretty good idea how shows like this could be edited. She had already been complaining to other contestants on the live feeds that she could tell how the show was trying to portray her based on her interactions in the diary room, and she wasn't pleased about it. Having a hunch that Braden's comments may not have made the air, she used another of *Big Brother*'s unique features to try to say her piece.

From the very beginning of the show, the eviction episodes have always been live. Contestants will plead their cases and walk out the door to Julie. Chima knew that if she wanted to make sure she was heard, she'd need to wait until the live show. So she did.

On the night of the first live eviction, Chima stood in front of both the house and America and said, "It amazes me how short some of the memory spans in here are, because my opponent here called both of my very good friends in the house 'b**s.' And he even called Julie a whore. Yes, he did. And so a vote for Braden is a vote for a bigot. Anyone who aligns himself with a racist and misogynist—you deserve to go home."[18]

In a panic, production cut the audio before she said "friends" and left it cut until she said "Yes, he did." America did manage to hear him be called a racist and a misogynist. They then subsequently saw that the vote came in 5–5, a tie that HOH Jessie broke to evict Braden.

After later being informed that her speech had been censored, Chima confronted production, telling her fellow contestants, "I said, I don't think it's fair because I don't think they showed when it first was said. And I was like, if someone's a racist, they should be portrayed as one. You shouldn't edit it to make them look good."[19]

She later allegedly claimed, "Production was *pissed* about this speech. I ruined their edit… They never let me speak live again. And I had a target on my back from the powers that be from that night forward."[20]

Later in the season it was Chima's HOH reign that was nullified by Jeff's coup d'état power. Instead of getting her target out of the game, her HOH was overthrown, she wasn't allowed to vote in the eviction, and her ally Jessie left instead. Chima was incensed. Knowing that the power was out there, she had told production that all hell would break loose on the live show if it was used to nullify her HOH. So for the first time ever, *Big Brother* decided to pretape its eviction episode that week, ensuring that Chima could not slip anything by their censors.

The following week saw Chima go up on the block as the target. She'd had enough of how she felt production had been treating her and she stopped playing ball with them. She refused to wear her microphone. When one was finally handed to her, she tossed it into the hot tub.

After she refused to go to the diary room, Allison Grodner's voice came over the loudspeakers, pleading with Chima. "I need you to come to the diary room now," she said. "Please come, OK?" Right as Chima walked in, she was told, "All right, no need to sit down. We're going to go out this way." Chima was then expelled from the game.[21]

Outside of the house, Chima found herself apologizing for her own racist comments toward Russell, a fellow contestant of Lebanese descent. *Today* reported her statement: "I used a phrase that was insensitive given his Middle Eastern descent, and I apologize to all who are justifiably offended with my use of that racially charged term."[22]

Despite all of this, the uproar over the behavior in the house was minuscule compared to what was to come during *Big Brother 15*. Producers clearly went out of their way to obscure and minimize these incidents as much as possible, despite the fact they were as clear as day on the live feeds. And it worked.

I was seventeen and losing interest in the show again. An entire year had passed since *Big Brother 10* blew me away, and there was nothing about season 11 that captured my attention. Admittedly, most of this went over my head at the time. I wasn't keeping track of what was going on in the forums, reading articles, or obsessively checking in on the feeds. It wasn't until later in my *Big Brother* journey that I learned about Braden and Jeff and many of the true events of the season.

It was the first time I ever felt like I had been genuinely tricked by the show. Jeff and his homophobic comments in particular really shocked me, because he is a hero through and through in the edit of *Big Brother 11*. It made me consider the other shows I watched and the ease with which I could be manipulated into liking or disliking a person based on how the show decided to edit them.

I wasn't the only one thinking this at the time either. Andy Dehnart wrote, "Obviously, we're aware of this because the live feeds reveal to us what we would otherwise not see on a reality show. Maybe other shows deliberately conceal their stars' horrific behavior and attitudes too."[23]

Since the beginning this had been the strategy for *Big Brother*. Other shows without live feeds got away with it much more cleanly, because by editing around things, they'd always been able to avoid getting too much heat for what happened in their house.

Responding to racist comments made against Kaysar in season 6, Arnold Shapiro said, "I'm appalled by any racial or religious slur, personally. You will notice that they do not end up on the television show… I wish that racial and religious slurs did not happen… Anybody on the internet knows the 100 percent truth about this thing. We and CBS do not want to put those kinds of comments on national television. There's a bigger purpose and picture here, and I wouldn't want my name on a show that was having those kinds of things spoken."[24]

When confronted about hiding the racist comments being made in *Big Brother 15*, Allison Grodner replied, "We really don't want to put hateful things out there in our edits. And so for the most part, when this goes down, we keep that out of the show."[25]

And yet, *Big Brother 15* became the first season to ever actively showcase the racist comments and behavior of its contestants to a significant degree. They no longer seemed to be hiding it. But why? What was it that changed the strategy they'd been using for over a decade? Grodner's explanation? "It was ultimately part of the story in the house." Her claim was that because other contestants were actively speaking out against the behavior, it "gave us a launching pad to be able to tell this story."[26]

The real reason? Most believe it came down to a fundamental shift in how society contributed to the cultural dialogue in

America. Put more simply, there were more people complaining on social media.

A lot more people.

Social media's ubiquity in American culture came about through the rise of popular sites like MySpace, Facebook, YouTube, Twitter, Reddit, and others in the mid-2000s. The niche forums and community pages that had populated the internet began to lose steam as these popular social media sites became the central hubs of online discussion.

With the rise of social media came the decline of anonymity on the internet. People were now choosing to attach their real identity to their online profile. A central gathering place along with public profiles meant that there were fewer barriers between fans and creators than ever. As more people signed up, social media slowly began to dominate every aspect of cultural conversation.

What this meant for *Big Brother* was that the voices of those discussing the show were gathering and growing louder. Instead of being confined to *Big Brother* sites like JokersUpdates.com or the many forums dedicated to the show, people were now creating Facebook groups, a subreddit was created for the show, clips of the live feeds were being posted on YouTube, and people were discussing *Big Brother* constantly using the hashtag on Twitter.

Twitter soon became the place to be for *Big Brother* discourse. The ephemeral nature of character-limited tweets coming and going on a timeline was perfect for the 24/7 live feeds, where there was always something new to be talking about. You could find people like Big Brother Daily posting quotes from the feeds as they were happening. Hamsterwatch made an account and started posting her jokes there in real time. All of this was happening in a space frequented by journalists, celebrities, and maybe even those working in production themselves.

Eventually this would come to impact the contestants as well. As they came off the show, they'd find themselves bombarded by social media interaction. Where before they might have gotten some emails if people were able to find their email address, now the only way to escape the horde of fans who were waiting to bombard them with opinions was to disengage from social media entirely and become an online version of a recluse—a self-imposed exile for the sake of their own mental health.

Social media and *Big Brother* fit perfectly together. It's a show where you have constant access to these people living their lives in the house. Out in the real world, we were getting closer and closer to voluntarily putting ourselves in the same position—broadcasting our lives to a world ready to consume and commoditize it.

Thus was the landscape of social media throughout the first half of the 2010s for *Big Brother*. Things were growing and expanding rapidly. Barriers were coming down, and fans were finding voices they never knew they had. It was this landscape that producers found themselves contending with as the events of season 15 played out before them.

It began like it always did: niche segments of the fandom raising the alarm that there were awful things being said in the house. A few news outlets picked it up and raised a fuss, but most people didn't see it, and it didn't make the episodes. No incidents on the live shows or anything either.

This was usually the extent of the controversy for *Big Brother*, but in season 15 the complaints continued to get louder and louder. More people were hearing about what was being said in the house on enormous platforms like Twitter. A common thing for the fandom to do in these circumstances was to compile a list of quotes to show those not watching what vile things were being said in the house. These lists were now circulating the big social media sites and gathering more attention. More attention meant more news coverage.

Then the big one. *Video* compilations containing many of the incidents were being uploaded to YouTube. One of these accumulated nearly 100,000 views in just one day, before eventually being taken down by Endemol USA.[27] The fire was spreading, and *Big Brother* couldn't contain it.

Mainstream news outlets were now reporting, "*Big Brother* contestants lose jobs due to racist, homophobic remarks."[28] First was Aaryn Gries, who was dropped by her talent agency and the magazine she worked for. "Aaryn, season 15 cast member of *Big Brother*, revealed prejudices and other beliefs that we do not condone… Upon much consideration, we have decided to release Aaryn from her contract."[29]

Next was GinaMarie Zimmerman, when she was fired from her job of five years at East Coast USA Pageant Inc. A statement from the company said, "We never knew this side of Ginamarie [*sic*] or have ever witnessed such acts of racism in the past. We are actually thankful that this show let us see Ginamarie for who she truly is as we would never want her to be a role model to our future contestants… When she returns from the *Big Brother* house we will be terminating her employment for her unforgivable behavior."[30]

It didn't stop there. More of the players lost their jobs, and they were all grilled as they came out of the house. The days of this kind of behavior being swept under the rug were long gone. This had some asking if the reaction had gone too far. Should people be losing their jobs for comments they make on the live feeds of a reality show? *Should* there be live feeds for a reality show? Surely anybody being filmed 24/7 for three months is bound to say or do something offensive, right?

This seemed to be the stance that the aforementioned *Big Brother Canada* eventually took. After a decade of streaming live feeds, they made the extremely controversial decision to remove them in 2023. "We are constantly looking for new ways to evolve the show to ensure we operate with the utmost duty of care and prioritize the mental health and well-being of the houseguests," Lisa Godfrey said in the press release.[31]

Big Brother Canada had already been known for its tight control of the narrative for their show, cutting the feeds constantly and attempting to hide any kind of controversy that occurred on them. It was no surprise when they ultimately decided to stop having live feeds at all. In the U.S., *Big Brother* producers are constantly dealing with pushback from fans about things they see on the feeds, and when they *could* hide the kinds of things that were happening on season 15, they did. So *Big Brother Canada* basically seemed to say, yeah, we don't want to deal with that anymore.

It must be asked, though, in talking about mental health, which Houseguests were being prioritized by hiding this behavior? I don't doubt that someone who can't help but sling racial slurs around in their free time would think it's a great call, but what about the Houseguests who are actually impacted by that behavior?

In season 15 the producers buckled and finally showcased the kinds of things that went on in their studio lot designed to look like a house. They first dropped a small montage in an episode, but things quickly escalated when they put out the most infamous scene of the season: the bed-flipping incident.

At the start of week 3, Aaryn and her allies Kaitlyn and Jeremy found themselves on the wrong side of the game. They were mourning the loss of another ally and knew that two of them would be nominated that week. They were in the minority, something they weren't used to in their normal lives.

"I feel like I'm back in high school but I'm on the other side," said Kaitlyn.[32]

"Like, on the losers' side?" Aaryn replied.

"Yeah!"

Aaryn, who had been lying in Candice's bed, got up, threw everything off it, and flipped the mattress off its base. Candice was the only Black woman in the house, and there had already been significant tension between her and Aaryn, along with many of the comments being made.

When Candice walked into the room to find her bedding scattered across the floor and her mattress on its side, she was confused. "To my surprise my bed is flipped upside down and all my pillows are on the floor and my clothes are just everywhere. It was very hurtful."

As she was carefully gathering her things and flipping the mattress back into place, another of Aaryn's allies, Jeremy, crawled into bed with Jessie, a woman in the opposing alliance. Jessie did not want him there. "I don't want any company right now. This is making me very uncomfortable and I'd appreciate it if you got off the bed," she said. He did not. He stubbornly continued to lie next to her. "Please get off the bed," she asked again.

Minutes passed as tensions continued to rise. Then Aaryn walked into the room. Candice confronted her, saying, "I know somebody got one more time to flip my bed, and it's going to be all hell in this house."

Aaryn's friend Kaitlin replied, moving her head back and forth and snapping her fingers, "Ooo! I'd like to see that. To see the Black girl come out of you!"

Aaryn also got in on it: "Whatchu gon' do, girl? Whatchu gon' do? Do something. Do it right now." She started moving and snapping her fingers while putting on her affected accent.

"I'm not making a fool of myself. Please believe that," Candice responded.

"Well then don't talk. And first of all, I wouldn't get in your bed anyway with all them crabs," Aaryn replied.

It should be noted at this point that due to the questions being asked in the diary room, the players were aware that the racial tension in the house was being put on the show. Fellow contestant Amanda even warned Aaryn specifically about the comments she was making.

"I think the people who are a different race are taking it, like, offensively," Amanda told her.

"That's the most obnoxious, annoying thing I've ever heard." Aaryn replied. "I wish that I cared more about this, but I don't."

Back in the bed-flipping incident, the only Black man in the house, Howie, had walked into the room, and Candice had quickly gotten him up to speed on the situation.

Aaryn continued mocking her, saying, "Whatchu gon' do, girl? Whatchu gon' do, class girl? Where's yo class?"

Howie stood there, watching this unfold. He stared at Candice and tried to beckon her to leave the room with him.

"You don't need him to protect you," Ginamarie—another of Aaryn's allies—declared.

"I didn't ask him to!" Candice replied.

Howie opened the door. "Candice, Candice!"

GinaMarie stood up and stepped to Candice, who got up in response.

"What do you want to say?" GinaMarie asked.

"I'm not going to say anything to you."

"You want the Black to come out?" GinaMarie retorted.

At this point, Howie carefully put his arm in between them, then literally grabbed Candice and carried her out of the room as they all continued to taunt her.

Once in private, Howie and Candice talked about the experience. Howie was frustrated. He was a gamer; he had come into the house to play hard. He was in a secret alliance doing his thing and just wanted to be able to play like anyone else. But in the house he was faced with these kinds of incidents. Part of him just wanted to ignore it; getting wrapped up in all of this would only hurt his game and thus his chances to win $500,000. On the other hand, he couldn't just sit back and allow these things to happen.

"You're not being weak if you let them have a bed; you're just being bigger," he told her. "The only way I'm going to leave this house is defending somebody. The only person I honestly have to defend is you and Helen. Because I fit in the same minority y'all are. That's the only button they've got to push. And they're going to push you, which pushes me."

"We have had racist remarks said to us. I have been called Shaniqua. They flipped my bed over, start talking ghetto talk to me, and I'm supposed to go and hide and sleep in another room?"

Candice started to break down in tears. Howie pulled her into his arms as he fought off his own wave of emotions and frustrations at the situation, evident clearly on his grimacing face.

"All she wants to do is stand up for what's right," he told us in the diary room. "Unfortunately we're not playing a game where we can do that."

"You came here to win. My battles are not your battles," Candice tried to tell him.

"It's just reminding me of where I'm from," he replied. "It's reminding me of what I heard. It's reminding me of all this stuff that we know that goes on. And now we've got to be in the room close with it?"[33]

It's a harrowing segment to watch, mostly because it's a window into a world of experience that many people would rather pretend didn't exist. It was one of the first times the general audience was seeing a glimpse of what it might be like to be an actual minority in the house. These stories and experiences had almost never been shown or focused on, and there's plenty of reason to believe that this segment itself would never have made an episode if not for the confluence of events that led to a social media uproar being something that the show could no longer ignore.

This segment changed *Big Brother* forever. They could never go back to pretending these stories didn't exist. They could never again claim that they weren't worth telling for the sake of respectability. That is, unless they decided to get rid of the live feeds like *Big Brother Canada*. And to their credit, they haven't.

Aaryn was evicted from the *Big Brother 15* house to an audience booing her. Julie pressed her on the various comments she had made in the house. Aaryn was stunned. This was not something that happened on this show; these comments were supposed to be hidden away.

Aaryn recently called herself one of the first people to be "canceled." *Big Brother* was once again at the bleeding edge of American culture, as by the end of the decade "cancel culture" would become a hot topic in political and sociological discourse. With hindsight, some fans bemoan the changes that the season forced upon the show. People were playing it safer now, being "more PC." The show was hiding more from the feeds themselves to try to avoid more controversy and seemed to lighten up on casting "controversial" people.

Over the years since season 15, there has slowly been a reduction in slurs being used but also screaming matches and fights in general. Regardless of whether one of those things necessarily follows the other, there is a portion of the fan base that feels the baby was thrown out with the bathwater, and they'd like to see a return to the more controversial side of *Big Brother*. This shouldn't be surprising, though, because the same conversation is happening in our culture at large. The one happening for *Big Brother* of course is just a reflection of that.

So what happened to players like Jeff and Aaryn? As social media continued to grow, other controversial figures from *Big Brother*'s past began to come to light. A post made on Reddit years after Jeff's seasons read, "Never saw this before. Jeff Schroeder being homophobic on *Big Brother*. What the actual f?"[34]

Eventually Jeff couldn't escape his controversial past. Despite the fact that he claimed that he's apologized "many times," fans of *Big Brother* had a hard time finding any kind of sincere apology for the bigoted mindset he showcased while on the show between the two seasons he was on, two years apart. As the people at CBS began to change, his defenders there lost influence. In 2020 CBS cut ties with

Jeff, withdrawing their offer for him to interview the cast for that year's *Big Brother* season.

"I felt gutted. I've said some things. People make mistakes and I've made mistakes, and I've apologized for those mistakes over and over again, but when do you let go of that? How many times can you be punished for the same crime?" he said on his podcast. "To turn your back on somebody you have that history with—and I did over a dozen shows with CBS Interactive—it hurt... I was canceled."[35]

Despite this canceling, Jeff has had a lucrative career in show business since his time in *Big Brother*, working with CBS for over a decade on a number of shows and having his own successful podcast. He is also a permanent cohost on the daytime talk show *Daily Blast Live*.

For Aaryn, though, her future looked much more bleak. She was fired from her job, dropped by her agency, and unlike Jeff's, her behavior was shown to the world in the episodes, blasted over countless mainstream news outlets.

Then, just two years after her time on season 15, Aaryn started a YouTube channel documenting the experience she was having with her pregnancy. It took off immediately. For close to a decade now, she's been running her very successful YouTube channel with over 300,000 subscribers.

In a recent interview she did with Lara Trump, Aaryn spoke about her experience with *Big Brother*. "Julie had immediately called me racist and homophobic, like right out of the bat. I thought I was going to be getting like, you know, clapped for... We have to remember that we were there twenty-four hours a day, every day... They took my worst moments."[36]

Lara Trump told her, "They tried to cancel you, but you kind of proved that you are only canceled if you allow yourself to be."

She went on to ask Aaryn if she regretted going on *Big Brother* as opposed to *The Real World*, which she had also made casting finals for at the time. If Aaryn had been on *The Real World*, because there are no live feeds there's a good chance her comments and behavior would not have made national news and may not have made a single episode.

Despite this, Aaryn replied, "I don't know, because I have this platform now that I wouldn't have had if it weren't for *Big Brother*."[37]

That is another angle of social media's influence on the show. With more attention, there was also more *opportunity*. For a long time reality TV contestants were ridiculed for trying to make a career off their fifteen minutes of fame. Now, the following they could attain on social media meant that they could create new careers for themselves. This was especially so for *Big Brother* players, who were able to develop deeper, more parasocial connections to their fans through the live feeds.

It was in this landscape that *Big Brother 16* arrived, fresh off season 15's controversy, to an audience that was now deeply involved on social media. The show capitalized on this by casting a self-proclaimed "social media mogul" named Frankie Grande. Brother of pop star Ariana Grande and with over a million followers, Frankie, they hoped, would bring in a new generation of viewers who were social-media savvy. The show was also finally upgraded to HD for the first time. It had been the final regularly scheduled prime-time TV program to make the change, largely because of the complete overhaul it required to rewire the entire set with so many cameras.

Big Brother 16 was set to be a new start for the show. What they got was the most dominant strategic game the show had ever seen—a culmination of new strategic innovations that had been developed over the years since Dan had mastered the game in season 10.

The strategy of *Big Brother* had shifted away from the story of an underdog overcoming a big majority. Now it was a game of numbers and dominance. There are many reasons for this, but it all starts with one man.

Back in season 12, four years prior, a self-proclaimed Mensa member had managed to crack the code of *Big Brother* and broke the entire game.

11

Cracking the Code

"An aspect that I enjoy about games or just life in general is a manipulation of the system without cheating. You're taking what exists and going, how can I look at it in a different way? Nakomis did that with what became the backdoor. That's sort of how I feel the Brigade went down."

Matt Hoffman[1]

Mensa member Matt Hoffman told us that he was a genius in the opening to *Big Brother 12*. He fell into the burgeoning player archetype that deeply compartmentalized the *Big Brother* experience foremost as a game. Importantly for Matt, it was a game where anything goes.

He's famous for his "sick wife" lie, where he pretended his wife was dealing with a rare progressive bone disorder in order to gain sympathy in the game. I wouldn't blame you if your first impression of the self-proclaimed diabolical supergenius wasn't a great one.

Still, for all the bluster in the diary room, Matt is very laid-back and easygoing in person. What's also clear is that he thinks outside the box when it comes to strategy. Whether it's going on national television and lying about having a sick wife to his fellow contestants or coming up with groundbreaking new strategic functions in the game, he was always looking for a weakness in the game structure that he could exploit.

Some ideas worked better than others.

Like many innovative players before him, he was a fan of the show and was particularly fond of Danielle and Jason's secret alliance from season 3. He wanted to replicate what they were able to do for his game. Instead he stumbled upon a strategy that cracked the very code of strategic gameplay that the show rested on.

Since Danielle and Jason's amazing run in season 3, making secret alliances had become the thing to do. Dan and Memphis had just implemented their own version of it with the Renegades. It was an incredibly effective way of finding success in the game. But it wasn't perfect.

There's one major problem with the secret alliance strategy as outlined by Danielle and Jason: there were only two of them. Sure, you can split up into two sides of the house, but what if there are more than two sides? Or what if one of the secret alliance members doesn't have enough influence to keep the other one safe? At the end of the day, the majority still rules in the house, and if you're not as skilled as Danielle and Jason were, your secret alliance will mean absolutely nothing.

There had been attempts to solve this problem before. Danielle herself tried to increase the number of people in her secret alliance in her *All-Stars* game. The Legion of Doom was a secret four-person alliance with her, James, Will, and Boogie. Increasing the number of people in the alliance meant they could have more influence, more chances to win competitions, and a much better chance at controlling the game.

Unfortunately for Danielle, the Legion of Doom was doomed to failure. More people came with more problems. There was no clear hierarchy in their group; it was just two duos: Danielle and James on one side, Will and Boogie on the other. This meant that if either duo wanted the advantage in the endgame, they'd have to turn on the alliance sooner rather than later.

This had been Maggie's strength in season 6. She'd positioned herself at the center of the maligned Friendship alliance. On *Survivor*, they'd come to call this an "onion" alliance, meaning that within a group of four, there was secretly a group of three, and within that group of three, there was secretly a duo that was really running things. The key to this strategy was in convincing each member of the alliance that they were the ones in the core. This allowed everyone to be working in conjunction for the good of the alliance because they all thought it was set up in their own best interests.

Dan eventually set this up in season 10, using his secret deal with Memphis to position himself at the core of his late-game alliance. But Dan is Dan. What he was able to do was not easy to replicate. Many have tried, and all have failed. This is where Matt Hoffman came in.

Matt was hoping to land himself a secret alliance and quickly found himself included in an early four-person bro alliance. These are pretty typical for *Big Brother*. The strong, athletic, good-looking popular guys come together and form an early majority alliance. These are the kinds of early alliances that all of the strategic innovation of the previous ten years had been built to destroy.

Matt wasn't exactly the usual bro archetype, but his laid-back attitude and head for the game got him a spot on the squad. It was him and three other guys. The competitive ladies' man Hayden; the good ol' boy Lane, who told us in the opening that he was looking for someone smart to do the thinking for him in the game; and the smooth-talking Enzo from Jersey.

Hayden was the first HOH, and he was approached by Enzo to start the alliance. "When you start the mafia, you've got to go to the guy in charge, which was Hayden this week," Enzo told us. "The next thing you got to do is have some brains in this operation."[2]

Enzo and Hayden approached Matt to join and then completed the alliance with Lane.

"Every mafia needs some type of a muscle, which I call him Lane," Enzo continued. "He's like a size of a tree, this guy."

They named their alliance the "Brigade." Enzo gave everyone nicknames: Hayden was "the Animal." Lane was "the Beast." Matt was "the Brains." Enzo was "the Meow Meow."

Don't ask.

"We formed this alliance called the Brigade. And I, uh, have no clue what a brigade is. It came out of Enzo's brain and he's from Philly or Jersey—I don't know where he's from, and you never know what comes out of his mouth," Lane told us in the diary room.

At first glance, this motley crew of dudes did not seem like they'd be the first alliance to properly steamroll a season of *Big Brother*, but Matt quickly felt an affinity for them and had a vision. "It goes against my greatest instincts right now to say that I trust anybody, but I do," he said. "I got this gut feeling that these guys have got my back. I'm going to venture to say that we're the strongest alliance in *Big Brother* history."[3]

Let me tell you, the audience was laughing at this line. This poor guy did not know what he was in for. Strongest alliance in *Big Brother* history? What a joke.

It wasn't long, though, before Matt and the Brigade found themselves in a nearly untouchable position, one that they were happy to help facilitate and maintain as they dominated the season.

"The only thing that was on my mind was the secret alliance of Jason and Danielle," Matt told me. "It wasn't until we were all up in that room that night, the four of us, that it all just kind of came out and clicked."[4]

Here's how it works, at least in theory. If you have four people who are secretly in an alliance, each of those four people can then choose one person *outside of* the alliance to link up with. Hayden, for example, got into a showmance with Kristen (who would later be told to grab a life vest by *Big Brother* legend Rachel Reilly, but that's another story). With Hayden publicly linked to Kristen, nobody would suspect that he was secretly more loyal to the other three guys in the Brigade. Additionally, if anybody ever wanted to target Hayden, they'd of course put him on the block next to Kristen and not any other member of the Brigade.

If you can avoid being put up against your own alliance member, you can have the full force of your alliance working to make sure you survive the eviction. And this is where the real genius comes in. Because each member of the alliance has buddied up with one other person, the secret alliance of four can functionally operate as if it's a secret alliance of *eight*.

This structure was tested in week 4 when Hayden *did* get nominated against his showmance Kristen. But Matt was able to influence his plus-one that Hayden would be better to keep, Lane was able to talk to his person, and Enzo… Well, in theory he had someone as well. The idea is that it's much easier to influence one person, a person who thinks that you're their number one in the game. This effectively doubles the alliance's influence in the house without the risk of creating an unwieldy big alliance that would be prone to people leaking or defecting. Half the people in the Brigade's sphere of influence were basically Brigade alliance members without even knowing it!

An added benefit of this structure was that it made the alliance nearly impossible to detect. It was a shortcut for maintaining secrecy. From the outside it looked like a bunch of separate duos were in the house with no big majority anywhere. It didn't even require much skill in the game to operate. As long as everyone played their part, the structure could basically run itself and was devastatingly effective. It solved all of the major issues that a smaller secret alliance had.

Unlike Dan's unorthodox methods that only a player of his caliber could pull off, this was a formula that could be replicated. And it was. More than once in fact. The game was officially broken. It wasn't exactly *easy* to run the Brigade formula, but it was so strong that if you managed to pull it off, you almost couldn't fail.

There was one other key ingredient to its success, however. The Brigade had something that the Legion of Doom didn't, a leader who created that little onion structure I mentioned earlier. Without each member of the alliance feeling like they would be set up for success in the endgame, they might take their plus-one and try to flip the game around.

To this point, *Big Brother* had always been the story of the underdogs, the outsiders who used their wits to overcome the "cool kids" in the majority. It's a huge part of what makes the show so appealing to so many. Matt fit into this archetype well. He stood out in the Brigade alliance, with his tattoos and smaller frame. He was the architect of this dominant strategic structure that allowed the Brigade to cruise through season 12. But Matt was not the one who reaped the rewards of his efforts.

Week 1 HOH Hayden, the ladies' man, was the one who kept the alliance together with his charm and charisma. He had each of them thinking that they were in the core with him, which kept even a smart guy like Matt loyal until Hayden decided to cut him.

"I never thought I was the guy Hayden was with, but I never thought I was the guy Hayden was against. So really, that's all that matters. He did a great job of doing that," Matt told me.

Hayden recognized that Matt was too smart for his own good and that if he wanted to win, he'd need to take Matt out of the game. So he initiated the first and only betrayal of the alliance to evict Matt from the game—three rounds short of making the Final Four with them. Satisfied with his remaining structure, Hayden led the Brigade down to the Final Three from there, where he took home the win.

Hayden hadn't known the show before playing. He was recruited by casting. But when his own competitive savvy, physical strength, and charisma combined with Matt's deep knowledge of the game, a new kind of player emerged. Matt had handed the keys to the strategic kingdom over to the popular kids, the majority players.

From there, majorities in *Big Brother* started adapting game knowledge and strategic development to help crush the outcasts of the game. The tools that were once used by players on the outside to infiltrate and usurp majorities were now being used against them. For over a decade after Hayden's win, no winner of *Big Brother* hadn't had some significant level of game knowledge or fandom of the show prior to entering the house. And a vast majority of those winners started the game as majority players.

The Empire had struck back, and the fans were not pleased.

To the fans on the burgeoning social media sites, season 12 was largely considered to be the most boring season of the show. The four Brigade members kept everyone in line, which limited drama, meant there were no power shifts, and HOH competitions barely mattered because it was all part of the one master plan. Newer fans might balk at the suggestion that season 12 could be considered boring given the iconic fights and characters that season produced, but that's more an indictment on the current state of *Big Brother* than a defense of the season as a whole.

A popular description of season 12 was that it was basically just summer camp for the players. They'd sit around and play pool all day, hanging out and joking around. This was especially true after the star of the season, Rachel Reilly, was evicted.

Despite this, there was a lot happening strategically. For a viewer like me, I was fascinated by how the Brigade's strategy functioned. More than ever I was craving active and lively discussion about *Big Brother* strategy. Even as social media was growing, though, it was difficult to find sources for it that would satisfy me.

I was slow to adapt to the world of social media. I was so late to MySpace that by the time I finally relented and created a page, everyone had already moved on to this new site called Facebook and had developed their own instant messaging lingo that sometimes felt like a foreign language to me. Maybe if I'd grown up watching *The Circle* (a reality show in which contestants only communicate via text), I'd have been better prepared.

Still, somehow I was the one who ended up making their living in this world of internet drama. Maybe I was smarter as a teenager.

All this *Big Brother* discussion on Twitter was completely lost on me. I'd created an account in my senior year of high school and then never touched the thing until after graduating from college in another five years. I came back to it for a very specific reason.

My very first tweet to someone was to a man named Rob Cesternino. It linked to a video of me promising I'd lie, cheat, steal, and backstab for a chance to speak with him about *Big Brother*.[5] That tweet changed my life.

Let me rewind a bit first though. Rob Cesternino is a legendary *Survivor* player who had first applied to be on *Big Brother 3* before casting decided he was a better fit for *Survivor: The Amazon*. In *Survivor*'s sixth season, Rob revolutionized the strategy of that show with his more fluid, *Big Brother*–inspired approach to alliances. *Survivor* host Jeff Probst called him "the smartest player to never win."[6]

After his time on the show, Rob tried to get work in the entertainment industry. Despite some success, he was finding that there wasn't a lot of demand for "reality stars," and he felt stalled out after years of work. In 2010, frustrated and without a creative outlet, he grabbed a microphone from the popular video game *Rock Band* and recorded a podcast with his future wife, Nicole. He called it *Rob Has a Podcast,* now usually abbreviated to *RHAP*.

Podcasts were another form of media rising in popularity as social media shaped the way people both consumed and created content. Here was this former *Survivor* player who was still just as much a fan of the show as anyone, watching every week and talking about the episode, giving his insight and having other former *Survivor* players on as guests.

It's difficult to describe how revolutionary this felt at the time. I didn't do social media, I never participated in the forums, but when

I discovered *RHAP* I knew it was exactly my thing. Reality television has never been an easy thing to talk about. Growing up, I'd occasionally get a friend or two temporarily hooked on the show, but only after a vetting period where I made sure I wouldn't be judged for being into it myself. I know many others in the community who have felt the same way, isolated in their fandom.

What Rob provided in his podcasts was a regular discussion in which it wasn't weird to like the show. He understood what made these shows special, and hearing him talk about it with others made you feel a little less alone and gave you a taste of what it would be like to be able to have a regular conversation about a show that you otherwise had to keep hidden away from the rest of the world.

There was an official internet talk show called *House Calls* that ran for a few years in the early days of the show, hosted mostly by Marcellas from season 3 and radio host Gretchen Massey. They would have former players on as guests, discuss the events of the week, and take calls from viewers. To some degree it resembled some of the bigger budget versions of these sideshow concepts for *Big Brother* that appeared internationally, and it was actually pretty great. However, it had some limitations because it was an official production of CBS, and it ultimately struggled to find a significant enough audience to justify its production.

Promotion was difficult before social media really started taking off. "At the time that we launched the show… I don't even know how you found the podcast if you weren't already a friend of mine in real life," Rob told me. "It wasn't like my stuff was going to show up in a search result in the very early days. We really were just putting it out there into the world and whoever could find it was going to find it."[7]

But as social media continued to grow, so did *RHAP*, as more and more people found their way to it. By 2014 it had become successful enough that Rob was able to go full-time creating podcasts for a living with the support of his listeners. It was an exciting time for the reality TV audience as we were finding more outlets for discussion, analysis, and community.

Big Brother was tough though. Rob started his *Big Brother* coverage in season 12, but despite my love for *RHAP*, I never got into the coverage for *Big Brother*. The show is unique and faces some particularly difficult challenges when you're trying to talk about it. A show like *Survivor* or really any other show, scripted or not, airs once a week. You watch the episode and talk about what you saw in those sixty minutes. Maybe if you're thorough you'll watch the episode more than once, you'll take notes, you'll pull clips. Rob did all of these things. But *Big Brother* is on 24/7; its audience fragmented into episode watchers, casual feed followers, and hardcore live feeders.

Rob didn't have the interest or ability to follow the feeds. How could he? It would basically require someone who dedicated their entire life to monitoring the game to be able to properly discuss it on a podcast. Besides, back in 2010 social media hadn't quite consolidated the *Big Brother* community yet. "At that point in time the live feeds were not as predominant as they are now," Rob said on his *History of RHAP* podcast. "Social media has made it so that when things happen on the live feeds almost everybody knows about it. It wasn't like that then. The *Big Brother* community was not as connected as it is now."[8]

It just made more sense to cover only the episodes. Those that watched the episodes considered the events of the live feeds "spoilers" for future episodes anyway. This method didn't quite work for many of the *Big Brother* fans who were invested enough to listen to a podcast about the show, me included. Without the knowledge from the live feeds, discussion points could be wildly inaccurate or irrelevant to the actual events in the game.

This eventually changed as Rob invited guests on as "correspondents" to keep him informed on the events of the live feeds, but I remained dissatisfied with the coverage. It was still primarily focused on the episodes and just couldn't properly speak to the strategy of the game like they could with *Survivor*.

Finding a place to discuss *Big Brother* strategy anywhere at all was difficult at that time. The way that the old forums and community sites were set up did not lend themselves well to any kind of in-depth analysis or discussion, and even the new social media sites like Twitter seemed to only exacerbate that issue. Between that and the fragmented audience, good strategic discussion was almost nonexistent in my eyes.

I'd resigned myself to this. At the time I was convinced I was an anomaly, someone who just happened to discover the show and appreciate it for reasons that even the show itself didn't seem to cater to. When I ventured out into the forums, I discovered all kinds of name-calling and fandom wars. Where I did find strategic analysis, it was often limited—as with *RHAP*—or just completely absent of any discussion about the feeds.

Then in 2015 Rob put out a call for a new set of people to help him cover the live feeds.

I had just spent four years of college finally experiencing the fresh start I'd always hoped for. I entered the dorms like I was stepping into the *Big Brother* house, quickly establishing a more confident identity, finding friends and allies, and feeling *free* for the first time in my life.

At least, I felt socially free. Financially, it was another story.

College was expensive, and despite the financial aid and scholarship money, I quickly ran up a debt higher than any sum of money I'd ever dreamed of having. To make matters worse, in the fantasy land I lived in, it was a great idea to rack up that much debt for the sake of a film degree.

By my senior year I was juggling classes, night shifts at a reality TV production house, and an unpaid internship at a point-of-sale tech startup. I was fueled by Red Bull and a crushing anxiety for what was going to happen to me after graduation if I couldn't find a source of income on my own.

It ended up being the unpaid internship that turned into my biggest opportunity (though this is far from an endorsement for the exploitative concept); they hired me full-time when I graduated. Making marketing and tutorial videos for a tech startup was the least creative of my endeavors, but the offer of a salary lifted a weight off my shoulders that I'd never fully recognized was there.

My whole life, I'd felt that financial disaster was always right around the corner, that mere survival meant struggle. Fresh out of college, I had the privilege to experience what it was like to exist without that constant state of dread occupying space in my mind.

Then, disaster. Less than a year into my working there, the startup was bought out and shut down. Just like that, the weight came back.

This time without the use of metaphor, *Big Brother* truly came to the rescue. I was doing freelance video work while looking for a job when Rob put out the call for people to apply to join him on the podcast.

I never thought I'd be good at this. I felt woefully unprepared, and I knew that my strategically oriented perspective was not a popular one in the community. Still, I understood how to make videos, and I figured it would be a cool opportunity to speak to one of my favorite *Survivor* players at least once.

I made a parody video of the preseason interviews they do for the show—complete with corny B-roll and a bland background with me amping my personality up like I was Dan Gheesling at a casting call.

It worked. I knew it would work. "Hey Taran," he wrote to me. "I really want you to be part of the live-feed team I'm putting together. I thought your video was fantastic!"[9] Making videos came easy to me. Poor Rob would be disappointed when I was live on a podcast with him. That's when he'd discover how boring I was. I pitched myself as the strategy correspondent, promising I'd break down every angle of the game. I honestly didn't think anyone would be all that interested.

The idea was for a few of the applicants to be selected and then do a trial run during a season of *Big Brother Canada*. After the season ended Rob would narrow things down and choose who he wanted to stay on permanently.

A week in and two podcasts under my belt, I got an email from him. "I thought you did a great job again tonight. As long as you want to talk about the feeds, you've got a place on the podcast."[10]

It's been ten years now and he's still stuck to that. As it turned out, I hadn't been an anomaly, and I wasn't at all alone; there was a huge appetite for the strategic analysis I had been craving. Luckily for me, despite being boring and social media illiterate, I fit right into that gap in coverage that so many people were hungry for.

Now I'm writing a book about the show. Weird, right?

On *Big Brother*, strategy was continuing to evolve in favor of big majority alliances. *Big Brother 12* star Rachel Reilly came back in season 13 along with her showmance Brendan, Evel Dick and his daughter Daniele, and Jeff and Jordan from season 11. The six of them with their combined experience and competitive ability were able to put up a strong showing even as the alliance itself disintegrated, ultimately ending in a controversial win for Rachel.

In season 14, Dan Gheesling returned to compete against Will's Chilltown partner Mike Boogie, Janelle, and another *Big Brother 12* standout, Britney. Of course, Dan once again dominated the game, pulling off moves that were even more wild and impressive than those he had managed in season 10.

Dan's season 14 game went against the modern metastrategy, as he intentionally weakened his own position so that he could build his way back up. This worked, but the mechanics of the season hurt him in some dramatic ways. The first of these was that he and his fellow veteran players were introduced not as players but as "coaches." To the other players, they weren't supposed to be competing; they were supposed to be guiding. This meant that when the producers allowed the coaches to enter the game proper, the new players felt cheated. They thought they were at the Final Eight of their season when suddenly people who had played before and *won* before got to enter the game, and now they were back up to twelve people. The new players were infuriated and made a pact to never allow one of the returning winners to win the game.

This caused a lot of headaches for Dan, along with the fact that something else seemed to be happening with the game structure.

Throughout most of the show's run, competitions had been difficult to win consistently. There was a component of randomness to them—meaning that anyone could win—and this dynamic made the game even more exciting because someone new could grasp power at any moment.

However, in season 13, Rachel was able to dominate the competitions, which led to her winning the game, and now in season 14 just two competitors, Frank and Ian, were winning at least one competition every week for seven weeks straight. Many of those weeks saw one or both of them winning both the HOH and the veto. This proved difficult to work around, especially because Frank was a sworn enemy of Dan, the Jerry of this season. Dan had planned to have Frank voted out earlier in the season, when a twist canceled his eviction. Frank held a grudge after learning that Dan had been planning to betray him.

Frank eventually had Dan in his crosshairs; he'd won HOH and he was determined to make sure Dan did not win the game. He nominated Dan against his closest ally, Danielle. What followed is the greatest strategic move in the history of the show, also known as "Dan's Funeral."

In the veto competition that week, players were forced to take punishments to win points. This led to Frank taking as many punishments as he could to prevent Dan from winning the veto to save himself. So Frank was dressed up in a punishment carrot costume when he helped lock Dan away for the punishment Dan had received in the competition: twenty-four hours of isolation—twenty-four hours when he could have been campaigning to try to get off the block or save himself. He was devastated.

"In the end, there's three things that I love in my life. My wife and my family, coaching, and playing this game. This game means so much to me, and I had so many opportunities to save myself. Letting it slip through my fingers is not easy to deal with," he said in the diary room.[11]

After taking some time to gather himself, Dan had a different outlook on the situation: "Although some people may look at twenty-four hours of solitary confinement as a punishment, to me it's a blessing in disguise. So when I'm in solitary confinement, the only thing I'm going to be doing is thinking how to get myself out of this mess and who I can stab along the way."

He walked out of isolation looking sick. He asked his fellow Houseguests to join him in the living room because he had something to say. As they gathered around, Dan began his speech.

"Honestly the last twenty-four hours for me have been pretty tough. When I walked out of there"—he began to get choked up—"and saw you guys sitting there, that meant the world to me... I'm dressing in all black for a reason. I want to welcome you guys all to my *Big Brother* funeral."[12]

It's important to emphasize how dead in the water Dan was. Frank had been after him for weeks, and nobody was going to vote Danielle out over Dan. Everyone had seen his season. They knew how much of a threat he was. They'd spent the last twenty-four hours making future plans that did not include Dan.

The quote that represents Dan the most over the course of his two seasons on the show was something he said early on: "There's always a way out of every situation as long as you believe you can get out."[13]

That just wasn't true for *Big Brother* though. Positions like this were unwinnable. I thought so. The players thought so. The audience thought so. I remember reading the discussions online. I had assumed Dan was done for, and then I saw people saying things like "There's nothing he can do. Whatever this is isn't going to work." I had no idea what they were talking about. Luckily I was able to tune in in time to watch Dan's show.

Dan went around the circle talking about each person left in the game, referencing personal conversations he'd had with them and talking about how much each one of them meant to him. Tears were flowing from every direction. This was the great Dan Gheesling's eulogy. For as much as they didn't want him to win, he had developed some good relationships in the house.[14]

He went around the circle until he got to Frank. He told Frank that he'd said some things in the diary room that he'd like to apologize for privately. He was trying to make amends before he left.

Then he got to Danielle. His closest ally in the game. His partner who he was sitting on the block against. This was bound to be the most heartfelt and dramatic of them all. She had already been sobbing listening to him so kindly talk about everyone else.

He turned to her and said, "Finally, there's Danielle. The last time I played this game I learned a lot of tough lessons early on. I learned that you've got to find one person and put one hundred percent of your trust in them. I thought if I picked you, you'd have similar qualities to Memphis Garrett. And through my own fault, I was wrong." Danielle went from teary-eyed to confused. "We don't need to get into it now, but in this game you'll never earn my trust back. You know what you did. And in this game you're dead to me. So don't come to me and ask about it, because it's over."[15]

Danielle's mouth shot open. People were wiping tears from their faces as they looked on in shock at what had just happened.

"I don't know what you're talking about, Dan," Danielle tearfully said.

Dan gave some quick hugs around the circle and concluded the meeting, leaving everyone to console an emotionally wrecked Danielle.

To us in the diary room he said, "Did I really go crazy in solitary confinement? Or did I come up with a master plan to get myself out of this mess?"

Of course, you know it's the latter. He grabbed Frank and took him upstairs to talk privately. There Dan exposed the inner workings of the alliance that had been working against Frank for weeks. Dan had allowed Frank to blame him for everything, holding in his back pocket the information that could potentially liberate him. After telling Frank that everyone was against him, Dan proposed that the only way forward for Frank was to work with him. And hey, everyone was going to hate him now after the big stunt he'd just pulled downstairs.

"If my plan works, think of this: I'm going to be off the block from a guy that put on a carrot suit, took an avocado bath, took a chum bath, *and* sat out of an HOH competition all to get me out. I may have a future in sales selling ice to Eskimos if I can pull this thing off," Dan said in the diary room.[16]

It worked. Everyone was shocked—the players, the audience, even production. We were all in awe of what had transpired. This just didn't happen in *Big Brother*. It just doesn't happen. It remains to this day as the most monumental save, the most anyone has ever managed to dig themselves out of such a massive hole in a single maneuver.

After speaking with Frank, Dan went downstairs and explained to the devastated Danielle that he couldn't tell her what he'd planned because he needed her reaction to be genuine. Infuriated, she demanded to know what exactly it was that he had planned. He explained that he had just managed to save both of them.[17]

With the house convinced that the two of them were now at odds, Dan could safely be taken off the block and Danielle would be safe against Dan's replacement. With this one move, Dan managed not only to save himself and his closest ally but also to snipe out the biggest threat left in the game at the time, Britney.

I could write an entire book just about this season and the moves Dan made. I've talked about them at length in other mediums, but suffice it to say, Dan pulled off some absolute *miracles* in season 14 that stand far above anything else that has been seen in the strategic landscape of the game.

Dan quickly turned around and stabbed Frank in the back, evicting him when he finally lost his first competition in six weeks. After that, Ian went on a monumental competition run, winning week after week and preventing Dan from eliminating his next biggest threat. Instead he was again forced to get creative.

At the Final Four, Dan managed to convince his ally Danielle, who had won both the HOH and the veto, to keep him off the block and allow him to choose who was evicted that week. Sounds simple until I tell you that Danielle did have someone in the game she was closer to than Dan: her showmance Shane. Dan convinced Danielle to use the veto on him, putting Shane on the block. Then Dan stood up and shocked them both when he evicted Shane from the game. Danielle has some pretty famous "shocked face" memes in the *Big Brother* community.

Dan then got both Ian and Danielle to throw part 1 of the final-three HOH competition to him, which placed him in a head-to-head against Ian in part 3. Ian won the competition and took Dan to the Final Two with him.

None of that really mattered though. As Britney would later describe, the jury that season would have voted for a bottle of ketchup if it had been sitting next to Dan.[18] They'd never forgotten their pact to prevent a former winner from ever winning again, and the lengths Dan had been forced to go to in order to survive that season had not helped his case. Ian was voted the winner of season 14.

With the end of Dan Gheesling's reign over *Big Brother*, the shift toward big alliances came back with a vengeance. Season 15 did not just have a racism scandal; it also was the first season where a large majority alliance was able to exploit the structure of the game in the same way that the smaller Brigade alliance had been able to, this time by exploiting the ill-conceived twists of the game.

In the Shapiro era of the show, most of the twists were focused on the casting of the show—secret partners, exes, rivals, Project DNA, etc. Starting with season 9, the twists began trying to alter the very structure of how the game was played. In season 9 the players competed as pairs for a few rounds instead of individually. In season 11, they introduced the coup d'état twist that allowed Jeff and Jordan to completely change the course of the game. In season 13, they brought back the "Pairs Twist" and played it out even longer.

Season 15 is when the players caught on to the fact that these twists often came with an exploit. The twist that season was called the "MVP Twist." It allowed America to vote for one player to have the power to nominate a third person for eviction that week on top of the two people the HOH nominated.

Fan-favorite Rachel Reilly's sister Elissa was cast for that season and had been an opposing force to much of the controversy that had been happening. She was far and away the audience favorite and won the MVP vote every week, allowing her to nominate someone of her choosing over and over.

The majority alliance that eventually formed that season quickly saw the value of this strategy. All they needed to do was pull Elissa into their alliance and keep her from being evicted. If they did, through Elissa they would have the power to nominate at least one person every week. Because they were the majority and had more numbers, this meant that they could then use those numbers to vote out the player they nominated every week.

It was a cheat code for the game. The people on the outskirts could win as many HOH and veto competitions as they wanted, and the majority could use the twist to nominate their target of choice and vote them out over the HOH's nominees every time.

And they did.

This exploit also had an interesting side effect. Because it was so unreasonably powerful, it heavily incentivized the majority alliance to stick together while it was still in effect. Where large alliances had been too unwieldy and cumbersome to operate successfully in the past, there was now a common cause giving them reason to stick together.

Once the twist ended that season, Andy—dubbed the "Rat Floater"—was able to brilliantly separate and dominate the rest of the game, following in Jun's footsteps as a floater who bounced back and forth between the factions that formed out of the wreckage of the previous majority alliance.

I remember tracking this strategy at the time, noticing how smart the players were becoming. Being a fan of the show was now the norm. Players like Hayden were competing without the need of a Matt to help get them up to speed with the metastrategy of the game. Meanwhile, the producers seemed to struggle to understand the implications of the twists they were introducing. It seemed as though every time they tried adding something to the game that would make things more difficult for the majority—and therefore exciting—it had the opposite effect. The majority would find a way to exploit it and frustrate the audience.

I wasn't personally frustrated at the time. I found it fascinating to see the strategy evolve so quickly as players adapted to these exploits. It felt new and fresh. Sure, it made for "boring" seasons when it came to drama or power shifts, but I was fine with that in the short term. I just wanted to study how deeply the game could be broken, and it felt like a race for players to discover the next new ultimate game-breaking strategy.

That finally brings us to season 16.

With social media in full gear, fresh off the controversial season 15, *Big Brother* upgraded its cameras, cast Ariana Grande's brother, and introduced the "Battle of the Block" twist.

The purpose of the twist was to take away some of the power of the HOH. How it worked is that instead of just one winner each week, *two* people would win HOH. They both would make their own set of nominations, and then their pair of nominees would compete against the other HOH's pair of nominees. The pair who won would be saved from the block and dethrone the HOH who had nominated them. The pair who lost would remain on the block, and the HOH who nominated them would remain as the sole HOH.

They hyped up the fact that you could win HOH and still go home that week! What a coup for the underdogs, right?

Not exactly.

Derrick Levasseur was a former undercover detective who had been a big fan of the show. He told the audience that he'd be going undercover in the house, and he hid the fact that he was a police officer from them for the entirety of the season. While Derrick hadn't intended to break the game, he found himself in a position to exploit the Battle of the Block twist to full effect.

An alliance of eight people quickly formed called the "Bomb Squad." Like the Brigade before it, the alliance was initially a joke to much of the audience. It was clearly too big and had some huge wild card players who were sure to break the whole thing wide open. Derrick also saw that this was true, so he started making contingency plans.

Along with his number one ally, Cody Calafiore, Derrick quickly and quietly took control of the alliance. He was a master of subtle influence, placing ideas into people's heads and then allowing *them* to convince *him* of the plan he had originally wanted. With this control, Derrick was able to create the ultimate onion alliance.

"I remember specifically there was a point when I was playing the game where the DR [diary room] called me in and said, 'How would you describe what you're doing?'" Derrick told me. "And at the time I said a Wi-Fi signal, right? Like, you have the biggest line at the top, and then as it gets closer to the middle it's just a dot... It's like that cone. But I think an onion analogy is probably even better."[19]

So within the eight-person Bomb Squad alliance, Derrick created a five-person inner alliance called the "Detonators." This alliance consisted of the most stable, reliable players from the big alliance. It made all of the Detonators comfortable and gave them an opportunity to still use the bigger "Bomb Squad Alliance" for numbers.

Within the Detonators alliance, Derrick had a few different final-three alliances, all of which included his ally Cody, and at the center of it all was that Final Two. They named themselves the "Hitmen."

In a strategy similar to the one in season 15, the big Bomb Squad majority alliance was able to exploit the Battle of the Block twist to crush any minority opposition. They now had *two* chances to win HOH instead of one, and as long as just one person from the majority won HOH, they could nominate people who were willing to throw the Battle of the Block competition, ensuring that the majority alliance member would remain HOH, then use the veto and their superior numbers to ensure that their actual target went up on the block and got evicted.

Derrick was the first to do this. He was one of the two HOH winners in week 3 alongside Nicole Franzel, a smart player who was not in his alliance. If she retained her HOH power, it could prove disastrous. So Derrick nominated a pawn from outside the Bomb Squad alliance named Jocasta alongside his ally Caleb. Caleb was willing to take one for the team and throw the Battle of the Block competition, ensuring that he and the pawn Jocasta would stay on the block and, more crucially, that Derrick would remain the HOH.

After that, the veto was used, and Derrick's target that week went up on the block and was sent home. If this sounds complicated, that's because it is. It's a level of gameplay that I enjoyed deciphering but that the producers did not seem to be capable of predicting. There are theories that producers put these exploitable twists in the game on purpose because they prefer seasons that are more "boring"—they're easier to edit into a coherent storyline—but that theory isn't supported by any evidence.

With the added safety of the Battle of the Block exploit, the alliance structure that Derrick created was that much easier to manage. Why ruin a good thing? From there it was just a matter of winning as many competitions as possible while peeling off each layer of the onion one by one.

"We slowly found ways to convince the larger alliances that we needed to decrease size and to not worry because if we got rid of one of the Detonators, that doesn't mean the Detonators are over; it just means we cut the fat, right?" Derrick told me. "You're still part of team Detonators; you're still in the core group. And before they realized they weren't, we tried to set it up in a way where there was nothing they could do about it."[20]

Derrick went on to win season 16 in a show of unprecedented force. It was the most dominant game the show had ever seen; never once was Derrick nominated, never once was he in trouble the entire time. If Matt Hoffman had cracked the code that broke the game, Derrick Levasseur shattered it into pieces.

Season 16 was lamented as one of the worst seasons the show had ever produced. The drama was nonexistent; the power structure that was put into place on day 2 was basically unchanged by day 97. There were no power shifts, no back and forth, no controversy, just a guy playing really well. And this was truly the shape of *Big Brother* to come, as nearly every prospective strategist who came to the show after season 16 hoped to replicate Derrick's success.

I remained fascinated at the progression of strategy in the game. It wasn't quite the underdog rebel story that the early seasons had been, but I was still seeing smart, adaptable players overcome the stronger, more popular ones. I was obsessed with solving the variables that were allowing the game to be so broken. I dug into the nature of the twists, the structure of the alliances, and the various strategies once used by outcasts now appropriated by the established power players of the game.

I eventually created podcasts dedicated to alliance structures where I geeked out with players like Matt Hoffman and Derrick Levasseur about strategy. The audience may have been frustrated with the direction of all this strategy, but they became ever more interested in consuming content that analyzed it. *RHAP's Big Brother* coverage was growing rapidly.

However, at first my role was only to fill in the gaps on episode recaps, making sure the discussion about the episode didn't stray too far from the truth of what was happening on the feeds. Then in the "spoiler" section in the second half, I'd go into full-on storytelling mode, explaining the latest developments and how they happened as succinctly as possible.

Still, it left me frustrated. There was so much more nuance to the events that were happening that I couldn't possibly fit in such a format. Like the episodes themselves, I was finding myself forced to condense the events of a few *days* of gameplay into maybe thirty minutes of discussion. I started feeling more empathy for the editors of the show as I learned how to pluck the most interesting and vital storylines while omitting things that I predicted would not become relevant enough to make the cut.

I was also new to the podcast and I felt incredibly self-conscious if I spoke for more than a minute or two without interruption. Like, who am I to monopolize the airwaves here? It's called *Rob Has a Podcast* for a reason; nobody is here for me. I also knew from experience that I really enjoyed explaining the events of the feeds a little too much. Friends of mine at the time were all too used to me recounting the day's events to them in excited tones as if they cared at all about what was happening on a random set on the other side of the country.

It was season 17 when I felt the most frustrated. After a lot of preseason hype, professional poker player Vanessa Rousso had gotten off to an awful start that season. She was outside of the majority alliance, and by then that was basically a death sentence in the game. Worst of all, Battle of the Block was back, which incentivized the big alliance to stick together and wreak havoc on the outcasts.

But there was one other twist that season, one they pulled from the Shapiro era. The Twin Twist was back. Contestant Liz was secretly switching places with her twin, and if the two of them made it far enough without being evicted, her twin would join her in the game.

But *Big Brother* players were far more knowledgeable about the show now than they had been back in the days of Adria and Natalie, and future star Da'Vonne Rogers spotted the subtle differences between the twins and started spreading it around the house. The Twin Twist is back! Liz is a twin!

The poker star Vanessa saw the opportunity. She quickly grabbed Liz (who was actually her twin, Julia, at the time) and explained that they'd been caught by Da'Vonne—a member of the majority alliance. "Liz" was panicked, of course, but Vanessa offered her support.

Vanessa didn't mind that she was a twin; in fact this was fantastic news. It meant that Liz was actually two players for the price of one.

Using the information to bond with Liz, Vanessa then used Liz as a bargaining chip to create new alliances that divided the majority. Who could pass up the opportunity to smuggle an extra ally into the midgame? Using Liz as her hammer, Vanessa cracked the game wide open and formed her own majority alliance out of the wreckage.

I recall trying to explain all of this in my limited spoilers portion of the podcast. I sounded like a child trying to explain how awesome my favorite toy was to my uninterested parents. I knew I had to get better at this. I knew there was something interesting here if I could just say it in the right way.

After Vanessa took control of the game, people began to recognize her brilliance, and she became a star of the episodes. But there was another player I had my eye on: superfan Steve Moses was the geek archetype incarnate. Early on he had a famous moment when he accidentally said "I love you"[21] to Da'Vonne as a goodbye like he was speaking to his mom. He was adorable. Harmless Steve had been left out of the early alliances, but Vanessa had seen his value. When she created her counteralliance, he had been a key part of it and had quickly become her number two.

What Vanessa didn't know, and what even the producers of the show didn't know for far too long, was that Steve was truly a wolf in sheep's clothing. Steve had read Dan Gheesling's book *How to Get on Reality TV* cover to cover. He even brought it with him to casting. He knew that his chances of getting on the show were not good by just being himself. Instead, he focused on building a character.

"I almost memorized [Dan's book] to the point where when I walked into my finals interview, I knew the name of every EP [executive producer]," Steve told me.[22]

Steve was one of my first friends from the show. He reached out after his season to thank me for my coverage of his game, and we kept talking from there. He'd been excited to be part of the *Big Brother* community at the time, though things had changed for him by the time I caught up with him for this book.

When studying how to get on the show, Steve had noticed that in episode 2 of every season since *Big Brother 10*, the "Previously on..." segment included a recap of the cast. It would go something like "Thirteen strangers from all walks of life began the battle for a half million dollars. *Among them*, a great-grandfather, a New Orleans socialite, a Catholic schoolteacher, and a preacher's son." He called these your "Among them..." In season 17, Steve's "Among them..." was the "Geek."[23]

"I tricked production into casting me. I don't think they would have ever cast me with me being myself," he told me. So Steve did everything he could to be the stereotypical geek—or at least the kind of stereotypical geek who could be cast on reality television. He bought a pocket protector on the way to his audition.

"I was the cocky, know-it-all, smartest-person-in-the-room jackass. Like, I was actively mean to every person I interacted with at finals week. I was a stuck-up know-it-all. I was a little prick. And I did that because I was trying to be the best archetype of the nerd with glasses as I possibly could be... I tricked them."[24]

Like Dan, as soon as Steve entered the house he changed and became the sweetheart nerd who wanted to lie low and couldn't fathom being rude to a soul. Production wasn't pleased. CBS CEO Les Moonves, now married to Julie Chen, was still taking a big interest in the day-to-day of *Big Brother*. He infamously was quoted in an interview with *Vulture* saying, "This wasn't a great year for casting on

Big Brother... Usually you have one or two disappointments. I think we had five or six disappointments."[25]

It was notable at the time because Moonves hadn't publicly derided *Big Brother* casting in such a way since season 1. When Steve got out of the house and saw the comment, he felt he knew who it was directed at. "They didn't get what they wanted from me at all. Les didn't say names when he said a whole bunch of the cast were disappointments, but I imagine I had to be disappointment number one. Because I was probably the biggest deviation between what they bought and what they got."[26]

So perhaps because they were annoyed at Steve, or maybe because they honestly didn't see what he was doing, Steve became the most underedited winner *Big Brother* has ever had. This meant that a lot of his content was not used in the edits for the show. To be fair to the producers, *Big Brother* has a unique issue that other competition reality shows don't have to deal with: it's all live. This means that they don't know who's going to win or what's going to be relevant to the long-term storyline. It's the problem I had to deal with when I tried to explain what was happening in my short window of time on the podcast: Was I giving all of the *relevant* information considering that I couldn't possibly predict what was going to happen in the future?

In this case, I knew Steve was doing much more than the episodes were showing. Vanessa was the focus of most strategic discussion that season, but I always made sure to say that people were sleeping on Steve, that he was, in my eyes, at least the second best player of the season and unlike with Vanessa, nobody could see it.

Vanessa was such a logical player. She was a poker star and lawyer. I loved watching her strategize. Toward the end of the game, she used Skittles to plot out every iteration of possibilities for the endgame, using each Skittle color as code for the other players. She was able to accurately predict what every person in the house would do at every step using this diagram of Skittles. That is, every person except for Steve. He had successfully convinced her that he was willing to bring her to the end, when in reality he had been plotting her demise for weeks, knowing that in order to win the game himself, he'd need to snipe her at the last minute and take the crown from her.

Much to the dismay of many strategically oriented fans, that's exactly what he did. These fans were furious that Steve—who in their minds had done nothing all game—had managed to take down Vanessa and win. I felt useless. I had been trying to advocate for him and explain what he had been doing all season long, but it wasn't in the episodes, and most people just didn't see it.

When Steve reached out to me after the season, I saw firsthand the kind of impact that an edit can have on a player and consequently how important the live feeds can be to them. I could feel the disappointment in Steve when I informed him that many of his camera talks hadn't made the edit and that many hadn't even been shown on the feeds.

I've sensed a deep desire from most contestants I've talked to for their experience to be faithfully represented or, at the very least, for their experience to be understood and seen. Of course, this isn't an easy task because everyone has different experiences and memories of how things went down. But when the only source of information comes from an edited show, it's very easy to feel slighted or hurt because of how the show chose to portray you and the events you experienced.

Many players feel their time on the show wasn't represented in the way that they'd hoped but that the feeds were at least a somewhat objective account of the reality they experienced. For some players, this is even more frustrating because they're less capable of claiming that there were things the audience didn't see that will vindicate them. A common phrase from alumni that will elicit an eye roll from fans is "The feeds don't see everything!" Nowadays the truth of Steve's strategic game is known to most strategy fans, but at the time I was feeling the futility of my position more than ever. There were so many stories being left untold on the live feeds. I wanted to do more.

Podcasting was a hobby for me then. I never imagined it could be a job for me. After the startup failed, I had been hired for video production at another company and was toiling away at a job that I didn't enjoy. Still, that crushing weight of financial anxiety had been lightened again, and that was more than enough for me.

I was happy to plug away at my real-life job while I dallied in the fantasyland of *Big Brother* podcasting. I wasn't ignorant of the fact that it was possible to make a living doing it, but that kind of dream was for other people, not me. Still, Dan's mentality had worked its way into the core of my being without my knowing it. All these years later, I asked Dan what he took away from his time on the show. His answer? "I was thinking about how I was before I went on *Big Brother*, because it really proved to me a lot of things I thought I believed in, like, hey, you can really win in any situation. It's truly never over."[27]

I can't say I ever truly believed in a world where I achieved my dreams, but *Big Brother* taught me to try as hard as I could anyway. It's why I went to college despite the debt, and it's why I worked as many jobs as I could. All you can do is maximize your odds of winning.

I was and still am uncomfortable with ambition. I enjoy games, but I don't like competing. Maybe that's weird to hear from someone who spends so much time analyzing games, but then again, there's a reason I enjoy breaking things down the way I do.

I expressed some small desire for more time dedicated to live feeds on the podcast, but I felt too uncomfortable with how self-serving that was to ever push for it too hard. What I wanted was a podcast dedicated entirely to the live feeds. I could talk about them every day, getting into the various stories and strategies that had occurred. It was what I had always done to my friends, talking their ears off about the events of the previous day, spending my mornings catching up on what I'd missed overnight. *That's* what I wanted to do on the podcast. But I didn't know how to ask for it.

I was extremely lucky to have stumbled into Rob Cesternino's world. He's not only been very kind to me but also has a great eye for content that syncs with my own. He approached me one day asking what I thought of the idea of a daily podcast where we'd briefly run through the events of the day on the feeds.

He wanted me to take the reins of this project, and I couldn't have been more ecstatic. This was everything I had wanted from *Big Brother* coverage since I'd started reading posts on JokersUpdates years ago. The challenge for Rob was that it seemed impossible for any one person to accomplish. There were a few superhuman efforts from people like Big Brother Daily, Hamsterwatch, Online Big Brother, and Madrosed among many others, but what we wanted to do was have a live show every morning that anyone could watch or listen to and get up to speed in order to watch the feeds that day.

The only way to accomplish this would be to make it your full-time job—not only staying on top of everything happening on the feeds but also being available every morning for a live show. The second Rob asked me to work on it, I knew what I had to do. The *Big Brother* coverage had been growing rapidly, and I really had faith in this concept. I dropped everything else in my life and committed to being there every morning, telling the story of the live feeds day in and day out.

So I did. And after over one thousand live-feed update podcasts, I've still never missed a single day. The updates drove our *Big Brother* coverage to new heights. Every morning thousands of people were tuning in to hear me retell the events of the live feeds from the previous day while providing context and analysis for what we saw. It soon afforded me the opportunity to live my dream and do this for a living. Luckily nobody has ever figured out that I would have done it for free.

The game remains endlessly fascinating to me, even when it's frustrating or disappointing. Without a detailed accounting from live feeds, other competition reality shows often feel as though they're just spectacle, an exaggerated summary of events. Every morning I dive headfirst into the depths of why things are truly happening and how they came to be. It continues to teach me all kinds of things about myself, our society, and the various ways that those two things interact with one another. I can't make the case that this is, or can be, true for anyone else, but the show has given so much to me.

Talking to Steve Moses after his season was the first time that I had come to understand that others found what I was doing valuable as well. It felt good that my understanding and recognition of his experience had given him any sense of relief, small as it might have been. Since then, some of the most rewarding experiences I've had doing this job have been the times that players have felt seen and understood by me as we've talked through their games.

And ultimately, that's how I ended up writing notes at 3:00 a.m. as I watched a person get out of bed on the live feeds, anxiously waiting for them to go upstairs to the HOH room to see if the entire game was about to flip on its head.

I was there, documenting everything as *Big Brother* started going through some of its biggest and most tumultuous changes yet. As dominant alliances started to reign supreme over the game, there was one alliance that was determined to dominate the game in a way that had never been seen before: They wanted to do it so thoroughly that it made a statement reaching all the way back to the very conception of the show.

12

The Cookout

In the era of dominant majority alliances, there was still something that seemed so impossible nobody thought it could ever be done. Every big alliance broke up and took out some of its own members in order for the most strategic players to gain advantage in the endgame. It's what Hayden did to Matt, and it's how Derrick whittled down his alliances. Despite the success of large alliances in this era, it only ever served to benefit a small few within that alliance, not the success of the group as a whole.

That is, until the "Cookout."

Taking season 23 by force, the Cookout became the first alliance ever to get every one of its six members all the way down to the Final Six of the game. It was so monumental that it made national headlines, not because of *how* they made it happen but because of *why* they made it happen.

The Cookout was an alliance that consisted of all the Black players on the cast, and by making it to the Final Six together, they guaranteed that a Black player would win *Big Brother* for the first time in its twenty-one-year history.

"Black players changed *Big Brother* forever. Fans say the show can't 'tiptoe' around it," read a headline in the *LA Times*.[1]

Azah Awasum, Derek Frazier, Kyland Young, Hannah Chaddha, Tiffany Mitchell, and Xavier Prather: six names that went down in *Big Brother* history. They inspired a whole new generation of players and fans who had otherwise been turned off to a show that had so often been mired in racial controversy.

The Cookout's dominance can largely be attributed to the strategic planning of Tiffany Mitchell. At forty years old, she was the oldest player in the house. Demographically she couldn't have been less likely to succeed in the game. Despite this, the longtime fan quickly found herself at the center of multiple power structures and was all but guaranteed to make a deep run.

Her primary allies included the comp beast Derek Xiao and superfan Claire Rehfuss. Using her magnetic personality and strategic acumen, Tiffany was able to infiltrate and demolish the initial majority alliance and supplant it with one of her own, all while remaining mostly under the radar.

But while all of this was happening, another game was being played beneath the surface. There were six Black players in the house—an unprecedented number—and they recognized what seemed like a once-in-a-lifetime opportunity. Their initial goal wasn't lofty; they just wanted to support one another.

"My strategy coming into the house was never about race or femininity, gender or my age. I didn't have a motive besides winning $500,000," Tiffany told me.[2]

Little did she know, it was during her season that they'd finally increase the prize money to $750,000. Doesn't exactly roll off the tongue anymore, but hey, at least they were starting to adjust for inflation.

I'd spent two days with Tiffany right after her season ended, diving deep into the specifics of her game. She has a powerful presence that draws people to her, and if you're lucky enough to be considered her friend, there's a fiercely protective quality to her. It's easy to see how she ended up at the center of the strategic play in the game.

So, naturally, she was ready to help however she could when I asked her to share her thoughts for this book.

"I think there is an underlying, unspoken human characteristic that when you enter an environment, especially if it's foreign, and there's someone that is recognizable to you, that is relatable to you, you gravitate towards that," she told me. "Walking into the *Big Brother* house and seeing more Black people than I had ever seen in the house at one time, it was like, 'Oh, well maybe I'll have a little more protection this season than what I've seen occur in other seasons,' because we all have watched *Big Brother* and we know immediately people of color go out first. There's no one there to protect them. There's no one who identifies, who relates."

With that, the Cookout was created. For weeks the players never even met as a group; it was a mostly unspoken agreement to look out for one another. But all that changed after Tiffany had a literal dream she called her master plan. It would send a message far beyond the scope of *Big Brother*.

The story of the Cookout begins long before season 23. In fact, it goes all the way back to the very first season of the show. While there was plenty of overt racism throughout the show's history, that wasn't the only thing on display in this game that mirrors how our own society works.

In discussing some of the racist comments being made in the house at the time, critics had already brought up concerns about the very makeup of the cast and the way that certain players were being portrayed.

Writer Joe Rhodes and attorney Lisa Hoffman were quoted in an article from *Daily News Los Angeles*, saying, "Rhodes and Hoffman also say that racism seems to be behind discussions among Eddie, George and Karen on voting in a bloc against Cassandra, the lone remaining African American houseguest. 'Cassandra is on their hit list because they don't relate to her,' Hoffman says. 'They don't relate to (Asian American) Curtis,' whom the houseguests had 'marked for banishment' last week… That, too, has not made it on the broadcast version of the show—or on the series' official Web site, which dwells on much other minutiae of the houseguests' lives."[3]

Further in the article, the founding director of the Center for the Study of Popular Television and Syracuse professor Robert Thompson said, "They have to take material and in a very short time work it into a pseudo-documentary. Editing film is a fictionalizing machine—you create characters and conflicts. No matter how pure their intentions may be, the general prejudices and biases of the culture have come out. Will 'Mega' was presented as dangerous, somewhat threatening, and aggressively male. They knew what they were doing with his depiction."[4]

"It didn't start in season eight or season fifteen," Cookout strategist Tiffany Mitchell told me. "In season one, Will Mega was targeted because of his Blackness. He was aggressive, or he was too assertive, he played too hard. And really, it was just that he was too Black."[5]

These criticisms would go largely unheard for years. If a player was portrayed in a certain way, fans would often argue that they gave the producers that content, so how could they complain? They'd argue that players can't say it's unfair or wrong to only include one or two Black players on each season because that's representative of the country; it's just the way things are.

So, it was the way things were. For years.

In season 8, amid all the other chaos, a segment about race made it through. Jameka was the only Black person on the cast that season, and she had gotten into a disagreement with Evel Dick.

"I said something about starving kids in Africa, and she got so defensive, like I was saying it in a racist way because I picked Africa. And that really upset me," he said in the diary room.[6]

When Jameka pointed out that there were starving kids in all countries, they sat down and talked about it. "Listen, I'm the only Black person here, so I am cognizant of how that is portrayed... I'm not saying it has anything to do with you... It's just a lot. Y'all don't understand because y'all aren't a minority, but it's a lot on my shoulders because if I act... I have to be mindful of how I'm portraying myself."

She apologized in tears for making him feel uncomfortable and said to us in the diary room, "To come into this environment, I felt as though I had to be what other people wanted me to be; I didn't feel comfortable being myself."

Evel Dick said to us, "When you're taking the weight of an entire race on your shoulders and being the representation of them to the world from this show—it has to be a hard thing, it has to be a personal thing, it has to be an emotional thing."[7]

Jameka's plight was not unique. She felt like she wasn't afforded the freedom to just be herself because she felt the weight of what she represented to her community. But it goes further than that. Even if she had decided to eschew the responsibility of representation and just be herself, that didn't mean that her fellow contestants, the producers, or the audience would just forget that she was the only Black person on the show.

Big Brother 24 contestant Taylor Hale explains, "It's good to have these competition reality shows where you have the opportunity to not be who you are in the real world. It's like Halloween for a lot of people. It's Halloween for your brain. Honestly, you get to experiment with being somebody else playing in a different way. And that's the sort of freedom that you might not get in the real world."[8]

That's what Dan did when he played. He was able to compartmentalize the game from reality and have fun maneuvering around the playground of this societal mirror. It's what Dr. Will did as he toyed with those around him. For someone like me, this is a big part of the appeal of the show. As a kid, I could imagine myself being whoever I wanted to be in the manufactured world of the show, conquering my opponents with my wits in ways that I would never do in real life.

For others, though, it's more difficult to divorce their real-life identity from their in-game identity. For decades the way that reality television portrayed minorities was fraught with stereotyping and prejudice. In season 1, Will Mega complained that his portrayal was unbalanced in comparison to that of his fellow contestants. "You only saw the intense, analytical, debated, confrontational, argumentative, issue-pressing 'Mega,'" he said in *Daily News Los Angeles*. "You didn't see 'Mega' who every morning would get up and pray... You didn't see Will Mega's poetry."[9]

Paul Römer retorted at the time, "There are people out there who say this show is boring. What would be boring is to show the lowlights."[10] Yet, the show was more reluctant when it came to the eventual winner's racist remarks and controversial statements, preferring to show his softer side.

It goes beyond individual examples, though; it's a pattern—one that was pointed out time and time again to an audience that didn't care to listen.

Then season 15 happened. There was so much pushback to the overt racism displayed that season that the show finally had to listen and portray it on the episodes. A major win for those looking to combat racism, right? After season 15, the show got a bit more careful about who they cast, and far fewer slurs have been slung around in the *Big Brother* house since.

But what if I told you that after season 15, Black players were consistently performing even *worse* in the game than they had in the first decade of the show?

As before, there were plenty of people trying to point this out at the time. Hugh Ryan wrote in the *Daily Beast*, "Aaryn Gries is a racist... Her actions have prompted CBS, for the first time ever, to publicly address offensive statements made on the show... But far from exposing racism on *Big Brother*, the maelstrom surrounding Gries (and to a lesser extent, fellow Houseguest GinaMarie Zimmerman), has had the ironic effect of hiding other, more systemic forms of racism that exist on *Big Brother*—and in reality television as a whole."[11]

"This goes on on other shows too," said Sistah J of the *Sistah Speak* podcast while being interviewed by Ryan. "But they don't show it overtly like *Big Brother* because there are no live feeds."[12]

Ryan went on to discuss an article coauthored by Bryan Denham called "Survival of the Stereotypical," which examines the various social stereotypes that these shows reproduce in the way they edit their characters and narratives. Denham doesn't believe it's intentional, but when producers—who are mostly White—cast and edit their shows, they're using their own preexisting assumptions about race.[13]

"The idea that by dealing with Gries we will 'deal' with racism on reality television is ridiculous. She becomes a sacrifice whose very punishment is the thing that allows us, the mainstream audience, to continue watching, snug and smug inside our own non-racist self-conceptions," Ryan wrote. "Turning racism into a story with a villain—instead of an underlying force of our existence—guarantees that any resulting conversation will go nowhere, mean nothing, and quickly be forgotten. Indeed, despite the anger at Gries inside and outside the house, all of the contestants of color have been sent home, while she remains." He continued, "Aaryn Gries is racist. But calling her out on her racism while ignoring our own? That's racist too."[14]

I mentioned at the start of this chapter that the Cookout's goal was to crown the first Black winner in the show's more than twenty-year history. Twenty-two seasons, twenty-two winners, and arguably Danielle Reyes from season 3 was still the closest a Black player had come to winning the game. But it was worse than just that.

In a paper written in 2019 called *"Big Brother's Diversity Problem by the Numbers"*, author Vince Dixon analyzed the statistics of the various demographics and their performance in the game. He confirmed that even when accounting for the fact that there were fewer Black players total, any given Black player was still underperforming in the game compared to a White player.[15]

This shouldn't be surprising to anyone, and most fans have long been cognizant of it without needing any data to back it up. The contention really comes down to the fact that there are people who don't see it as a problem worth dealing with.

In the paper, Dixon actually cites my own theory that these outcomes were being made worse by the direction in which the twists had taken the game—namely that with the format of the game being altered to benefit larger majority alliances, the underlying systemic issues around race were being more blatantly exposed.

As America's Player Eric Stein explained to me, "There's a game called Huggy Bear that's often played at bar mitzvahs. Basically they yell out a number and it's like, 'Huggy Bear nine!' And you have to immediately grab nine people and anybody who's not in a group is eliminated, and they say, 'Huggy Bear five!' 'Huggy Bear seven!' You do it again and again and again until nobody's left. I feel like that's how *Big Brother* is played. Week one it's Huggy Bear eleven; you grab the first eleven people that are standing next to you on the dance floor that remind you of back home or whatever the case may be. For the other five people it's like, tough shit, you're not in my group."[16]

Of course he goes on to explain that there's more to the game than just that, but it is one of the biggest and most impactful elements of *Big Brother* strategy. Overcoming those initial groupings is the foundation that the show was built on. But as time went on and as the format and twists started changing, it became more and more difficult to accomplish.

Stein continues to explain: "A big part of *Big Brother* is that all the action of the week is so consolidated into those first few days."

How a week on the show works is that the HOH competition happens right after the eviction, nominations take place the next day, and then the veto competition happens the day after that. After the veto competition, there's a period of four days or so when the only thing to do is formalize the decision by the veto holder in the veto ceremony, then prepare to vote for one of the two nominees.

"You basically spend the next five days living in the aftermath. That allows the anchors of power to dig in even further," Stein described. "When you are in charge and the week has gone your way, you are not scared for your life, you can speak freely, you have allies that know they're safe. This gives you an additional five days to operate and forge bonds. Whereas the people who are already on the outs don't have those five days because they're in danger and spending their time trying to survive. If they say the wrong thing, it's being lorded over them that they could be put up and voted out so they really have no choice but to play the game of the people who put them in that position. It ends up being this sort of never-ending cycle of hell for people on the outside because they can't ever maneuver their way out of that."[17]

If unchecked, power snowballs in *Big Brother*. Initial power that stems from being part of the early majority can be translated into more power as your majority wins more competitions, exploits the twists in your favor, and forces anyone on the outs to play the game of the majority rather than their own.

What we started seeing from around season 15 on was that when one group got out to such a massive lead, the others started seeing the game differently. There was more groupthink and ostracism of those in the minority. In response, players on the outside were less and less likely to rebel against the power, feeling it was hopeless. They'd often betray each other for the hope of a little favor from the majority. With just a few small changes to the format, the game was spiraling in an incredibly lopsided direction.

This is where the initial foundations of *Big Brother* strategy came in. Secrecy, floating, divide and conquer. These were techniques that could be used to get out from under the oppressive nature of how power works in the game. But now the majorities were adapting these strategies for their own use while they continued to exploit the twists to work in their favor.

As outcomes started to get worse, the problem became more and more clear. Even in places like Reddit there were posts popping up like the one by user EmpiricalMonarch: "This show is the primary piece of evidence that I have ever been exposed to that people are treated differently because of their skin color... What I have learned is that racism is not only outward discriminatory opinions, viewpoints, or statements made to another person on the basis of somebody's race. This is more concrete and visible to us in society, so we often think this is what constitutes somebody being racist. Instead, it can manifest in more subtle ways: subconscious biases, non-purposeful ignorant remarks, even exclusion... This post is not about racism in the *Big Brother* game. It's about racism in the world, highlighted by the microcosm that is the *Big Brother* game."[18]

Season after season, players from the initial majorities won the game. Season after season, those majorities just so happened to either not include Black players or eliminated them quickly. By season 21, no Black player had even placed in the top half of a season for *eight years*. They finally broke that barrier in season 22, when David Alexander managed eighth place, out of sixteen players.

The Cookout played in season 23.

Let me catch you up. In season 18, Derrick Levasseur's rival Nicole Franzel returned and won a fairly dominant game of her own, controversially staking a claim to become one of the top winners of the show. The following season saw another returning player—Paul Abrahamian, fresh off their loss to Nicole in the Final Two of the previous season—completely dominate the game using Derrick's formula, only to lose *again* in the Final Two because of how poorly they treated their fellow Houseguests.

During that season, I hosted a podcast discussing the psychology of the cult-like tactics that were becoming commonplace on the show. By then it had become abundantly clear that Derrick's strategy was here to stay. Not only was it a culmination of all the strategic innovations that came before it, but it was a clear formula that anyone could attempt to replicate. *Big Brother* continued to implement exploitable twists, and big alliances continued to exploit them.

The audience was frustrated. Even my enthusiasm for all the strategic innovation was dwindling. It was exciting to see people crack the code, but watching people just follow that formula over and over again season after season was getting dull even for me. This was especially true given the fact that this strategy meant fewer power shifts, less drama, and, worst of all for me, a stifling of further strategic innovation.

After the golden age for ratings during the Dan Gheesling era where the show had been growing in popularity, the ratings started to drop again. Soon they fell below the previous low of season 9 and continued dropping each subsequent season.

Season 20 saw a brief reprieve from the lopsided dominant play that had plagued the back half of the decade. The house very fortuitously divided into two even sides at the start of the game. The audience hadn't seen a split house like that since Kaysar versus Maggie in season 6. To make it even more exciting, both sides were trading off HOH wins back and forth, taking shots at one another and keeping the sides even enough to maintain the tension.

The tension broke when, of course, a twist was introduced into the game that one side was able to exploit to take control. From that point forward, they crushed the rest of their opposition and many felt the season lost its steam.

That brought us to season 21. To kick off the game that season, there was a twist where the players all voted for a "Camp Director" on the first night based mostly on first impressions. The winner of the vote was Jackson Michie, a twenty-four-year-old from LA who was square jawed, charming, and extremely fit. He was also White. As Camp Director, Jackson was tasked with choosing four people to banish from the game. Those four would then have to compete against each other, with the loser becoming the first person evicted from the game.

Once again this choice was intentionally meant to be based on first impressions. Somehow, the producers didn't seem to see it coming when Jackson declared he would be banishing three people of color along with the oldest Houseguest in the game. Three of them had volunteered themselves for the position of Camp Director but hadn't received the votes to win against Jackson, so he felt they were easy targets for banishment. In the episode, it was implied that Jackson's fourth pick was based purely on the fact that the player hadn't even bothered to talk to Jackson after he won the vote. Seems pretty reasonable I guess.

There's an important note here though. For most of the show's run, the live feeds have started a few days late. This is because they pretape the premiere episode and don't kick the feeds off until after it airs. This means that we miss the first few days of initial impressions and bonding. This was the case in season 21, so when the episode heavily implied that one of Jackson's picks hadn't even talked to him, there was nothing to contradict that information.

That is, until we later heard from multiple contestants that it wasn't at all true. The pick *had* talked to Jackson; he just didn't like the conversation. "I don't have much to go on besides the first impression, and your first impression wasn't all that sweet," Jackson told us in the diary room.[19]

To this day, most *Big Brother* fans believe the simple narrative presented to them by the show. Why wouldn't they? It's perhaps a small detail in the grand scheme of the game, but it's these "small" points of contention that can end up being very important to individual players who have to deal with these misconceptions from fans for the rest of their lives. This is why so many players I've talked to have lauded the live feeds as a layer of protection despite their invasiveness. In this case, this point of contention became even more important as the season progressed.

The player who ended up being evicted first was none other than David Alexander, who would return in the next season and become the highest-placing Black player in nearly a decade at eighth place. But the season's race troubles had only just begun.

It wasn't long before the season started to feel like another season 15, as racist comments and behavior were being captured on the feeds. One of Jackson's closest allies in the game (named Jack—no, I'm not kidding) was grilled by Julie about his comments after he was evicted.

Another twist in the game did more to highlight the issue than anything that had come before it. Producers introduced the "Camp Comeback" twist. The idea was that the first three players evicted from the game would be dressed up in "camp uniforms" and be sent back into the game to live in a sparse "Have-Not Room." They weren't real players and had no power or amenities in the game. At the end of the week, they'd compete with the next person to be evicted, and one of them would be able to return to the game in full.

It might be clear to you by now where this is going. If you're a fan of the show, you've likely already seen the image. The first three people evicted from the game were all people of color, and they sat on stage in their camp uniforms, looking dejected as they spoke to Julie. The image made the statistics real to many people who had been able to ignore what had been happening. From there, once again, discussion started picking up in the mainstream press.

In addition to the Camp Comeback situation and the racist comments on the live feeds, CBS was getting heat from *Survivor* contestant Julia Carter. "First and foremost, I will call attention to the elephant in the room, RACE. No one ever wants to open the can of worms, stir the pot, and there is certainly less incentive if you find yourself in the majority. I was that person a long time ago, even though I am Black. Growing up in predominantly White communities where you are made to feel like you do not belong can indirectly teach you to silence yourself," she wrote in a piece she published about her experience on the show.[20]

She goes on to explain that in her first night on the *Survivor* beach, she was shocked to hear someone say the n-word. She was the only Black castaway on the beach. She said she didn't feel prepared to have to fight against racism and bias when she was hoping to just play *Survivor*.

After someone said the word again a few days later, a White tribemate spoke up against its usage, which led to a lengthy discussion about race in the tribe. Julia had a significant confessional following the discussion where she, in tears, expressed how she felt about the whole situation and the difficulty of being the only Black person on the beach. She said the camera crew and producer there were crying by the end as well and offered her an apology for what she was dealing with.

None of this made the edit. At all. In fact, Julia didn't have a single one of her confessionals make the show until episode 5 of the season despite every other contestant having at least one in the first two episodes. In the edit, she was one of the most underrepresented contestants in the history of the show. Unlike with *Big Brother*, there were no live feeds to fall back on; she was a lone voice telling a story that seemed to conflict with the official narrative. When she tried to speak out on Twitter, she was met with significant backlash from fans.

"I went on *Survivor* knowing I may be a role model & inspire someone to play despite NOT fitting the archetype. Therefore, in S38, in which there are only two Black castaways, it's disheartening to see the lack of equitable airtime defeating my goal," she wrote. "But we have A LOT of S38 left! Hopefully, CBS can strategize in the future, taking into account that fans want to see more of us. As for now, for those at home not seeing many people who may look like you on the show, continue to watch! And trust me, you can do it."[21]

Fans replied, calling her boring and ungrateful and claiming that she was pulling the "race card." If she wanted more airtime and attention she should have been more entertaining.

After the season, she wrote her piece about the show and ended it with a message to CBS: "There is a significant difference between diversity and inclusion. Casting a few Black faces each season simply isn't enough. Include them in the story. Stop giving them stereotypical edits that perpetuate the same stereotypes that many of us come on the show to combat."[22]

This was 2019. CBS president Kelly Kahl and senior VP of programming Thom Sherman—two White men—had gone to the Television Critics Association that year to tout their latest diversity statistic: 53 percent of CBS's writers and 50 percent of directors for its scripted series were women or people of color.[23] Instead of being impressed, however, the press at their panel grilled them about the racial issues happening on the unscripted side of production.

In response to the *Big Brother* Camp Comeback controversy, CBS had already released a statement saying, "At times, the Houseguests say things that we do not condone. We share some of the viewers' concerns about inappropriate behavior and offensive comments, and producers have addressed specific incidents with the Houseguests involved. However, there is absolutely no truth that the casting of the show is racially motivated, that the Houseguests' behavior is predetermined or that the outcome is controlled in any way."[24]

The issue is that in addition to the other controversies, it was revealed on the live feeds that a diary room producer had prodded a Black contestant to behave in a more stereotypical way. "They were like, 'Oh, why don't you wag your finger and be like, *Uhn, uhn, girlfriend*.' I'm like, I don't even talk like that... I literally don't talk like that so what are you trying to do?"[25]

Reporters grilled the CBS president and his colleague about all of this. Margeaux Sippell of *The Wrap* wrote, "This summer, *Big Brother* producers have asked their only Black female cast member to act and talk in a more stereotypical way. They've edited out hateful and violent things that White men have said about her and editing her seems rather crazy. So I guess my question is, is it acceptable to, in your two top reality shows, allow this behavior to continue to perpetuate stereotypes through the choices that producers are making in editing and in production?"[26]

Sherman responded by saying they had learned a producer had overstepped while trying to get a sound bite and had since been reprimanded and gone through unconscious bias training, as all producers on the show did. He went on to say, "I think the vast majority of people who come off the shows are very happy with the way they're represented… There are thousands of hours that are condensed down to forty-two minutes per episode and we're simply not able to show every single thing that happens on the show."[27]

Eric Deggens of NPR pressed the issue: "You guys have been in situations before where people have tried to talk to you about your lack of diversity in programming… We are now telling you that you have a problem with your reality shows. Why can't you take that criticism and do some substantive looking at it rather than trying to spin it?" He continued, "This year you had a situation where your three people of color were stuck in some sort of camp situation where they had to live in lesser circumstances than the other Houseguests. The people of color have been systematically eliminated from the show. People are talking about racism on *Big Brother* and you're telling us that one producer got some kind of training."[28]

CBS president Kelly Kahl finally replied, saying, "We will absolutely—after the season is over—take a look at the show."[29]

Two seasons later, Tiffany Mitchell had just taken the Cookout from a loose agreement to something vying to become the most dominant force the game had ever seen.

Throughout the first few weeks, members of the Cookout often found themselves struggling with the alliance. It was great to keep each other safe, but their interests were quickly conflicting. They all had allegiances and power structures outside of the Cookout alliance, and they weren't sure how far to take their pact.

What made it more complicated was the uniqueness of their situation: six Black players in a single season, combined with the state of the country at the time—just one year removed from George Floyd's murder.

Nobody felt this tension more than Tiffany. Her win condition was tenuous. The competitions in *Big Brother* were becoming more physical, especially in the endgame. This meant that in order for someone who wasn't athletically gifted to win, they needed to have a rock-solid plan for how to make it to the end and win without the aid of winning competitions.

In other words, Tiffany's margin for error was very small. Her allies Derek and Claire were key to her success and she knew it, but it was becoming more and more clear that if she wanted to move forward with the power structure that was best for her, she'd need to break away from the Cookout.

Kept awake at night trying to decide which direction she should go in the game, she found herself wavering back and forth. Should she go with the most strategically advantageous path, betraying the Cookout and risking their opportunity to make history? Or should she forgo the optimal structure in favor of one that maximized the odds of overcoming the decades of racial bias that had been holding Black players down? The two paths were too much at odds. Every member of the Cookout had their own allies that they wanted to keep around. It just couldn't work.

That's when she saw it—a way to all but guarantee the Cookout's success. It went all the way back to when Matt Hoffman broke the game in season 12.

She called it her master plan. She woke up the next morning and explained it to each Cookout member. Each of them was to continue to publicly buddy up with an ally from outside of the alliance. In doing so they could influence that person, thus bolstering the Cookout's numbers. It would ensure that if any of them ever went on the block, they would be up against that plus-one ally and not someone else from the Cookout, in turn ensuring that they'd have the numbers to keep them safe.

The Brigade had done something very similar a decade prior, but with only four people instead of six. And even within those four, their hierarchy had failed them and Matt was sent out early. The Cookout, though, had *six* members and could barely get along sometimes. In order for this to work, each of the six members needed to believe wholeheartedly in their mission and be willing to sacrifice part of their own individual game to make sure they didn't waste the opportunity that was given to them.

It wasn't a coincidence that there were six Black players in the house that summer. The opportunity was created by the hard work of advocates in the reality television community who sought to combat the racism found in these shows.

As 2020 hit the world like a sack of bricks, there was change in the air. The global pandemic led to the cancellation of *Big Brother Canada 8* just twenty-five days into production. Still, they managed to fit a whole host of racial controversies in before it ended, including the decision to remove a Black player from the game because some of the White Houseguests felt he was too "threatening."

Then in May, George Floyd was murdered by police, and the issue of racism in America reached a boiling point. In July, *Big Brother Canada* host (and lovely person) Arisa Cox became an executive producer for the show and announced that it was her goal to ensure that at least 50 percent of every future *Big Brother Canada* cast would be Black, Indigenous, or another person of color.[30]

"There is a reason *Big Brother Canada* and I are aiming for at least 50 percent BIPOC on our next cast. BB is a numbers game. If we want every player to have the same chance to succeed, we must evolve past the idea that minorities in the country must remain minorities in the house," she wrote on Twitter. "Leveling the playing field is critical to making sure that reality TV can move into the future as an entertainment medium, and not be left behind as a relic that upholds the status quo. This is why we are changing the odds that have legitimately frustrated so many Reality fans."[31]

After this change, *Big Brother Canada 9* produced the show's first Black winner. In the U.S., nothing had changed. Camp Director Jackson had gone on to win *Big Brother 21* after completely dominating many of the now-numerous physical competitions.

Big Brother 22 had the show's second full *All-Star* cast, and of the five people of color in the house, only David's eighth place managed to score in the top half of the season.

Undercover detective Derrick Levasseur from season 16, who was still the pinnacle of dominant majority gameplay, watched at home as his partner from the season 16 "Hitman Alliance," Cody, went on to dominate season 22.

Unfortunately, by then the issue of competitions had become insurmountable for anyone who wasn't extremely athletic. Cody, in addition to having an intimate understanding of how to play in the majority, also recognized how the competitions could be exploited. By gathering up all the best competitors into one alliance, they were able to effectively shut out everyone else in the game.

Cody's strategy wasn't new per se. The Four Horsemen had tried it back in season 5. But now the competitions really could be won only by the strong, athletic people. So Cody's alliance simply won them all. Like, actually won every single HOH competition that season and nearly every veto as well. Cody himself was an athlete and won eight competitions in just that one season, nearly tying the all-time record. Just one season prior, Jackson, another athlete, had also won eight competitions in a single season. The season before that saw yet another athlete, Kaycee Clark, win the game after winning seven competitions. Between her and her two closest allies, Tyler and Angela (also both athletes), they won nineteen of the twenty-nine total competitions that season. What was supposed to be a once-in-a-generation statistic was becoming commonplace, and it was beginning to look like only athletes were capable of winning *Big Brother*. Somehow the show that took place in a studio designed to look like a house was requiring more physicality to win than *Survivor*.

Speaking of *Survivor*, just one season after Julia called out the producers for their editing practices, they had one of their biggest controversies yet. Contestant Dan Spilo was the first person to ever be ejected from the game due to an "incident" of inappropriate touching that involved a female crew member. Despite the fact that multiple contestants had already spoken up about Dan's inappropriate touching starting from the very first episode, nothing was done about it beyond a "formal warning" until he was ejected on day 36, twelve episodes into the thirteen-episode season.

CBS was not unfamiliar with sexual misconduct by that time. In September of 2018, during the final weeks of *Big Brother 20*, *Big Brother* host Julie Chen's husband—CBS CEO Les Moonves—had stepped down after six women accused him of sexual harassment and assault. Moonves had been instrumental in the acquisition of *Big Brother* and had championed the show throughout its eighteen-year history to that point. He had married its host, Julie Chen, and allegedly had a heavy hand in finalizing the casts each season.

Earlier that summer, Ronan Farrow had written a piece in The *New Yorker* detailing the accounts of harassment and assault levied at Moonves.[32] Within two months Moonves had stepped down from his role as CEO and eventually forfeited his $120 million severance package as well. He had been one of the highest-paid CEOs in the country at the time.[33]

Following her husband's resignation, Julie was absent from her usual TV appearances on CBS and later resigned from her own position on *The Talk*. But there was a *Big Brother* live show coming up at the end of the week—a double eviction in fact. Fans were wondering if this would mark the end of her time as the host of *Big Brother*. Then on double eviction night, she showed up and hosted the show as usual. Everything was normal except for one small detail: she signed off at the end of the show as "Julie Chen Moonves." It was the first time she'd ever included her husband's surname in her sign-off, and she has continued to do so to this day.

So it was with new leadership that CBS navigated the waters through a tumultuous 2019 into 2020. After the murder of George Floyd, many people were sick of tiptoeing around the issue of race while they watched the same issues continue to plague every corner of our society. More Black *Survivor* players started speaking up, expressing their dissatisfaction with how they were portrayed by the show and explaining the ramifications of only casting a few Black people at a time.

"We go on this adventure just like everybody else, but we don't even go with the same freedom," explained Earl Cole on a panel of Black *Survivor* players hosted on *RHAP*. "We're carrying something else. We've got to code switch all the time, we've got to do this, we've got to do that, just to make sure that we are not hurting someone's feelings or making them feel uncomfortable. You know, with the fragility. That's part of our game, and it sucks that we have to do that. So when we win or get to the end, man that is a testament. That we actually had to be another person to be accepted once again to make it all the way to the end. And then most of the time we get voted out first or second anyway."[34] Earl was the first Black man to win *Survivor*.

The movement grew quickly. Black *Survivor* players from nearly every season of its two decades on the air were speaking up and being heard. Dr. J'Tia Hart, a former *Survivor* contestant, started a Petition for Anti-Racism Action, which called for CBS to take action, with a list of ten steps to follow, to combat racism on *Survivor*.[35] It quickly gathered thousands of signatures. This followed another successful petition started by the Bachelor Diversity Campaign that called for action to combat racism on *The Bachelor*.[36]

J'Tia helped organize a collective of former *Survivor* contestants called the Soul Survivors Organization. The group included Julia Carter, who had spoken up the year before about her experience on the island, and Brice Izyah, host of the *Purple Pants Podcast* on the *RHAP* network, who had competed on the same season as J'Tia.

"We came together and were like, what can we do as our part to make this space that we're in better? We can't change the world, but we can change a show that we know can directly impact other people," Brice told me.[37] Brice is an endless reserve of positive energy, and I'm reasonably certain that it's impossible to speak to him without at some point having a goofy grin on your face. But he also can speak passionately about serious topics when the situation calls for it.

"I think that with CBS specifically, it was a blind spot of theirs," he continued. "Let's be real. The world is a White man's world, and a lot of the executives that run these shows are White men. A lot of the producers behind it are just telling a story from their perspective, and if we hadn't called them out on it to have this conversation, they wouldn't have seen it."

This group and others were able to utilize the petition and the media coverage they were getting to send a letter to CBS letting them know that the former players would like to have a conversation with them about the state of things. CBS responded, setting a time and date for them to meet. While there were different ideas for how to approach CBS, the overarching message was the same: something has to change.

"Of course we wanted more representation in front of the camera, but we want it behind the camera as well," Brice told me. "Only a Black woman can tell a Black woman's story. We need more people behind the cameras telling better stories. If you are editing this Black man to be aggressive, to be nasty, to be mean, it's crazy."[38]

A few months later, CBS announced that all future unscripted programs were to have "At least 50 percent of the contestants being Black, Indigenous and People of Color (BIPOC)."[39] The new CEO, George Cheeks, said, "The reality TV genre is an area that's especially underrepresented, and needs to be more inclusive across development, casting, production and all phases of storytelling. As we strive to improve all of these creative aspects, the commitments announced today are important first steps in sourcing new voices to create content and further expanding the diversity in our unscripted programming, as well as on our Network."[40]

On *Big Brother 23*, Tiffany's master plan operated flawlessly. Week after week, the Cookout got closer and closer to achieving their goal of getting all six of the alliance members to the Final Six. For Tiffany, it worked *too* well.

It was at her hand that her closest allies outside of the Cookout were sent home. In the case of her friend Claire the superfan, Tiffany was the HOH who had to nominate her. It was a deeply emotional conversation when Tiffany had to break the news to her.

Nobody had realized what was happening with the Cookout, and Tiffany couldn't say much, but Claire was enough of a fan of the show to understand the history and importance of why she was being sent out of the game by her closest ally. It had been her dream to play the game, but even in the midst of the betrayal she was able to see the reasoning behind it.

Claire had her own happy ending when she and Tiffany's other ally, Derek X, fell in love in the Jury House, were on *The Amazing Race* together, and became the second team of *Big Brother* players to win that show's million-dollar prize. They're also lovely people.

So the Cookout had done it: all six of them had made it to the end together and guaranteed that a Black winner would be crowned for the first time in over two decades. I do want to note that Tamar Braxton had won *Celebrity Big Brother 2* in 2019, becoming the franchise's first Black winner overall. But for the regular edition, this was still a massive deal.

"I was thirteen when season 17 aired. Da'Vonne was the reason I dreamed of going on *Big Brother* to be the first Black winner because Da'Vonne wasn't able to do it," a podcast listener told us during one of our weekly Q&As that season. "Now watching the season, I'm really happy. People don't understand, for me, how important it is to see the Cookout."[41]

She wasn't the only one. All season long, fans were coming out in support of the Cookout, inspired by what they were doing.

At the same time, there was pushback, mostly from White fans who felt threatened and offended by the very concept of the alliance. How would people feel if this were an all-White alliance with the goal of ensuring a White winner? How was it fair or right for the White players on season 23 to have been discriminated against due to the color of their skin?

"Since the beginning of Black America's existence, there's been a fear of Black people teaming up and working together because of what we could do if we unite. Because together we would have the power or capability of shattering the control that has been used to keep us controlled," Tiffany told me.[42]

"Black people have to stick together to *survive*," said Brice Izyah in my conversation with him discussing his campaign for more diversity on *Survivor*. "We're not making this up! It's documented. We can see it, we can talk about it... Then people will be like, 'Does everything have to be about race?' Those are the comments that always fluster me the most, and we got that a lot in *Survivor* when we were making this initiative."[43]

"Coming into the *Big Brother* house, even we were apprehensive and a little anxious about what the perception would be of us working together," Tiffany said. "Why do we have to carry the burden of what someone else thinks about us working together? It's an embedded fear in Black people amongst our community because for so long in America, us working together has been a negative thing. We've gotten killed, amputated, hung—everything you could think of has happened to Black people because of their unity."[44]

"What the Cookout said is, 'Fuck you. We have each other and we are all we have. And we have one shot of trying to work together,'" she continued. "It can be viewed as ostracization, racism, reverse racism, whatever. We finally viewed it as this is family and family sticks together. If you saw that negatively, that's your perception, not ours. And we weren't against non-Blacks and we weren't against White people. We just were for each other getting to our goals. It's just about us having a fair shot, a chance in history, a place in this show that at that point had been on for twenty-two seasons... The only thing we wanted was an opportunity for us to not be cast out and forgotten with another year of no chance of us making it anywhere because we're Black."[45]

What *Big Brother* had done was accidentally shine a spotlight on the ways in which structural racism can subtly influence outcomes while placing the burden of combating it on the people it victimizes.

By casting just a few people of color in the game at a time, the show placed a huge burden on those players to represent their communities while also having to navigate a game where they stood out. This is a patently unfair starting position for a social game, but because it's baked into our culture and it's the way the game has always functioned, it might seem normal and fair—just something players have to deal with.

Then, as twists and other game structures shifted the game to be even more about first impressions and big majorities, outcomes got worse even as the more "visible" racism got better. So as writer Hugh Ryan had pointed out, we were able to feel virtuous by decrying the racism of someone like Aaryn while then ignoring the real harm being done by the very structure of the game.

This makes it difficult for these players to advocate for themselves because voices of opposition will try to shoot them down for "making things about race." When players like Jameka try to speak up about certain aspects of her role on the show, it's her responsibility to make sure that the White people around her are comfortable with the topics she brings up. If she's not careful, they'll think she's calling them racist, and that would make *her* a bad person in their eyes.

After all, there are no racists in this particular season, nothing bad has been said, the Black player is even included in some of the alliances! And look, there have been a couple of winners of color throughout the years. Isn't that enough? Aren't they just complaining because they're not better at the game?

What goes overlooked is that the game is rigged from the start.

We all know this; we've just come to accept it as normal. It can be difficult to admit that we all participate in a system that is inherently unfair to others, that even with one's intention to treat others fairly, that may not be enough to prevent your perpetuation of the system that causes such harm.

Does that make you racist? Different people may have different definitions.

"I don't believe people are innately racist," Brice told me. "I believe that people are innately ignorant because you know what you know, and you don't know what you don't know. But when you are old enough to have the wherewithal to educate yourself, that's where you need to do a better job."[46]

Conversations like this were popping up all over the community with no end in sight. For some, the show had almost become too real, and they pined for the days when these issues weren't talked about. It was too late for that though; *Big Brother* could never function as a pure fantasy, removed from the society that had created it. We learned that right away in America, and over twenty years later it still rings true.

In season 23, Tiffany's master plan had worked for the alliance but not for her. She was the first member of the Cookout to be evicted from the game as the two athletic men from the alliance—Kyland and Xavier—won seven of the last eight competitions and all but locked Tiffany out of the game. Still, she went on to win the "America's Favorite Houseguest" prize and remains active in the community to this day.

Xavier went on to win the season, and he represented it well. He had also been a big fan of the game and had arguably been the social glue that held the alliance together in moments of turmoil.

"Being the first Black winner in *Big Brother* history is an honor. And it's something that the individuals of the Cookout came together to make happen because we felt it was something bigger than the game. Representation is important. We wanted to show that with this season, and we accomplished that," Xavier told *Ebony*.[47]

Brice made it clear to me, though, that this was not the end. "For me it's like, there's still so much more work to do," he said. "Intersectionality is a thing. I am a Black man and I'm a gay man. I'm part of this LGBTQ+ community and I want more representation for my trans sisters. I think there is just a lot more awareness that we can bring to a community that is not shown enough love, a community that is being ravaged."[48]

Trans men and women have had their own journey with *Big Brother* and *Survivor*. Audrey Middleton was the first trans woman to appear on a North American version of *Big Brother* and had a short but memorable stint on the show. Julie Vu was then on the Canadian version but was voted out first.

Meanwhile, contestant Cody Nixon was caught unapologetically making transphobic comments on the feeds. They of course didn't make the episodes, and he went on to win the $25,000 "America's Favorite Houseguest" prize. He then went on to compete on another CBS show, *The Amazing Race*, where he and his partner Jessica were the first *Big Brother* players to win a million dollars on that show.[49]

"I did think in that moment, well, maybe next time someone can come into this house and play this game and won't have to feel like they have to sacrifice themselves and their opportunity to make any sort of statement," Tiffany told me when we discussed how she felt about the decision to prioritize her mission over her game. "But I'll tell you, I think that's just not true. And it doesn't have anything to do with race. There'll be a really old person that wants to come in and do it for the really old. There'll be a gay person that wants to do it for the gays. There's always somebody who wants to do it for their community."[50]

Still, it was in a post-Cookout world that *Big Brother 24* began, a world that promised that the landscape of the show would be different now. Reporter Mariah Espada wrote in an article for *Time*, "For many BIPOC viewers who saw themselves represented in this year's cast for the first time, this season was a step forward, but also a call for the industry, and other popular reality shows like *The Bachelor* franchise, to do better when it comes to including and recognizing people of color among their casts… Now future houseguests and viewers will anticipate what this unprecedented season could mean for next season's casting, house dynamics and gameplay strategy—and how it might even help change the landscape for reality television."[51]

Season 24 will be our last stop in this book, one final *Big Brother* story to touch on everything that came before it. There was more hope and anticipation for that season than any other in recent memory.

Less than a week into filming, people from all corners of the fandom were calling for its cancellation.

13

The Rules of the Game

Taylor Hale was not a fan of *Big Brother*. "I thought *Big Brother* was a dying dinosaur that nobody watches," she told me.[1]

She was a pageant title holder, a winner of Miss Congeniality, and an attractive prospect for a reality TV casting producer.

Longtime casting director Robin Kass had left the role a few months after the announcement of the diversity initiative. Despite outward appearances, there's not too much reason to believe her departure was directly correlated to the initiative, as she'd already been casting with a similar directive for *Big Brother Canada* and continued to do so after leaving *Big Brother U.S.*

Still, there was a new guy in town, and his name was Jesse

Tannenbaum. Jesse had experience casting for *Survivor* and had been responsible for casting a short-lived spin-off of *Big Brother* called *Big Brother: Over the Top*.

It was Jesse who reached out to Taylor Hale asking if she was interested in competing on *The Amazing Race*, an invitation that she declined. He was determined, though, and asked her if she was interested in other shows, like *Survivor*. She still said no. It wasn't until he brought up the idea of her going on *Big Brother* that her interest was piqued.

We've gone into detail about the casting process and the lengths to which players have gone to make it on the show. This is the other side of that process—what it's like to be recruited. For some fans, this is a turnoff, especially if they've been trying to get on the show for a long time. Recruits also aren't exactly known for their game savvy. Hayden Moss in season 12 was the last person to win the game as a recruit who didn't know the show very well. For over a decade, it was basically a requirement that you knew the game inside and out if you wanted a chance to win.

What piqued Taylor's interest in *Big Brother* was that, despite thinking it was a dying dinosaur, she had heard something remarkable about the latest season.

"A hypercut of Tiffany putting together the Cookout came up on my TikTok and I was like, ooh something is going on here. I texted my friend and I was like, you need to watch this show *Big Brother*," Taylor explained to me.[2] "I'm sure you've heard of it; nobody fucking watches it. The tone is wacky and stupid, but this is the smartest show I have seen on TV. I was like this is an incredible game of strategy, manipulation, and maneuvering. This is the first time they've had more than two Black people in one season. They created this thing called an 'alliance' to navigate the game and make sure we get the first Black winner ever. They are all sacrificing their best interest until they get there together, and that is remarkable."

She watched some of the episodes until she saw them succeed in making it to the Final Six, at which point she moved on with her life.

"I also immediately knew that it could never be replicated; it can only happen one time. And I knew all Black people in the future were *fucked*," she said. "Black people and minorities already have to overcompensate to make White people feel comfortable in a world that is designed for them to be comfortable already. Now you're in this game, which is a pressure cooker and a microcosm of society, and when you put race in there it can get very ugly and murky very quickly. When I was watching the Cookout, I said, OK, good job. That was fun to watch. I will not be watching *Big Brother* ever again. Goodbye, good times. Then I got the DM."

Jesse had her hooked: she was interested in *Big Brother*. She went through the rest of the casting process and watched more seasons to prep for the game. "They tell everyone to watch the show, especially recruits," Taylor said. "A lot of people don't listen, but I'm nosy and I like to win."[3]

So she did her research. "I just searched on Spotify: *Big Brother* podcast. It really surprised me just how broad the game is. Surveillance is the name of the game, but what is it like when you step out of that surveillance and people analyze all 24/7 hours of the game." What she found was my four-hour deep dive interview with Tiffany Mitchell from the previous season, going through the intricacies of her game. "There were so many things in that interview with Tiffany that made me learn about the mechanics of the game... Hearing you two break it down was like, OK, there's a lot more here. I need to watch this a couple times," she said.[4]

Still, she felt self-conscious about going onto the show without the depth of knowledge that most fans would have. The podcasts were helpful, but she also went back and watched a few seasons in the time she had before going on the show.

The last season she managed to see before entering the game was a special one for her: it was season 3.

The last thing Taylor Hale saw of *Big Brother* before stepping foot in the house was Danielle Reyes—a Black woman and the queen of secret alliances and strategic innovation herself—losing a jury vote back in 2002.

I want to take us back there one more time, to 2002. Danielle's loss was the closest a Black woman had come to winning the game in the decades the show was on the air. It had been so impactful on the audience that production had decided to change the rules of the game in response to it. From that point forward, juries were sequestered so they couldn't see each other's diary room sessions before casting their final vote. But that jury vote on *Big Brother 3* goes deeper than just frustration at Danielle's diary room sessions.

The thing is, to the best of our knowledge, Danielle was *never* winning *Big Brother 3*, regardless of her diary room sessions. Dr. Will had just won his season a year prior, insulting the jury in his final speech, but Danielle's brand of strategic gameplay was not ever going to be rewarded in the same way. There are of course many reasons for this that we can examine, but the biggest reason they had such animosity toward her is actually very simple:

Danielle broke the rules.

Her diary room comments had been one thing, but this crime they could not get over.

She *lied*.

Of course, it's not against the rules of the game to lie—in fact, it's encouraged. But the producers can only determine the rules for the rigid frame that the game exists in; it's up to the players themselves to determine the rules of their own warfare.

In *Big Brother 3*, the rules of the game were that you weren't supposed to lie. I wrote about how a big alliance formed early on in season 3. This big alliance was led by a guy named Roddy. Roddy was handsome, he was smart, he was fit, he was charming, he was the picture of desirable masculinity. On top of it all, Roddy was *honorable*; he was *honest*. Being at the top of the food chain in the house, Roddy spearheaded a culture of honesty and integrity; this season's cast would not make the mistakes of the season 2 cast—they would not have a Dr. Will succeed this time.

Danielle would later go on to famously refer to Roddy as the "Devil" in her diary room sessions.

He was not a fan of that.

I remember being a young boy and idolizing Roddy even though I was rooting for Danielle. It was different from the way I liked Dr. Will or Danielle or Jason, who were players I felt I could relate to; Roddy was someone I felt I was supposed to aspire to be. He was the man who society wanted me to be.

Keep in mind, this is coming from the eyes of a ten-year-old boy. But I felt guilty rooting for Roddy's downfall. It felt subversive to want him to fail; it felt *wrong*. I don't know if I've ever fully escaped that feeling. When I wrote about Dr. Will's machinations, I couldn't help but think about the way it must look to someone unfamiliar with the show, the way that I describe my young self in awe of these feats of deception and manipulation.

How can I reconcile the fact that I cheer for the liars and manipulators while rooting against the honest people? As I think about it, that's how much of the fan base operates. It's a common refrain that those who consider themselves the "good people" on any given season are usually the most hated. Players who try hard to be honest are usually liked the least. Isn't that wrong? Roddy certainly thought so.

Of course, this culture in season 3 didn't stop the majority of the players from lying anyway; it's just that Danielle was the most successful at it. In an episode of *House Calls*, Marcellas and season 3 winner Lisa discussed the jury vote that season.[5]

"If they did the Jury House with my season, I still would have won," Lisa declared.

"Ding, ding, ding!" replied Marcellas. "People always say that if you hadn't watched the diary rooms—Danielle's diary rooms did not matter in the least to me... What we talked about our season in the house was not rewarding a Will and rewarding somebody good."[6]

Roddy and his culture of honesty lasted deep into the game that season. To be clear, it wasn't only Roddy; he just had the most influence for much of the game. Openly strategic discussion became focused on who was the most clean and honorable. Anytime someone was nominated, it was because they had done something wrong. Of course, Roddy was the most honest and honorable, so he found himself surviving even as his allies were picked off by Danielle's scheming, exposing them for the lying game players they were along the way.

Roddy made it to the Final Six bereft of allies. At that point, Marcellas had his sights set on sending Roddy out and, in the context of how they played the game that season, justified it by saying Roddy was guilty by association after all his former allies were exposed as having been liars and game players.

"There was a power structure around you. People who are around you who are doing bad. They are doing bad and it's benefiting you. But that power structure is what splashed back on you," Marcellas said to Roddy after nominating him.[7] The culture of integrity had turned around on Roddy. Still, he fought back in that language.

"You talk about a nest of vipers? *You're* the jackal doing that! You saying that this was this way and this was this way; you telling me to my face that you a hundred percent trust me when you had a different story going on. *That's* the nest of damn vipers!"

"Then you're the victim of all, and I'm sorry," said Marcellas.

"Then that's the case. You've made a bad choice, and I'm fine with it," Roddy said. "I totally one hundred percent forgive you. I swear I truly do. I don't think the right choice was made, but there's nothing else I can do about it and that's fine."

"OK, that's fine." Marcellas started to walk away.

"And you should be a little more accepting when someone tells you they forgive you," Roddy said. Awkwardly half laughing, he continued, "You should react with a little more appreciation when I tell you I forgive you."

After some more back and forth, Marcellas finally walked away, and a confused Roddy vented to Danielle, "What the hell was that? I was being a big man and offering love when someone was being— when they might have made a mistake. Offering them friendship."[8]

Roddy was honestly perplexed. He had been honorable, he had

been the bigger man, he had been honest. Why was it that the people around him weren't responding with gratitude? Why was it that *he* was the one being targeted at the Final Six? That's not the way the game was supposed to go for him.

While Marcellas had managed to find a way to justify breaking his word to Roddy, there was still one more string for him to pull. He had extracted a deal from Amy, who was on the block next to him that week, that if she were ever to win the veto she'd use it on him. She made it clear to everyone that if she won the veto, she would have to stay true to that deal even though it would lead to her own eviction. This was the strength of the culture in that house.

"When Amy told me that, I went, oh sweet Jesus Lord, have mercy, is he ever going to die?" Danielle proclaimed in despair.[9]

Hopefully it's now easier to understand how Marcellas came to avoid using the veto on himself in that fateful ceremony later in the season.

Once again, though, Roddy became trapped by his own rules. When Amy told him she would use the veto on him, she wanted to know that he'd at least repay the favor and vote for her to stay against the replacement nominee. Roddy knew that the replacement nominee was likely going to be his closest remaining ally and the eventual winner of the season, Lisa. He wasn't going to vote Lisa out. Still, it was an easy lie. His vote wouldn't have mattered anyway; Danielle and Jason were always going to control who stayed that week.

But Roddy had to follow the rules. He couldn't blatantly lie to her, so he told her that although he would want her to stay, he couldn't promise that he'd vote to keep her if Lisa went up. Amy was flabbergasted. "He had me willing to sell myself down the river to keep him here."[10]

Wouldn't you know it, Amy *did* win the veto that week. Despite everything, Roddy still expected her to sacrifice her own game to save him. He had played by the rules, and if Amy played by the rules as well, that meant he should be safe.

Of course he wasn't. Amy didn't use the veto on him, leaving him to his fate. He was "disappointed" in her. "I just feel like sometimes kindness can be taken advantage of," he told her.[11]

In Roddy's eyes, he'd played by the rules to the detriment of his own game, sacrificing the easy play for the integrity of the hard truth. What he got for it was a whole lot of nothing. How unfair, right? It's everyone else who failed him by breaking the rules of the house and being lying, manipulative game players. Right?

Except there's a reason Roddy seemed to expect things to work out specifically for him if everyone else followed those rules.

Think about it. If everyone in the game plays with complete honesty and never goes back on a deal, who benefits the most? With no intention of taking away from Roddy's charm and charisma, he starts with a massive advantage just by the nature of who he is and the people he's cast with. If everyone plays honestly with integrity and honor, Roddy wins that game ninety-nine times out of one hundred.

It's structured that way. He'd enter the game, find himself in a majority alliance full of people who looked up to him and respected him, they'd win most of the challenges, and he'd be brought to the end because he'd be deemed the most worthy.

Of *course* he had the most incentive to create and reinforce cultural behaviors in the house that helped strengthen that structure.

To my knowledge, nobody on the season 3 cast harbors any ill will toward Roddy, but intentional or not, his "honesty" and "integrity" are ultimately self-interested behaviors, ones that reinforce the social structures and hierarchies that keep outsiders down. It may seem paradoxical to say that, when Roddy found himself sacrificing his own positioning to maintain his honesty, but I truly believe this is the strength of these structures.

Roddy honestly believed that he could get away with telling Amy he wouldn't vote for her to stay and she'd *still* use the veto on him. It's the same way that he expected Marcellas to be more grateful when he "forgave" him for being nominated. That's supposed to be his reward for being honest, for being forgiving, for being the bigger man—for reinforcing the social structure that's designed to benefit him in the first place.

The same cannot be said of Danielle Reyes. "I was really concerned that no one came to me with an alliance," she said. It was the end of *Big Brother 3*, and Danielle was somberly explaining her experience in the first week of the game. "If people don't come talk to you, that means that you're part of the plan to be picked off sooner or later."[12]

Danielle's experience would be echoed across decades of gameplay for many other Black women, other people of color, or really any kind of outlier to the show's main casting demographic.

It's not always so straightforward, but the point is that those who find themselves left out don't have the luxury of following the rules set by the majority, rules that may appear noble but that truly benefit only those already in positions of power.

This has become my refrain when thinking about the ethics of lying on the show. Lies and manipulation are tools that the outsiders can use to disrupt the oppressive majority. We like and root for the liars when they're the underdogs working to dismantle a system designed for them to fail. Is it right to call that wrong? It's basically the entire foundation that the show rests upon. If it's easier for Roddy to be "noble" because he's used to that working out for him, doesn't it undercut the nobility a bit?

What *Big Brother* started to teach me in a very practical sense was that the morality of your actions isn't only determined in a vacuum. If you're unaware of the context and systems surrounding you, you're equally unaware of the actual impact of what you do and say. Societal structures are tricky, and over the years many *Big Brother* players have consciously and subconsciously worked to create and reinforce social structures that benefit themselves using morality as their chisel and shunning those who don't abide. In a vacuum they might be correct, but when you look at it in totality, you start to see it's not that simple.

After cutting Jason to bring Danielle to the Final Two, Lisa began to regret her decision when Danielle confessed all she had done to make it to the end of the game. Lisa was convinced she would lose just like Nicole had lost to Dr. Will the year before. She felt she had been fooled into taking Danielle to the end not knowing how strong a player she was.

But at the jury roundtable, Jason found himself as the sole Danielle defender. Despite a general acknowledgment that Danielle had played a better game than Lisa, there was a lot of animosity for the *way* she played the game. In the eyes of someone like Roddy, the game would have been a lot easier if he had just played the way Danielle did, lying at will and doing whatever was most convenient for her in the moment.

"There were no rules to this game," Jason said to them.[13]

Marcellas was disgusted that he'd defended her and got up from beside him on the couch to move away from him. "It was very difficult for me to sit next to the Christian virgin and have him, sort of, glorify meanness," he said.

In the jury questioning, Danielle was asked to rate her ethics in the game on a scale of 1 to 10. She answered, "With ethics in this game, I was probably a one. I was a very, very bad person in this house. But with ethics, playing this game, I'll just say this: I didn't break any rules."

It quickly became clear to Danielle that she had no chance of winning based on the tone of the questions she was receiving. "I can sit here and say that if I played this game honest, I probably would have gotten the $500,000. But if I did play honest, would I be sitting here? I don't think I would have been."

By the end Danielle was in tears. Jason was the last to go. "I just want, Danielle, to say thank you. And I love you."[14]

The vote came in 9–1. It was September 25, 2002. For many years it stood as the most lopsided jury vote the show had ever seen.

There are no rules to *Big Brother*, but Danielle Reyes had broken them nonetheless.

That was the last thing Taylor Hale saw before she entered the *Big Brother 24* house decades later. It stood out to her, knowing that no Black woman had ever gotten closer than Danielle had to winning the game. She hoped to follow in the footsteps of Danielle and Tiffany from the Cookout, to play a fun and strategic game to come away with the win.

There were a few things standing in her way. First, we have to talk about the challenges again. *Big Brother* is not known for its competitions. For much of the Shapiro era, they consisted of quizzes, small carnival games, and other silly activities. In some ways this didn't make for great television, but in others it was perfect for the show.

A popular term in the community nowadays is "equitable competitions." That's what the early-era competitions were. Anybody could win almost any given competition. This was fantastic for the show because it led to more power shifts and bold gameplay.

Intentional or not, there was a distinct shift once Grodner took over the show. Competition wins started bunching up into the same group of players every season. This meant that as the game was being broken by big alliances, it became easier for them to hoard all the power in the game. It was already more likely that the people in the majority would win competitions by sheer numbers alone, but when the competitions became more predictable and winnable by a specific kind of player, things got even more lopsided.

As if there weren't enough incentive already, more physical competitions encouraged athletic players to group up and stick together because doing so meant they could basically control the game for sometimes months at a time just by trading off wins.

The other (likely) unintentional side effect of this was that a big gender disparity was starting to develop. Keen-eyed readers might have noticed that while women were winning the game at a fairly even rate with men in the Shapiro era, as soon as season 8 hit, men started winning much more frequently. This coincides almost directly with the rate at which women were winning competitions in each era.

To keep this brief, calling the challenges "more physical" is a generalization. That's certainly a large component of the issue, but there are other factors. "More physical" means that not only will more-athletic contestants reliably do better but the *kinds* of physicality being tested are often very similar as well. And while there are still quizzes and luck-based competitions that can be won by anyone, the more you introduce a category of competitions that only a select few players are going to win, the more imbalanced the numbers will become.

For instance, take one very athletic player and one average player and make 10 percent of the competitions physical enough to give a massive edge to the athletic player. That athletic player will pretty reliably win every one of those athletic competitions while also still having a relatively equal chance of winning the remaining 90 percent of competitions. So you might expect them to win roughly 55 percent of all competitions against their average opponent.

That sounds pretty reasonable. To some, it might also sound pretty reasonable to make 50 percent of the competitions overtly physical, which makes it fair because it's even. However, take those same two players and now all but guarantee that the athletic one wins all of the athletic competitions. They still have an equal chance of winning the remaining 50 percent of competitions against their average opponent, meaning they will now be expected to win about 75 percent of all competitions while their average opponent will win only 25 percent.

I apologize for the math, but this is exactly what has happened with the game of *Big Brother*. In seasons 9 through 20, men went from winning 50 percent of all competitions to roughly 64 percent—almost twice as many as women. Then in the more modern era (seasons 21 through 25) that percentage has gone up to nearly 75 percent of all competitions, meaning that in any given cast of modern *Big Brother*, you can expect the men to win three times as many competitions as the women in the cast.

These percentages also exactly correlate to winning the game. In seasons 2 through 8, a nearly equal number of men and women won the game. Then in seasons 9 through 20, twice as many men won, eight to four. Then in seasons 21 through 25, four out of the five winners were men.

All of this was despite the fact that an almost exactly equal number of men and women have played the game in each era and an almost exactly equal number of men and women have competed in each competition. (So no, this isn't a case of men doing better in the game and therefore competing in more competitions than women; and yes, I went through and counted each competition for every season—don't judge me.)

Again, though, "more physical" is a generalization. The best female competitors in the modern era were season 20 winner Kaycee Clark and her ally Angela Rummans, both of whom were extremely talented athletes. This suggests that the competitions are simply skewed to the more physical contestants and it's casting that's to blame for the gender disparity in competition wins. If women are cast for athleticism at a rate that is considerably less frequent than men are, that could be a significant factor for this widening gap.

So is the solution to cast more athletic women? Maybe. The issue with this growing divide isn't just the proposed unfairness of it; it's also that it's just *boring*. It's how Cody dominated the game in the second *All-Stars* season with his alliance winning every single competition. If everyone on the cast was capable of winning all competitions, things could become much more exciting again. So yes, that could mean making sure that all competitors are at a baseline level of fitness, but that would exclude some extremely entertaining characters and turn the show into something that it's not. In my eyes the easy fix is to rework the way they build their challenges to ensure that they're winnable for every cast member and not just an elite few.

As with the twists, though, this is a trend that continued to get worse even as the fan base had been pointing it out for years. Many people in the *Big Brother* community perceived a deep sense of apathy from the higher-ups of the show. What had once been a grand experiment and labor of love seemed to have become rote to them, a summer obligation where they were forced to go through the motions to collect their paycheck. They didn't seem to have any interest in reworking systems or making things any more difficult on themselves than they needed to be.

It's fascinating to watch as seemingly minor changes to the structure of the game have long-reaching consequences that spiral out over the years. These changes alter who succeeds in the game, which then changes the way new players approach it. As more players approach the game in this new way, the culture of the game shifts in that direction. Before long, players who haven't won at least four competitions aren't considered to be good at the game anymore.

Then it just so happens that women who are cast on the show are considerably less likely to win at least four competitions, and now not only are women winning the game less frequently, but they're less likely to be considered "good players." Much of this seems to happen beneath the notice of fans and producers alike. Feeling the shift in culture must be a natural phenomenon despite our ability to clearly trace it to decisions that have altered the structure of the game.

Now there are fans who think that altering the competitions to be more like they were before is unfair, that it would be artificial interference in the game structure in order to prop up inferior players. To them, the current structure is what is normal and natural, and anything else is dishonest.

Of course, this issue with competitions had only continued to push the game deeper into the broken territory—fewer power shifts, more majority steamrolls, and so on. It was becoming more and more difficult for outsiders to break through. By season 24, there hadn't been a winner who didn't start in the big majority alliance of a season in seven years when the Geek Steve Moses had overcome the majority that season with the help of poker mastermind Vanessa Rousso. This is the game Taylor Hale walked into.

Things did not go well from there.

Taylor's problems started before the season even began. There were leaks going around that there was a "pageant girl" cast on the season, and some of the season 24 contestants had seen those leaks before being sequestered. Immediate judgments were being cast about what kind of personality that archetype was likely to have.

Something really interesting happened here, though. On season 24, the live feeds started immediately. Unlike season 21, where narratives were created by both the players and the show that seemed to contradict the firsthand accounts of what had happened in the first week, we were about to witness every first impression, prejudgment, and relationship development right from the very start.

It didn't take long before people regretted having to watch it.

On the very first night, completely unprompted by anything other than some very small initial interactions, a group of women got together with the purpose of excluding Taylor. In mocking tones they called her a "pageant girl" who they needed to avoid. They said she was a "boy's girl" and therefore couldn't be trusted because they were "girl's girls."[15]

Are you regretting it yet? Here's the irony: Taylor's entire game plan had focused on working with the women. She may not have known the show very well, but she was always quick to pick up on sociological trends and other social dynamics. She understood that her race and gender put her at a disadvantage, even after the Cookout's success. She had no intention of repeating the Cookout's philosophy of playing the game with a mission to the detriment of her own success, but she did want to band together with other disadvantaged players to help counteract the larger trends that were encumbering them.

So of course when the other women finally talked to her the next day and she told them about how she wanted to work with them, the misunderstanding was cleared up and she joined what was now dubbed the "Girl's Girl" alliance.

No, I'm kidding. That's absolutely not what happened. What actually happened was that they didn't believe her and decided that she must be a spy working for the men.

An observable phenomenon that occurs on the show is how quickly things can spiral out of control. The prejudgment of Taylor led to a willful lack of generosity when it came to interpreting her words and actions. If she told them that she wanted to work with the women, that must have meant that she was secretly spying for the men. This expressed itself in a number of different ways.

Players don't always start the game with all of their clothes. There are various checks and other production-related things that need to be done to clear items of clothing. So after a few days, Taylor received some of her dresses, including the one she had brought to wear on finale night if she was to make it. This is a pretty common practice; lots of players bring outfits for live shows and a special one for their hopeful finale-night performance.

When Taylor received her clothes, other women in the house egged her on to show off the dresses. Taylor was happy to oblige, trying them on and offering them to her fellow contestants to try if they were interested as well.

When she put on her finale dress, they told her she just had to show it off to the rest of the house. Reluctantly, she agreed. "When they said, 'Oh my God, let's take you out and show you off to everybody,' I was like, ehhhh. Fine, I'll be a team player because I want to have fun with everybody. I just want to get to know people. I don't want to say no and have people think I'm not a good time," she told me.[16]

After she was paraded around the house to show off her finale dress, the comments started rolling in. How arrogant of her. She's never making it to finale night so why bother? She's obviously just trying to seduce the men.

This is the narrative that was brought to the episodes. In episode 2, Taylor is shown "seductively" playing pool with the guys while in her bathing suit. In the diary room she tells us that she agreed to play pool with them in the hopes of bonding with them. She feared that there was already a guys' alliance.

While she explains this, they play clips of her seeming flirty, and they replay one particular clip of her sitting up on the pool table to do a behind-the-back shot. It's played multiple times as though it happened more than once. The one moment is spread across the entire segment like that was what she was doing the whole time she played pool.

They then cut to diary room segments of other contestants like Monty saying that Taylor was really attractive and Paloma saying, "My initial impression of Taylor is she wants to use her beauty to allure men. Which is a strategy that is so like, old. Like, her demeanor comes across even more cocky when she's not trying to make an effort with women. She's just digging that hole for herself with the girls."[17]

The reality? The behind-the-back shot was again something that was egged on by others. "People were egging me on, saying to 'do it, do it, do it.' I'm not going to say no and have people think, 'She doesn't want to be a good time or have fun.' But I just fell into the traps and that gave people fuel to build a fire," Taylor told me.[18]

We don't just have to take her word for it either; we saw it all on the feeds. In the episode, this seductive-bikini pool segment was followed up by the Girl's Girls alliance meeting where they made fun of Taylor for being a pageant girl and decided to exclude her. As though that heavily recontextualized moment was the cause of this alliance's justified wariness and suspicions. Except we knew from the feeds that the initial alliance conversation happened on night one—before any of the bikini shots, before nearly *anything* had occurred. What happened was that, from a storytelling perspective, they had no concrete reason for why Taylor was becoming a house pariah, nothing that would make for compelling or scintillating television. So they just made one up. They took something from later on, slapped on the unfair interpretation given to them by the other players, and used it as the narrative to justify their treatment of Taylor. And the casual audience ate it up.

Most episode-only viewers saw Taylor as a seductress who got caught wanting to work only with the men. I shouldn't need to tell you that a Black woman who was clumsily trying to use her sexuality to manipulate men was not popular with the general audience.

Things only got worse from there as Taylor's comments and actions continued to be spun into monstrous behavior. She made an offhand remark about the modeling industry's unrealistic expectations for women's weight that was maliciously interpreted as her calling another woman fat. She asked another contestant if he'd be willing to do his dishes, and it sent him off on a tirade. It wasn't long before everything she did was wrong in the eyes of the house; they even made fun of the way that she *walked*.

We watched it all happen from the very start. People's initial judgments need to be justified, so they scrutinize everything until they find something they can pull on and use it to invoke further judgment and hatred. When others were confused about why nobody liked Taylor, the answer quickly became something vague—oh so many things. I couldn't even explain it all.

This is a common way that *Big Brother* house cultures work: find a scapegoat. It goes all the way back to the biosphere and the psychology of isolated and confined environments. Ostracize, ridicule, and strip every ounce of power away from the scapegoat. It's sometimes done as a deliberate strategy in the game, but more often it seems to be an instinctual response to the way power is hoarded in the modern era. A scapegoat like Taylor has extremely limited options for recourse; everything about the way the game design shifted has dug the hole deeper for outsiders—and for scapegoats that hole is impossible to climb out of.

Once Taylor became the house pariah, it wasn't just the Girl's Girls who were intentionally misinterpreting her actions; it was *everyone*. Even the people who initially liked Taylor found themselves annoyed by her. She asked me to do my dishes? How dare she? But if someone with a little more social capital asked them to do their dishes, the response would not be the same. This is how exponentially deep that hole gets. Every benign interaction is another opportunity to fall even deeper without knowing it. You can play a perfect social game with zero mistakes and make no progress because you're still just sitting in a hole. And if you actually *do* finally screw up? It's curtains.

On day 4, Taylor had a game conversation with Monte, a big, strong guy who was already in multiple alliances. Taylor had continued to be iced out of any strategic discussions with the women, and most people wouldn't talk game with her at all. Monte's willingness to talk to her was her first real opportunity, so she tried to give him some minor information as a show of good faith, letting him know that some of the girls were a little concerned that the men up in the Have-Not Room might be forming an alliance. She didn't think it would be a big deal because it was just idle chatter and she didn't think anybody really had an alliance yet. She was, of course, very wrong. There was already a girl's alliance, and those men in the Have-Not Room had discussed working together. Intentionally or not, Taylor had now screwed up in a tangible way.

They finally caught her. After four days of icing her out, making fun of her behind her back, convincing the entire house she was an actual bad person, they finally had concrete proof that she was a Guy's Girl, a snake. How *dare* she?

Girl's Girl leader Paloma went on a warpath when Monte told her. Taylor ratted out the women just like Paloma always said she was going to! Paloma was in tears, telling everyone what a bad person and bully Taylor was. There was no girls' alliance! Taylor was just a rotten liar! All of the previous pieces of evidence were thrown in for good measure as the entire house was whipped up into an anti-Taylor frenzy as they chivalrously defended poor Paloma.

None of this made it back to Taylor. She had no idea that she had screwed up. She had no idea how deep the hatred was for her in the house. But the fervor was so intense that night that she could catch a distinctly unfriendly vibe.

"It is so palpable in that house when something shifts in the air," Taylor told me, "I would walk into a room and there would be dead silence or people would physically turn their backs to me. It was deeply painful because I really didn't do anything to deserve any of that and I was so intensely ostracized that all I could do was… I went into the bathroom and there was just silent, empty house. I could feel the weight of isolation on me in that bathroom, and that's when I just folded over and let it all out."[19]

Thousands of people watched her break down and cry by herself in the bathroom while all kinds of insults and nasty rhetoric were being spewed outside. It wasn't a completely unique situation for the show, but it was one of the most jarring, especially because we had watched from the very start and knew that Taylor had truly done nothing to deserve an ounce of their ire.

When it came time to make a replacement nominee for the week, HOH Daniel was convinced to make Taylor the primary target. One of the decisive arguments made in favor of the move was that because the week was already over, they'd have to deal with Taylor "blowing up" on them only for a couple of days rather than a whole week. This is an unfortunately common line of reasoning when it comes to targeting Black women. They're often expected to be explosive or aggressive. The same was true for Taylor—to the point that it was used as a reason to target her in the first week.

When Taylor was nominated, the complete opposite was true.

"The replacement nominee is Taylor. It has come to my attention that you have been rubbing the house the wrong way a little bit," HOH Daniel said when nominating her. "So you're in the position now where you can rally the votes and maybe even apologize for some of the things you've said in the house."[20]

Most players in this position immediately get defensive. But not Taylor. Her instinctual response to being called out was to self-reflect. "The final piece? To be told that you are making people feel unwelcome? I never want to be that person," she said in the diary room.[21]

Her response was reflected in how she conducted herself around the house. She spoke to people individually, apologizing for lacking the awareness to know that she had been making them uncomfortable and asking how she could do better in the future. Of course, she hadn't really done anything to anyone, and most people told her as much. Something like, well, you didn't really do anything to me, but I know others have felt a certain way was often the response she would get.

Despite this, it was too little too late. Taylor was slated to be the first person evicted from *Big Brother 24*. But it was worse than that. Social hierarchies and unspoken cultural rules are what had crushed Danielle Reyes's game back in season 3. They continued to have an enormous impact on the game well after she lost.

Since the show's inception, one of the biggest unspoken and unrecognized social components of *Big Brother* has been that it is an incredible disadvantage to be nominated in the first week. Even if you survive the vote, the first impression everyone has of you will always be that you are of a lesser social status than them. This impacts your game on a number of levels. First, it's harder to make allies because you don't have as much value as other players. Then, if someone takes a chance on you and you disappoint them in any way, they're much more upset because you should have been grateful that they reached out their hand in the first place. And even if you do somehow make it to the end, you're so much less likely to win the jury vote. The list goes on.

Facing the first eviction vote was so potent a disadvantage that in over twenty years of *Big Brother*, both in the U.S. and Canada, spin-off shows and regular seasons, no week 1 nominee who faced an eviction vote had ever gone on to win the game. It just wasn't done. That is, until the great Kevin Jacobs accomplished it in *Big Brother Canada*'s final season before the live feeds were canceled, which ultimately led to the show's cancellation in 2024.

For Taylor, though, this wasn't even a normal week 1 nomination. There's never been a player in a worse spot socially or strategically in the game. Fans were calling out for her to be removed from the game for the sake of her mental health. I'd never seen the community rally around someone so universally.

Of course, this meant that the show needed to catch up. They had been portraying the narrative of the rest of the house while ignoring Taylor's true story. This meant they needed to buckle down and show more of the nuance that was happening. To this day, many episode watchers who consider themselves to be Taylor fans might still tell you that they didn't like her at first when she was trying to be all flirty with the guys, but then she turned it around. The reality is that the edit turned around, not Taylor.

Now, there was one other small exception to the rule of first nominees. Our favorite geek, Steve Moses, had been nominated in the first week, but crucially he had won the veto and saved himself. He was still often looked down on as a player in the game, but that was part of his strategy. It was important for the perception he maintained in the game to have that win under his belt. He went on to win six total competitions that season, which made it easy for the jury to vote for him.

Luckily for Taylor, there was a twist slated for the first eviction that would give her an opportunity to save herself by winning a competition. This could have been what she needed to win some respect in the game. Before that could happen, though, there was a major blindside for the whole house. Paloma, who had been the root cause of Taylor's ostracism in the first place, had left the game under mysterious circumstances. Her behavior had been a bit erratic in her last few days in the house, and it ultimately culminated in her leaving the game.

Everyone was sobbing at her departure. She was loved by many of the players in the game, including HOH Daniel. In some ways, this was a gift for Taylor, who was free from Paloma's rumor campaign. But in other ways it was so much worse for her. Players like Daniel began to foster genuine feelings of hatred and resentment toward Taylor. They blamed her for Paloma's breakdown and couldn't stand the fact that Taylor had outlasted her.

Additionally, the twist was canceled, which meant that Taylor no longer had the opportunity to save herself; instead the perception was that Paloma's exit was what had saved her from eviction. We know the opposite is true because they reused the competition that was supposed to be for the twist, and Taylor did in fact beat the player she had been likely to face off against in her battle to stay in the game.

Still, Taylor had survived the week. There were plenty of Taylor fans who weren't happy about this. As I mentioned, they were concerned for her mental health and genuinely wished her to be free of the people who were tormenting her. She obviously was never going to win the game after what was probably the worst start in the history of the show.

14

The Sword

Reality TV has a long and dark history of mental health challenges.

In 1997, before anyone in the U.S. had even heard of a competitive reality show, a group of sixteen castaways on an island in Malaysia participated in the very first elimination vote in the history of this competitive reality television format. The first person to be voted out in one of these games was named Sinisa Savija. Like everyone else, he had applied to be on the show in the hopes of winning 500,000 krona.[1]

A month after they wrapped filming, he took his own life.

This was the very first iteration of *Survivor*, called *Expedition: Robinson*. UK television producer Charlie Parsons had been trying to get this concept made into a show for years before Pia Marquard at the Swedish state broadcaster SVT decided to take a chance on it.

Savija's wife was adamant that the show was the cause of his suicide. "He became deeply depressed and agonized. He felt degraded as a person and didn't see any meaning in life. He was a glad and stable person before he went away, and when he came back he told me, 'They are going to cut away the good things I did and make me look like a fool, to show that I was the worst and that I was the one that had to go.'"[2]

Things hadn't gone well for Savija on the island, and he'd had a very real fear that he would be portrayed unfairly in the edit. He and his wife were refugees from Bosnia, which meant that his experience in the game would echo what many future players would experience when they didn't fit the majority of the casting demographic. Police officer and eventual winner of the season Martin Melin described it: "He didn't get on with so many people. It's a social game, that's how it works. I think I won because I was friends with everyone… It works the same way as it does in the country as a whole. If you are a refugee and you don't know the language and the culture—well, you're not in the group. You're different."[3]

The backlash was intense after Savija took his own life, and Marquard, who had taken a risk on the show, resigned her position and left the country. Despite this, the show became a huge success and continued in Sweden for many seasons before eventually becoming the juggernaut hit it was destined to be in America. Swedish producers would later claim that Savija "wasn't fit in his head" and blamed his marriage and his experiences with the Bosnian war.[4]

Savija was the first, but he was far from the last. At least forty reported suicides have been linked to a reality TV show. In the U.S.,

Survivor contestant and WWE star Ashley Massaro took her own life in 2015.[9] Najai Turpin took his own life shortly before the show he competed on, *The Contender*,[6] began airing. In Japan, the big hit show *Terrace House* was canceled after cast member Hana Kimura took her own life following a wave of online abuse that her mother felt was the responsibility of the show's editing.[7] *Love Island* has been struck by multiple tragedies as well.[8]

Unfortunately, the list goes on.

Big Brother does not appear on this list, but that doesn't mean that the show is without its issues. It's one of the longest and most intense commitments in reality television, with contestants trapped for a hundred-plus days in a confined space. In the U.S., this is one hundred days of paranoia, backstabbing, and stress. Under bright studio lights with only limited "backyard" time, some contestants have had a hard time adapting to it all.

Big Brother 24 had already seen an example of this. Once out of the house, Paloma wrote, "I left because of an ongoing mental health battle I faced which began once inside the walls of an idealistic utopia of a reality set... FOMO consumed my every move. I would get 2–4 hours of sleep at night... I did not see the sun for five days so I began to lose touch with reality."[9]

It doesn't end once you get out of the house either. As I've already discussed, online hate has been with the show since the beginning, but with the onset of social media it became more and more difficult to avoid. Some fans will simply say that players shouldn't go on social media at all. But that's much easier said than done in a culture where it's so ubiquitous.

Hate isn't the only thing that can impact a player out of the house. I spoke to season 17 winner Steve Moses about his experiences coming out of the game. "There was fifteen minutes of fame. When I got back home they did this whole parade for me with these fire trucks and the police," he said. "People lined up my hometown street and the whole shebang. It was a lot, which was cool at first, but it kind of got old quickly because I was never a big attention person. Like, in the weirdest way I almost felt trapped when I got home. I didn't sleep in my childhood bedroom on my first night home. I slept on a couch in the finished basement because I liked that there were no windows."[10]

He went on to describe the paranoia that hadn't left him. "The next morning I wanted to sleep in and I heard my parents having a conversation upstairs. Especially when you're in that Final-Three environment you can never ever, ever, never leave the other two people alone together. All it takes is two minutes. I tried to force my logical brain to understand that it's OK for my parents to be having a conversation upstairs without me. That's OK. But I couldn't get my heart to listen to my brain. I had to go get up to eavesdrop on the conversation… I couldn't help but think, if winning fucked me up as bad as it did, what the fuck would losing do to me?"[11]

Steve had, like me, watched the show since he was a kid. He remembered being devastated when Lisa won the final-three HOH that led to Danielle Reyes losing the game. He was also a fan of the podcast and thought that he would take a big role in the community after coming out of the house. But after trying to watch the season that followed his, he realized he just couldn't. "It just hit me differently because I knew exactly how I would feel if I was there and it was too real."[12]

Dan Gheesling himself also struggled a bit coming out of the show. "When I got off the show for the first time, I was one hundred percent in some kind of ozone daze for like, six months. It takes a while to get out of it, especially when you're not prepared for it. You're definitely in this daze where you think you're something special. It's really bizarre. So the second time I'm like, no problem, I know what's going to happen after the show; I'm prepared for it. This time I'm not going to go through that decompression period where things are really weird mentally for you. And sure enough, the second time comes around and you think you're prepared but you're not... It has an impact on your personal life, no matter how prepared you are."[13]

What Dan told me echoed what I've heard from many players, both winners and losers of the game. It's a challenge coming out of the house and finding your identity in flux. You've just gone through an incredibly intense experience that some would categorize as traumatic, and there's almost nobody else in the world who can truly relate to it. It can be isolating. While that's happening, you're being barraged by fans left and right wanting a piece of you or just wanting their pound of flesh. They have opinions about everything you do, every person you interact with, every post you like or don't like.

Neda Kalentar was a star of *Big Brother Canada*. She was loved by the fans but still had trouble adapting to life after the show. "I've had a problem with internalizing a lot of stuff. Even though you get like two hundred really amazing comments, you get that one mean comment and that's the only one I would concentrate on... I had never dealt with anxiety until after my season. I've read up on it now and it does usually set in in your twenties from traumatic experiences. It set in heavy, like heavy, heavy anxiety. I never realized the show could affect me like that."[14]

Fans dug into every aspect of her life, scrutinizing her relationship with a fellow contestant. It got even worse after they broke up.

"When you first break up with someone, you don't want to have them literally thrown in your face over and over again. Like, this is a private matter, but people feel like they have the right to it because it started on a national scale and because we had shared photos of each other on Instagram. So they just felt like they had the right to say what they wanted."[15]

Many of the players I've talked to have dealt with stalkers who range from uncomfortable to dangerous. It's hard to know if that's something specific to *Big Brother* or something that comes with the territory of having so many eyes on you. To my knowledge, reality stars from other formats with similar follower counts tend to experience a similar amount of scrutiny. The difference, perhaps, is that *Big Brother* seems to outperform its weight class compared to similar formats when it comes to players' ability to garner a following post-show. It's easy to imagine this stems from the intense level of parasocial connection and the voyeuristic nature of the show.

One of the missions for Brice Izyah during the diversity campaign was to fight for better mental health services for contestants. "CBS does a better job now, but we can even still do better. Before it was like, 'Thank you for your services. Enjoy!' It wasn't until people had to reach out and be like, 'Hey, I'm struggling!' Then something would be offered," he told me. "Now there are packages, but it could still be better. I think it should be mandatory. Not like, hey it's here if you need this; here's two or three sessions. It should be mandatory. When you come out there's so much to process, and there's so many things that an individual person may be traumatized by. People wear trauma so differently."[16]

Taylor's trauma was being broadcast to the world. She was nominated again in the second week. She was such a consensus house target that one of the men who had pushed the HOH to target her the previous week felt comfortable volunteering to be the pawn that sat next to her on the block.

As we all know by now, pawns go home unless you're Dan Gheesling. The rest of the house saw the opportunity to take out a bigger player and decided to blindside him, leaving a toothless Taylor in the house. She was no threat to anyone at that point.

There *was* a bit more to it than that, though. I mentioned that despite the frankly racist assumptions that she would "blow up" on everyone when she was nominated, Taylor did the exact opposite. Despite not even being at fault, she took responsibility for how she had made people feel and started treading very carefully in the house.

This of course did not stop Taylor from being at the other end of a propaganda machine designed to make her out to be an awful person, but she *did* make it harder for that machine to function properly. This helped her finally get a small in with the remnants of the Girl's Girls alliance, promising them that she was truly for the women and was looking to target Monte, the man who had ratted her out and caused the biggest outbreak of Taylor hate to spiral.

It was a believable story, and since Taylor was no longer a true threat in the game, it's what convinced the women to want to keep her around for at least another week. Some of them even started telling her that they had been planning to tell her they didn't think she was a bad person in the goodbye messages they recorded. How magnanimous.

Still, the men weren't happy with this arrangement. Monte didn't like that Taylor was suddenly feeling comfortable in the house—after all, she was supposed to be a pariah. He and his ally Kyle tried to flip the vote against her, but the women held strong, feeling that it was more important to take out a man than get rid of Taylor just yet. Despite not liking Taylor, they recognized her strategic value as someone who could make bold moves they weren't willing to make themselves.

Frustrated by the women not budging on the issue, Monte was in just the right headspace to be receptive when Taylor boldly made another attempt at bonding with him. This was risky because not only had he ratted her out the first time she tried to talk to him, but she'd been telling the women she wanted to target him for days, and he'd been trying to take her out for days.

So instead of campaigning and trying to get his vote, Taylor advocated for herself as a person rather than a player. The house narrative to that point had been that she was a bad person, of poor moral character. Having investigated where this all came from, Taylor was reasonably certain at this point that she truly had done nothing wrong and there were some other factors at play.

She spoke to Monte about her understanding of how race can be portrayed on reality TV, how there might be some unconscious bias in the house that was preventing her from having the space to open up and be herself. While he still felt like she had to own the responsibility she had for the situation, he agreed that there could be some unconscious bias going on in the house.

"It's not lost on me that the two darkest people in the house are the two largest threats," she told him.[17] Part of this segment made the show. "Growing up and experiencing colorism, specifically from people that you're closest to, can really negatively affect you and the way that you view the world. We all come in different shades, but sometimes people within the same race will still treat people with deeper skin tones as less than. This isn't an issue that's specific to the Black community; it goes across all races, but the more that we talk about it, the faster we can be the change that we need to see."[18]

This conversation had a huge impact on her relationship with Monte and her position in the game. "Hearing Taylor's story and learning a lot about why she is the person that she is and why she hasn't opened up as quickly as all of the other Houseguests has definitely brought me closer to her."[19]

After this conversation, Monte spoke with his ally Kyle and they agreed to stop trying to push for Taylor to leave that week. This came down to a couple of factors. While she had been telling the women she'd target Monte, she had now bonded with him and convinced him she would instead target the youngest player in the house, Turner. Turner was the safest target for Taylor because he was the closest ally to the person sitting next to her on the block and the person most out of the loop on the week's events.

On top of that, having opened the door to be able to talk to some of the other men in the house, Taylor started spending more time with them. She and Monte continued to bond while she also got to work on his ally Kyle. With just a small amount of social reinforcement from Monte telling him that Taylor was actually kind of all right, Kyle quickly grew to like Taylor from their conversations and was convinced that everything that had been said about her was unfair.

Kyle also quickly caught on to the fact that every time he spoke to Taylor, there was a whole group of people who would come and question him about it later, angry that he'd been treating Taylor like a human being.

Monte and Kyle were part of the majority alliance that season.

But this tension around Taylor became a major sticking point to them. First they wanted her out and they were denied what they wanted. Then they started liking her and got in trouble for it. By the end of the week, they were preparing to jump ship from the alliance and shift the power in the house.

It had been on Taylor to convince these men that her reputation for being a bad person was unfounded, that she was a worthy and valuable player and human in the game. To this end, she was incredible.

This wasn't the way Taylor had intended to play the game; it's not really a way that *anybody* had played the game before. She had to convince an entire house of people that their rule set for the game was wrong.

This kind of sociological rule setting had always been a tool of the majority. The majority always makes the rules. Danielle Reyes learned that the hard way. Over the years, the majority had co-opted every one of the outcast strategies that had once made the game a level playing field. On *Big Brother 24*, Taylor stole one of theirs.

She was so successful that she had managed to take the majority alliance to the edge of destruction, not through using strategic machinations alone but through simply advocating for herself and starting to change the social dynamic in the house. It was brilliant.

And it was ruined by a twist.

There's something we need to address. *Big Brother* has never been an overly serious show, but over the years it has drifted further and further away from Shapiro's more documentary-like approach.

Starting in season 8, players started wearing costumes as punishments, competitions got goofier, and over time the twists and themes started following suit as well.

I will admit that things like a quiz competition where they add fart clouds and sound effects to clips from the house or a butt-kicking machine that players are forced to use in the Have-Not Room are not really my thing. Still, I won't begrudge anyone who enjoys the camp of it all.

There are plenty of reasons it can be tough to recommend *Big Brother* as a show, from its controversy to the time commitment required to follow it. Honestly, though, the biggest hurdle I've found is the goofiness. It tends to smack you in the face as soon as you tune in to an episode and it's turned off more prospective fans I've tried to recommend the show to than anything else.

All this to say, in *Big Brother 24*, when they introduced a twist that demolished most of the work Taylor had done to dismantle the majority, the name of it was a true twist of the knife.

It was called the "Festie Bestie" twist.

Those are the moments that remind me that for as much meaning as I can find in the game, it's still just a silly reality show and it's really not that deep.

Festivals were a theme of the season, so the idea was that at the "Festie" you'd have a "Bestie."

The Festie Bestie twist saw the players sorted into pairs. They'd compete as pairs, be nominated as pairs, etc. As with nearly every major twist in the previous ten years, the majority quickly saw a way to exploit it to their benefit. They could choose who they were paired up with, so all the majority needed to do was have each of them choose someone on the outside and it would guarantee they'd be on the block with an outsider who they'd have the votes to stay against. It was like a built-in Brigade structure.

The advantage was too enticing to pass up. The majority alliance that had been on the verge of self-destruction came back together in order to exploit the twist. And players like Taylor—who had been slowly gaining ground by portraying herself as a valuable asset in the game—were now relegated back to disposable pawns useful only to act as shields that protected the majority.

Knowing this, Taylor was chosen to be Nicole's Festie Bestie. Nicole was the number one ally of the week 1 HOH, Daniel. The two of them had actually been some of the more reluctant players to believe in the "Taylor is a bad person" narrative. But Daniel loved Paloma, and after she left the game, he blamed Taylor for the decline of Paloma's mental health. Nicole chose Taylor knowing that she'd be the easiest person to be up on the block against. It was a lock that Taylor would be voted out before anyone else.

On top of it all, the person who won HOH happened to be Turner, the person Taylor had said she would target. It was easy for the majority to convince Turner that Taylor was the reason his number one ally had gone home the week before, and she quickly became the target.

With Taylor as the target, Nicole was happy to throw the veto competition so that Taylor wouldn't have a chance at winning. They had to compete as a team, and that meant that Taylor couldn't win without Nicole's help.

Things took a turn when Nicole came out of the diary room in tears shortly before they were to play in the veto competition. Taylor worried that she may have received bad news from home about her mother, who'd had some serious health concerns.

This did not seem to be the case. Nicole spent hours cooped up with Daniel in her bedroom after her diary room session talking about how much they hated Taylor and how they'd better not look like bad people for everything they said. Meanwhile, Taylor was letting everyone know that Nicole might have learned some bad news from home and was trying to organize a prayer in support of her.

When they finally left the room, Taylor attempted to console Nicole by expressing that Nicole shouldn't worry about her at all and should do whatever she needed to do, even if that meant tapping out of the upcoming competition.

Nicole took this to mean that Taylor was trying to manipulate her into quitting the game, just like she had done with Paloma.

"I'm pissed," Nicole's ally Daniel said in the diary room. "Taylor tells her she can leave this game anytime she'd like. Taylor is trying to manipulate and capitalize in this moment while Nicole's in a vulnerable state. As I do think she tried to do with Paloma. I'm fuming now."[20]

Taylor was still completely oblivious to the situation. When she walked into a room with Daniel, she was smiling and carrying her big bag of Lay's chips.

"Just stop. From this point on, just stop," Daniel told her.

Confused, Taylor replied, "With the Lay's?"

"No, with your fake bullshit."

Taylor still thought this was a bit.

"This guy hates me!" she said jokingly.

"The same shit you did to Paloma you're trying to do to her. You can fuck right off. You don't think America's watching all that?"

"This is getting intense now," Taylor said.

"You don't think so? From here on out, do not speak to me," he declared before storming off.

"I thought he was joking—is he serious?" she asked the room.

They informed her that yes, he was being serious. She followed Daniel into the living room to ask him what it was all about.

"Daniel?" she asked.

"No, stop! I will never forget what you did to Paloma," he replied. Taylor's face contorted in shock and confusion as he continued. "You think she didn't spiral because of you? You didn't add to that? Now you're trying to do it to Nicole? Mind games?"

Pain written across her face, Taylor said, "That's not fair…"

"Do not speak to Nicole like that. Ever again. *Ever again.*"

"What?" Taylor stood there, dumbfounded.

"Just give him some space, Taylor," another player told her.[21]

When other people in the house tried to explain to Daniel that they didn't think she'd said anything with ill intent, Daniel replied that it didn't matter.

This blowup was the result of weeks of Taylor being used as a scapegoat, being seen as less than the other players. She was so easily misinterpreted in the least generous way that it was beginning to stretch the limits of credulity. And this time, it had gone too far.

Taylor got back to it, advocating for herself once again. This time, she was able to take the offensive. It was clear to anyone with eyes that she was in the right. They had all been there as she led the prayer circle with more concern for Nicole than anyone. To have Daniel blow up on her so publicly while throwing Paloma's exit in her face was a bridge too far.

Others in the house were starting to see it as well and were saying so in the diary room. "Personally I have never once witnessed a concrete instance in which Taylor bluntly disrespected somebody. It makes me feel bad. She doesn't deserve it."[22]

She started explaining to people how ridiculous it was that she was being treated this way. Just a year earlier, she had literally won Miss Congeniality in a Miss USA pageant, and in this house she was being made out to be the devil incarnate.

Inch by inch, she started making progress again. The entire incident was a reminder to players like Kyle and Monte that they didn't like the people they were working with. But the twist had locked them into this structure. To break it, they'd be abandoning near guaranteed safety for *weeks*. It was a hard ask.

They started slow, talking to the HOH Turner and Monte's Festie Bestie Joseph to form an all-guys alliance designed to give themselves numbers against the rest of their majority alliance. Joseph wasn't content to be an add-on, though; he wanted this group to become the new power structure in the game. Kyle agreed, and in one chaotic night, they all gathered in the HOH room hyping themselves up and recruiting more players to their cause. With two additions, including Michael, the strongest competitor in the house, this new alliance was set to dominate the game.

While they were upstairs celebrating, Taylor was downstairs in the diary room discussing the incident with Daniel. It would be a massive opportunity for her if she could make her way upstairs and get involved with the new alliance. They were open to it. After the Daniel incident, they knew she'd be on board to join their cause and be a valuable number for them moving forward.

It's tough, though. *Big Brother* can be all about timing. If Taylor didn't make it onto the ground floor of this alliance, bonding with them and celebrating its creation in the excitement of their rebellion, she might never truly be considered a member—if she ended up getting the invite at all.

The live-feed audience was tense. We'd been here before, on the precipice of something grand, only to have it snatched away from us. For Taylor to find a reprieve from the treatment she received would be a reprieve for us all. So imagine how stressful it was as the hours ticked by and the energy of this new alliance started to die down. Taylor was still in the diary room.

"Production hates us!" cried out the feeders on Twitter. It felt like they were holding Taylor hostage, preventing her—and us—from escaping the hell that these first few weeks had been. Kyle was posted outside of the diary room, ready to grab her as soon as she came out, but was eventually distracted by other cast members. By the time Taylor finally came back, Kyle had left, and an oblivious Taylor stayed downstairs to talk with the enemies this new alliance had sworn to combat.

By now there was a new problem. In order to bring Taylor into the alliance, Kyle felt that Monte had to be there so they could clear up the Paloma stuff. If Taylor and Monte couldn't get over that incident in week 1 when Monte had ratted Taylor out to Paloma, she wouldn't be able to join the alliance. But it was late now, and Monte had fallen asleep.

Hours continued to pass. It was 3:00 a.m. on Saturday and there we all were, watching Monte sleep, waiting and hoping that somehow he would wake up and they would find a way to get Taylor into the HOH room. We *had* to be here for this.

This was *Big Brother*.

Monte finally woke up, but Taylor was still not taking the hint that she should go upstairs. More time passed before she finally made her way up. The boys watched as she walked through the house, cheering as she made her way up the stairs. "It's like watching a movie!" one of them proclaimed.

Taylor entered the room and sealed the deal. She would be the seventh member of this new alliance. An alliance designed to combat the unfair narratives created in the house. An alliance that would reshape what it meant to play *Big Brother* in the modern era.

"Taylor, I hate to say it, but the first week I remember so vividly you were standing by those damn laundry machines out there with your arm posted up and your sunglasses on, and I'm like, 'How are you feeling?' And you're like, 'I'm trying to talk game!' And I see this badass woman, about to make some moves. And I look at you now and I'm like, you have so much more potential in this game,"[23] Kyle told her. "I feel like you've been treated so poorly by so many people in this house, and I'm honestly sick of it. That's why I'm so passionate about this. I think we have the opportunity to change the narrative and take control of this game...and you're a key element. I'm sorry to say it, but we want that fucking girl at the laundry machines that's a badass that'll win some comps and dominate this game!"

"I miss her too," Taylor replied.

"We got three weeks of *their* Taylor, beating you down. Let's give them three weeks of badass Taylor coming out and winning shit and not yelling at your ass!"[24]

I was one of the thousands of people sitting in the darkest hours of the morning, illuminated only by the light of my computer, losing my *absolute* mind watching this. There's nothing that compares to the experience of seeing these moments play out in real time. It makes years of disappointment all worth it for these brief moments of glory. I was back to being a thirteen-year-old boy watching Kaysar. "I sealed your partner's fate." It was now time for Taylor to seal her Festie Bestie's fate.

Yeah, the name still doesn't do it for me.

I reenacted the whole ordeal on the live-feed update the following morning with glee.[25] The rest of the week the entire community felt invincible. We finally had a win. A group of outsiders had come together to overthrow the majority and stand up for those who had been mistreated.

They called themselves the "Leftovers."

> "I know this might come as a surprise to a lot of you. There was clearly one target this house had, but I don't feel like that's best for my game and I really don't want to add to the dogpile I feel like has been going on in this house. And I'm sorry about that. Behind closed doors a lot of you say some crazy things about individuals. And I really don't want to draw a line in the sand when saying this, but as the youngest one in this house I don't feel like I should be the one to say that it's not OK. But here I am."
>
> Matthew Turner[26]

"I knew who was going on the block, but I didn't know that Turner would make a point to stand up for what's right and I didn't realize until that moment how much I needed—in this house—someone to do that for me. I just feel like this is the right crew for me. They're going to take care of me and I'll take care of them," Taylor had said in the diary room after his speech.[27]

She had burst into tears while the HOH Turner stood in front of everyone and called them out for their treatment of her. He had blindsided the people who thought they were in power by not nominating Taylor.

The house erupted.

The former majority didn't know how to respond. They were

pissed that things had been turned around on them, but they had simultaneously been called out for bullying, which triggered a moment of uncertainty—were they the baddies?

No, certainly not. "It's crazy, because I've been defending her!" one of them protested.[28]

The soul-searching quickly turned to a hunt for a new scapegoat. Who was the real bully who was making them all look bad? Their minds turned to an incident when a player had very openly called Taylor a bitch. Everything else had been mostly behind the scenes in their minds, so surely that's what Turner must have been referring to. For a little while they were venting their anger on that player for getting them all in trouble.

Many people believe that in a social game like *Big Brother*, standing up for what's right is not a good move, that morality has no place. Many players have argued that they've stood by and watched as bad things went down in front of them because it would have been detrimental to their game if they had stood up and said something.

There's certainly some truth to this. As Danielle Reyes herself would always say, it's best to keep your mouth shut and your eyes open. However, I'd argue there is some value to opening your mouth once in a while. Turner calling out the bullying in the house while he held power forced the people he called out to go on the defensive. They started fighting among themselves looking for a scapegoat.

If the rest of the Leftovers had followed suit and stayed on the offensive, the remnants of the previous majority would have shattered and a whole new paradigm for how to treat one another would have developed. This is how rules are made in the house—by the majority. They get to set the standards. If they felt that Taylor should have been treated better, all they had to do was make it against the rules of their minisociety to treat others that way.

But that's not what happened.

Now that the Leftovers were in power, their priorities had shifted. Sure, they could support what Turner had said and encourage everyone to treat Taylor better, but everyone hating on Taylor was still kind of useful.

The former majority members were worried that hating Taylor was no longer the popular thing to do, no longer the majority opinion. But when they started asking around, members of the secret Leftovers alliance would respond with confusion and support, insisting that they were just as confused as everyone else—Taylor being bullied? No way! This whole thing seems blown out of proportion!

It just made sense to the Leftovers that they should continue to pretend they didn't like Taylor; otherwise, it would blow their cover. Taylor was a nice distraction for them, which meant they didn't have to risk any of their relationships with the people they had just turned on. And hey, Taylor could take one for the team, they figured, because they had done her a favor by including her in the first place.

As the former majority started to find that nobody seemed to actually agree with Turner, they stopped their infighting and realized that the problem really was Taylor after all. Here she was crying to Turner, exaggerating stories and getting him to target them when it was supposed to be her! Hate for Taylor didn't decrease; it started somehow reaching new heights.

So despite everything, the following week Taylor found herself as the house pariah *again*—this time half of it genuine from her enemies, half of it orchestrated by the people who were supposed to be her allies. Needless to say, she was frustrated.

If you've ever wanted to see concrete examples of power corrupting, *Big Brother* will deliver. Fan-favorite underdogs can often find themselves hated villains if they ever actually succeed in overturning the power structure. This is in part due to the nature of how we watch the show—rooting for the Rebels, not the Empire—but it also often comes down to how the players change as they gather power.

A term that has been created in the *BB* vernacular is "HOH-itis." It refers to the shift in behavior that is all too common when someone wins the Head of Household position. Suddenly they're calling people to their room to interrogate them, walking around the house in their special bathrobe expecting people to suck up to them. Add in a healthy dose of paranoia, and the recipe spells disaster. The HOH is an incredibly powerful tool to succeeding in the game, but as with the Targaryens in *Game of Thrones*, it's almost as though fate flips a coin when each person wins to determine whether they'll use the power effectively or allow it to go to their head.

Then it goes even deeper. The outcasts who once decried the overuse of power and stifling culture that the majority forced upon them will often find themselves using the same tactics and rule enforcement that was used on them once they find their way to the top of the food chain. The community tends to split pretty contentiously on these kinds of players, with some feeling the righteousness of subjugating the former majority with their own methods while others feel even deeper disgust for their actions due to the hypocrisy of it all.

The Leftovers was a rare case of the community all coming together to support a common cause. In the same way that Taylor had served as a common cause for the players to rally around, the disparate ends of the *Big Brother* community all came around to supporting her as well. But this never lasts for long.

Almost as if the community had won the power for itself, it began infighting soon after the Leftovers came into power. There were Monte and Kyle fans, who loved the strategy they implemented to overturn the house. There were Michael fans, who appreciated his unprecedented competition prowess. And biggest of all, there were still the Taylor fans, frustrated with the whole endeavor as she found herself nominated and blindsided *again* just one week after the Leftovers formed.

> "We have to be the oppressed and we have to be the teacher. We never get to go in there and only be ourselves."
>
> Brice Izyah[29]

As I mentioned, the fact that Taylor was a house pariah turned out to be too valuable for the Leftovers to just give up willingly. So they played into it, allowing the former majority to blame her for everything that had happened the previous week. Then they used her as a decoy target to keep everyone calm before enacting a plan to put her on the block as a pawn against her Festie Bestie Nicole. The intent was to send Nicole out, but due to some last-minute changes, Taylor wasn't even told she'd be going on the block before it happened; she was an afterthought for them.

Frustrated and hurt, Taylor was realizing that despite what Kyle had told her, she'd never be able to play the game the way she wanted. She'd wanted to play like Danielle Reyes, badass and cutthroat. But like Danielle Reyes, she was running into the brick wall of the rules and expectations others had for her. After all, in the end, Danielle had also been forced to play a certain way to make it to the end, a path that the jury then punished her for.

If Taylor wanted to survive, she'd have to adapt. There was no alliance to take care of her; she'd need to stay on the offensive and continue to advocate for herself. She couldn't afford to take her foot off the gas at all.

So she made her case. Using the Leftovers' own words against them, she explained how it wasn't right that they were using her in this way. She told them that she understood the strategy behind it, so she didn't blame them for the decision but she hoped they could understand that she was not willing to be used in this way anymore.

I often say that guilt is a trap on *Big Brother*. Many players instinctively reach for guilt-tripping as a tool in their strategic repertoire thinking that if they make someone feel guilty, they'd be less likely to screw them over. In reality, this often has the opposite effect. A player experiencing guilt tends to resent the person who's causing that negative emotion. They find themselves either hardening in response to it or feeling a desire to remove the source of it entirely. The result of this was that the more you tried to guilt-trip someone, the more they wanted you gone. *Big Brother* is a zero-sum game. Guilt and fairness have no place in it.

This is what made Taylor so good at her brand of gameplay. She worked hard to prevent her marks from feeling guilty about what they'd done to her. Instead, she did her best to invite them in and feel inspired about doing the right thing. Kyle's speech to her up in the HOH room when they formed the Leftovers didn't come from nowhere; it came from her many conversations with him where she left a trail of breadcrumbs for him to follow.

This kind of sociological strategy is difficult for some fans to recognize. Taylor is fairly unique in her success with it, so to some it may look like things just happened for her and she got lucky. While luck always plays a large role in the game, it's easy to follow the through line of Taylor's methods when you know what to look for.

So once again, Taylor was able to successfully advocate for herself and finally found herself in a position of relative power. After the Leftovers blindsided Nicole and the rest of the former majority, they stopped using Taylor as a scapegoat. This meant that Taylor's former enemies could no longer freely blame her for all of their problems. This didn't stop a determined few from still doing so, but Taylor now had the support of the majority; she had crawled back from the depths of being a social pariah.

I want to reiterate how unheard of this is. We'd seen people like Dan come back from strategic dead ends, but the social part of social strategy is so much more difficult to manipulate. Taylor still had a long way to go before she was back on equal footing with everyone else, but she was now free to exist as a full-fledged person in the house.

Taylor's troubles weren't over yet, however. She may have crawled out of the hole that was dug for her, but nobody in the house was going to easily forget where she came from. She had fought hard to survive, but how would she truly solve the Danielle Reyes problem? No Black woman had ever won the game, and no woman at all had won since Kaycee—the athlete—had after winning seven of the last eleven competitions she played in four years prior. Taylor was not an athlete.

Then there was Kyle. One of the primary drivers in the creation of the Leftovers, Kyle eventually let the paranoia of the game get to him. Having just seen the Cookout dominate the season before his, Kyle feared that all of the "minorities" were secretly plotting against him. When he told this theory to a couple of his White allies, they exposed him to the house (contentiously—this came a few weeks later when it was more convenient for them to expose this information). After being exposed, Kyle was quickly sent packing by one of his closest allies doing the will of the house. Yet again, the sociological forces in *Big Brother 24* were overriding the strategic ones.

The next hurdle was Michael, the competition beast. He wasn't exactly an athlete, but he was tall and well built for most modern competitions. He knew all the best strategies to win and was extremely skilled. It frustrated a player like Monte—who was more of an athlete—that he was consistently coming in second place to Michael in competitions that in any other season would be a near guaranteed win for him.

Monte became so distraught at his inability to beat Michael that he nearly gave up trying, feeling as though if he couldn't beat him, he'd have to just join him. However, after their rocky start, Taylor had developed a good relationship with Monte and was able to convince him to take his shot when he had the chance.

Soon, Michael finally lost a competition and was evicted. With Michael gone, Monte was able to dominate the rest of the competitions. He remained immune for the rest of the game. This is typically how it works in the modern era. A small group of players win all the competitions, and even when you take out the top competitor, the gap in equity is so large that the next best competitor *still* dominates the rest of their competition.

As their relationship blossomed, Monte began to promise Taylor that he'd take her to the Final Two. But he also had a Final Two with Turner, the HOH who had once stood up for Taylor. Taylor knew that, like Michael, Monte needed to be evicted if she wanted any chance of winning the game. He was a big, strong guy who'd won a bunch of competitions and been in a position to drive more of the strategy than her.

The jury made it clear that the smartest thing anyone could do was take Monte out. Monte was instrumental in forming the Leftovers: Monte overcame Kyle, Monte took down Michael, and Monte was dominating the endgame competitions. Even Taylor's former allies on the jury were arguing that she wasn't a very strategic player and that Monte had more control in the game. Taylor had only two competition wins; no jury had given their vote to a player with so few competition wins under their belt since Maggie back in *Big Brother 6*, seventeen years prior.

Of course, beyond all of that, much of the jury had spent the game hating her, scapegoating her, isolating her, and not respecting her as a person or a player. Everything else just piled onto this fact. If Taylor wanted to win, she would need to beat the two men in front of her and take herself to the end.

Things went from bad to worse when Taylor lost both parts 1 *and* 2 of the final-three HOH competitions, locking herself out of winning her way to the end. Her fate was now in the hands of Monte or Turner. Monte had promised her he'd bring her to the Final Two, but even if he was telling the truth, her chances of beating him were much worse.

Then there was the "if" part of that statement. Turner was easily the better option to bring to the end. He did technically have one more competition win than Taylor and hadn't spent the game being hated by the jury, but Taylor at least had a compelling story to tell; Turner was far too much of a yes-man, just going along with whatever people wanted him to do. The jury didn't respect his game at all. For Taylor to win, she knew she needed to sit next to him in the Final Two.

When Turner and Monte faced off to determine the final HOH winner, Monte predictably came out on top. Taylor's hopes were dashed. The best she could hope for now was that Monte would stick to his word and take her to the end despite Turner being the better option. To that end, she had been putting in as much work as possible, playing up his competition wins, trying to convince Monte that Turner played a game pretty similar to his.

Ultimately, though, the decision was Monte's. Turner pleaded his case. "You know that every single big move I've made, you were behind it… You know it's going to be unanimous. I have the worst jury management I think in a decade, so I'd be bamboozled if I wasn't taken."[30]

Taylor's response was equally defeatist. "I respect all of the game moves you have made, and frankly my biggest game move was done when I lost that second part of the HOH. So if you sit next to me, you know it's an easy win."

Monte stood and made his decision. "When I look at my résumé, the only thing that I can think that the jury sees missing is a big move made, so today I feel like this is my opportunity to make that big move. Turner, I'm sorry but I have to evict you, brother."[31]

Turner took it well. He told Monte that he had nothing but respect for him and understood the decision. And just like that, Taylor had somehow—*somehow*—made it all the way to the Final Two. That was about as much as anyone could have hoped for given the start she had.

> "Monte is every winner you've seen since the competitions became more physical, and I don't mean that as a dig. He's someone that

both the audience and his fellow contestants recognized as the biggest threat to win from the second he entered the house."

Me on my final *Update* before the finale[32]

Taylor's journey is representative of the state of *Big Brother* in the modern era: the issues it has with racism, sexism, groupthink, and bullying and the ways in which the structure of the game has come to encourage and exaggerate these things. Taylor valiantly fought back, but one person just isn't capable of overcoming systemic disadvantage without the support of the people around them.

By the time Taylor was preparing to face the jury, fans knew how the rest would play out; they'd seen it time and time again in the modern era. The game had become about having big majorities, athletically winning competitions, and using all that power to "make moves."

I tell Taylor's story here at the end of this book because it touches on so many of the things that *Big Brother* has become while also reminding us that seeds of the modern era have always been present in one way or another. The last thing Taylor saw before entering the game was Danielle Reyes getting eviscerated by a jury that didn't respect her.

Danielle Reyes is a legend in the community. She broke ground on the most fundamental component of *Big Brother* strategy. She set records that went untouched for more than a decade. Every single player who has ever stepped foot in that house to play that game is standing on a foundation that she built. And the jury still didn't give her the win because she had broken their rules. Never mind that they were rules designed—intentionally or not—to prevent a player like her from succeeding in the first place; she had still broken them.

So now Taylor sat there in the Final Two, in the same position Danielle Reyes had been in, wondering how it is that a player like her is supposed to win the game if the rules are designed to keep you down and you're not allowed to break them.

Taylor was frustrated at the game, at a culture that sought only to reward one particular kind of play, one particular kind of person. She was frustrated at the rules that had been put in place by her fellow contestants from the moment they met her, rules that made it clear she had no value as a player, had no value as a person, and was not allowed to play the way everyone else could.

When she lost the final HOH competition, she lost her only chance at winning by the rules others had put in place for her. She'd have made the "big move" Monte was talking about by cutting Monte and proving to the jury that she really was a player after all using a language that was well established in the world of *Big Brother*.

Now sitting there against Monte in the Final Two, there was only one option left to her. One that she'd been trying to do all season.

Taylor had to *change* the rules.

> "For someone given such a small margin of error socially, Taylor managed to be the player who made the fewest unforced errors in the game.
>
> Above all though, it's her resilience that stands out. And that translates through her gameplay and her jury management. She never gave up on a relationship, no matter how damaged it was or how much the person had wronged her. Don't mistake it; she had to advocate for herself before anyone else stood up to do it. Through that, she gained allies. Those allies gave her the social credibility she needed to eventually counter the culture that put her down, forcing those responsible to disassociate themselves from 'Taylor hate.' She then welcomed them with open and

forgiving arms, turning bitter enemies into people that said their biggest regret in the house was not being closer to Taylor *before they left the house.*

It's this resilience, grace, and empathy that could be the key to one of the most unlikely wins in the history of the show."

Me on my final *Update* before the finale[33]

After the Leftovers continued to use the narrative that Taylor was a house pariah, she knew she couldn't afford to take her foot off the gas. Taylor had relentlessly continued to advocate for herself even in the face of players who did not respect her. She'd have long talks with them about her place in the game and the position she'd been put in. She was never accusatory; she just worked to help them understand her point of view while hoping she could change theirs.

While Monte and everyone else were playing *Big Brother* the way it had been played for years now, according to *those* rules, Taylor was slowly convincing the entire jury that they could play a different game, one in which someone like her could not only climb out of the hole they were put in to start but go on to flourish and forge their own path in the game.

Monte had done everything right. He'd played by the rules, made the correct decisions at nearly every turn, won a bunch of competitions, and taken the former house pariah to the end with him. But he hadn't realized that Taylor had changed the rules right out from under him.

Wearing the finale dress that had once been the source of so much scrutiny, Taylor stood in front of the jury and pleaded her case as though her life depended on it.

"Monte may have more blood on his hands than me, but as someone who has sat on this eviction block *six times* on eviction night,

I have bled out the most in this game," she said.[34] "But I have bandaged myself together every single time, and gotten up and continued to fight. Because like so many other women in the world, that is what we have to do to get to the end; we have to take care of ourselves and put ourselves first while also looking out for the rest of the ones behind us." The women on the jury nodded along to this as she continued.

"I have been falsely accused and unjustly accused of using someone's mental health as a piece in this game; as someone's sick mother as a piece to use in this game," she continued. "I have been called the b-word so many more times in this house than I have in my real life. Not to mention there was an attempted all-White alliance formed and I had to sit on the block—left on the block against the person that tried to form that alliance." The camera panned across the faces of the people on the jury responsible for some of these things as they watched her before returning to Taylor.

"I have overcome so much in this game," she declared. "And I have come to understand that I am not a shield, I am a *sword*. I am not a victim, I am a *victor*. And if there is one word that is going to describe the entire season, it is resiliency. If you are to ask yourself who the most resilient person in this season has been, it is me.

"We can have the same *Big Brother* wins that we've had in the past, but I am challenging you jury members—I thought I would humbly ask you for your vote—but I am challenging all of you to decide: What type of winner you want to have this year? Do you want the same thing where we see evictions and comp wins be the path to success? Or do we want a winner where we choose *resiliency*, we choose *persistence*, as the reason to win this game. I have *never* given up on myself, and I refuse to do it tonight when I am sitting next to such a strong competitor.

"Jury members, I am challenging you to make the hard decision and change the course of this game. And choose progress for the course of this game. I *can* be the winner of this season. And I *promise* you will not do it in vain if you choose me tonight."[35]

I was in tears by the end of this. I cried for Taylor and everything she'd overcome. I cried for the incredible speech she'd given that reflected my own final analysis of her game. But I also cried for *Big Brother* itself, this show that I've come to love and that had so often reflected the worst parts of our society.

I'm sometimes overwhelmed by it—spending a hundred days at a time immersed in their world, seeing the same outcomes occur season after season with production deaf to the impact of their decisions. It can feel after all this time like the show has reached the limit of where it can go and what it can teach. But then someone like Taylor Hale will show up and change everything you thought you knew.

This moment was everything *Big Brother* promised consolidated into one speech: a reflection of society where an individual has the power to overcome the structures built to keep them down. It's a show meant to cater to our basest urges, a game meant to trap us in this competitive and cutthroat environment we live in.

But occasionally we get a glimpse of what it would be like to escape our golden cage.

Taylor Hale won *Big Brother 24* by a vote of 8–1 on September 25, 2022.

It was the twenty-year anniversary of Danielle Reyes losing *Big Brother 3*.

15

The Mirror

"I know some people out there are not happy with how this show went down, and they blame that on me. But the simple fact of the matter is, if you're not happy with this show, maybe you're not happy with reality based–TV in general. And if you're not happy with reality based–TV, maybe you're not happy with...with, as the name suggests, reality."

Dr. Will Kirby, winner of Big Brother 2[1]

Will said this in the final moments of season 2. I always considered it to be bluster, the arrogance of a man in love with himself. Rest assured, it is certainly that. But I wanted to bring back his quote at the end of this book because it also feels poignant to me as the first true winner's speech. Sometimes I *do* have an issue with this show, and while I don't think that reality based–TV is always representative of reality, my biggest complaints often stem from things that are at least reflective of reality.

It's also why I love this show, this mirror that captures a slice of humanity. I'm under no illusion that *Big Brother* is unique in this regard. I first grew fond of the concept of media functioning as a mirror to society in high school when I read that Ingmar Bergman's

Scenes from a Marriage had caused the divorce rate in Sweden to skyrocket. Causation was debated, of course, but one way or another the miniseries had reflected a moment in the culture that resonated so deeply it was attached to a larger societal trend.

The same can be said of *Big Brother* and the massive cultural impact it's had around the world. Did *Big Brother* inspire the wave of reality TV that swept the globe soon after its success, or was *Big Brother* simply an inevitable step in our reality television journey? From *The Real World* to the Biosphere 2 to JenniCam and more, *Big Brother* is at least as much a result of the existing culture as it has gone on to inspire more. In its wake were the rise of shows like *Keeping Up with the Kardashians* and *The Apprentice*.

Through the ubiquity of the reality genre and the democratization of video equipment, YouTube became the new frontier of reality content. Kids were now filming *themselves*. Then with Twitch and other platforms, we started live streaming ourselves. During every episode of *Big Brother*, I partake in my own taste of the show by live streaming myself watching it—an act of narcissism, a reflection of a culture that *Big Brother* helped create.

Now YouTubers and streamers are also getting in on the competitive reality television game. MrBeast is the largest creator in the world and hosts competitions of all kinds, some resembling *Big Brother*—a show that's now been around since before most of his audience was born.

Some of this online content is genuinely interesting, compelling, and innovative. *Jet Lag: The Game* is a show inspired by *The Amazing Race* and *Taskmaster* that has pushed the idea of reality competition game design and presentation into whole new areas of innovation that eschew the trappings of deceptive editing practices and manufactured drama.

There's so much more that can be said about reality television, from the dark secrets of its trade to where it came from and its place in society. From all that I've been able to gather in my time covering *Big Brother*, I've found that if you're looking for good gossip or scandalous secrets about production, there are far more interesting shows to read about.

Part of the fascinating nature of this show is how different it is for everyone aware of it. From the perception of those who are only mildly aware the show exists, to the fans who watch it on their TV when they happen to catch it, to the hardcore fans who follow every detail of the live feeds, the show means wildly different things. Even beyond that, many hardcore fans could write this book and tell entirely different stories about the show, painting a picture of what it means to *them*, because there are so many stories to tell and so many things you can take from the show.

I want to emphasize that this book has been an examination of my own experience with the show, an invitation into the perspective of someone who has dedicated their life to this absurdity. The fandom is far too large and diverse for me to be their voice.

The *Big Brother* producers themselves seem to portray the show they're making as completely separate from the *Big Brother* that many of the viewers actually consume. They advertise it with promises of more twists, more wacky competitions, and more *slime*. Much of the loyal, hardcore fan base of the show simply eats up the side effects of a show not designed for them, accepting the scraps for what they are, hoping for that rare moment when the show accidentally produces something truly great.

In the meantime, we're forced to try to explain a love for something that by all appearances is meaningless drivel. Maybe this book is part of a Sisyphean effort to explain my own passion for a show that feels utterly absurd. Or maybe I'm just trying to convince you that sometimes it's not creepy to watch someone sleep on live feeds. Would it help if I told you most people aren't actually *watching* the person sleep, because they're really just waiting for them to wake up?

Yeah, I didn't think so.

Creepy or not, the live feeds are the lifeblood of the show. When reality television was first born, there was a lot of discussion around how "real" it could really be. In 1973, *An American Family* was part documentary, part proto-reality television. Critics were skeptical of its "reality" bona fides, commenting that the very presence of a camera must alter the natural state of reality and that any form of editing at all is storytelling, making choices about what part of "reality" will be shown. If this is true, *Big Brother*'s live-feed cameras hidden behind every mirror with their live and unedited broadcast to the audience must represent one of the most honest representations of reality within its own context—at least comparatively.

"Yes, there can be a little bit of editing where let's say they take and chop up a sound bite from the diary room… But for the most part, if something happened a certain way, the fans will hold the show accountable if they were to misrepresent it in editing," *Big Brother 3*'s Jason Guy told me. "That was the scary part about going on television for me because I had worked in production. But there's some comfort in the live feeds, knowing that if I am who I am all the time, the audience will see that, and there's nothing the show can do to change that. I think it's a great thing for the players."[2]

Most players I've talked to share his opinion, but that doesn't mean there aren't those who disagree. "If you're not being a good human then you're not going to like what people are saying about you and what happens after you leave the house, but you know what you're getting into, you know what you're signing up for," Jason said.[3]

"It was my dream to be on the live feeds," my podcasting cohost and *Survivor* player Rob Cesternino told me. "As somebody who has done thousands and thousands of podcasts, I'm sure I've slipped up and not said things exactly the way I wanted to say them at different times in the past. But I really believe that if your heart is in the right place, people are understanding. If someone is being intolerant in the house and then gets caught on the live feeds having no remorse, those are the types of things that rightfully get called out in real life."[4]

Taylor had been recruited for a few other shows before being offered *Big Brother*, but she told me, "It was the live feeds, one hundred percent," that convinced her she could do the show. "I got recruited for other reality shows like *The Bachelor*, which is notorious for editing people to be the complete opposite of what they are."[5]

That decision turned out to be a crucial one for her, and she's become a big proponent of the live feeds for how important they were to her own journey and how important they have been for players like her in the past. To borrow her quote from the beginning of this book, "My stomach churns when I think about living in that house without 24/7 live feeds. I am genuinely afraid anyone could have a similar experience to me, and not be believed leaving the house. Sunlight is the best disinfectant. Live feeds are the sun."[6]

The live feeds are a weapon given to both players and the community to fight against the tyranny of the kind of producer overreach that has plagued reality television from its conception. As with the game of *Big Brother* itself, we're given this tool to combat the very nature of this show.

Between issues with casting, controversial production decisions, and attempts to control the show's narrative, the community has been playing *Big Brother* against the producers from the start. While it feels as though we've made steady progress over the years in forcing change, the show seems determined to stay in the past, often taking one step forward only to take two steps back.

It's surprising to find how many things in everyday life can find connective tissue to components of *Big Brother*. The Cookout's Tiffany Mitchell explains, "One of the reasons I specifically felt drawn to playing the game of *Big Brother* is because I felt like in my real life I had been playing the game of *Big Brother*, whether it was the way I moved through social circles in school, whether it was in my relationships, or specifically I felt a really powerful *Big Brother* dynamic being a small business owner. It was like I was the HOH of my business, but I also need the support, trust, and relationship of my employees to succeed."[7]

I asked Tiffany about this because I remembered her talking about it on the live feeds during her season. At the time, it really resonated with me, how often I would compare situations in my life to things I had seen on *Big Brother*. It echoes what Dan told me about how he'd use "*Big Brother* tactics" in high school. Similarly, I found myself using my *Big Brother* knowledge in college as I was trying to manage a film crew that was feuding among themselves.

There were two sides to a particularly contentious argument about the short film we were making and I was the guy both sides got along with. I found myself thinking, "It's like I'm being a floater right now," as I went back and forth and from side to side trying to make sure they both felt heard. Of course, instead of stoking the flames, I was doing my best to extinguish them.

Later when I was working in an office, I reluctantly accepted the necessity of playing office politics by thinking of it in *Big Brother* terms. When I was an unpaid intern, I knew I needed to create a perception of myself that was competent and important so that they'd see me as valuable enough to bring into the alliance—I mean *company*—proper. Then when I was hired, it was important for me to find allies from different parts of the company who would be willing to speak highly of me so I wouldn't get evicted—I mean *fired*.

Honestly, I hated it. I love watching *Big Brother*, and I enjoy playing low-stakes games of social strategy and deduction. I even liked that I was capable of being a good mediator. But when it starts translating to real-world social hierarchies or power dynamics, I want it to stay in the fantasy world of reality television. The problem is that reality television is just a mirror of our real world.

"I definitely see the correlation in the microcosm of *Big Brother* the game versus real life. I think that is why it focuses so much on our personal idiosyncrasies and how we relate to other people more than any other reality show. I don't care if you watch *Survivor*, *The Circle*, *The Challenge*, whatever, even *Real Housewives*; you've probably never seen them brush their teeth, wash their hands, go to the bathroom, eat their food, cut it up, whether they snore, talk in their sleep. None of those things are highlighted about a person's personal life like they are in *Big Brother* because with *Big Brother* we are supposed to be able to relate to our real-world experience," Tiffany told me.[8]

So should the show exist? I'm not really qualified to answer that question for anyone else, but for me it has to. I am arguably more a product of *Big Brother* than anyone. I could no more argue against its existence than I could argue against my own.

Still, the show isn't without its warts. *Big Brother* was born in controversy that has only ever continued to evolve with the show over time. From racist remarks and behaviors to threats of violence, expulsions, attempts at censorship, and more. The live feeds have at least functioned as a safeguard against the worst the genre has to offer, but there's still plenty of room for improvement twenty-five years in.

It's clear to me that in today's competitive reality market, *Big Brother* still exists and has the relevance it does for a couple of key reasons.

First is its legacy. As one of the original competitive reality shows, *Big Brother* captured the hearts and minds of many people in a way that cannot be replicated because it was so utterly unique for its time. That kind of impact has staying power and helped create entire subgenres in response to it. As the shows it inspired come and go, the *Big Brother* brand is still powerful enough to launch more versions and make careers all over the world.

What is *Big Brother*'s true legacy though? Is it the genres it inspired? The culture of reality television it prompted? Trash heroes? Certainly it's all of those things. But it's also the other key part of its own survival: its voyeuristic transparency.

Back when John de Mol was trying to sell the concept for *The Golden Cage*, he was met with skepticism and a lack of interest purely because it was so wildly different from anything that had come before it.

To combat this, they actually interviewed Jennifer Ringley about her experience with JenniCam and put together a promo tape to help prospective buyers understand what they were trying to pitch. In the video they showed clips of Biosphere 2 crew members describing the breakdown of trust in their time in the sphere. They showed clips from their interview with Jennifer and said, "They'll be stars of a series written by life itself. Wherever they are, whatever they do, whatever they go through… Every breath will be recorded and broadcast."[9]

The voice-over continued, "'*Big Brother* is watching you' is never truer than in *The Golden Cage*. What does being constantly observed do to you? There's never been a TV project with so unpredictable an outcome and so glorious a victory… Observation. Manipulation. Hope. The naked truth of *The Golden Cage!*"[10]

This promise remains all these years later. There's *still* nothing else that exists on television that can sate the voyeuristic hunger that JenniCam exposed in us in the way *Big Brother* can.

I spoke to UK contestant Raph Korine about the removal of live feeds in the UK, and he had this to say: "It's literally the only thing that makes *Big Brother* different from all the other shows. What's so beautiful about *Big Brother* is you can actually feel like you're in the house with them at that exact same time when you're watching live feeds."[11]

Even in the UK and other countries with more limited live feeds, the live and raw feeling of the show is important to its success. Raph goes on to explain, "I think the diary room is the most interesting thing about what makes *Big Brother UK* different from the U.S. because in *Big Brother U.S.* you're told to talk in present tense. So something happens and you have to reiterate it as though you're still in that moment. You'll also be fed lines; they'll be like 'say this again' or 'say this in this way.' When I was on *Big Brother UK*, I was never told one time to say something in a certain way. The diary room was actually just a confessional. I went in and just had a chat as though I was chatting with a therapist. I was never told to say anything."[12]

As *Big Brother U.S.* episodes have gotten wackier and tackier, other *Big Brother* versions have stuck to a more raw feel for their episodes, perhaps in part to make up for the lack of live feeds. For me the message is clear one way or another: the live, raw, voyeuristic feeling of transparency is a key element to the success of the show, and any version of *Big Brother* that abandons this concept quickly finds itself failing to compete in today's market.

Of course part of this is voyeurism, but I think it's also because we're all searching for something *real*. That sounds ridiculous to say in the context of reality television, because what we really want is something real that's within a completely contrived scenario. *Big Brother* is something ridiculous that we get to see *real* responses to.

It's why Americans wanted a more cutthroat game. It's why the rawness of the show is so important in the face of how fake so many other shows feel. It's why Dr. Will was able to stand in front of a jury of his fellow contestants and tell them that if they didn't like how the show went, they had a problem with reality.

For better or worse, *Big Brother* is real; it's us. *Big Brother* is us when it's at its worst, exposing the various facets of racism and other oppressive structures.

Big Brother is also us at its best when Taylor Hale overcomes overwhelming odds to find success.

It's us when Dan Gheesling masters the game and wins, and it's us when he does it again and fails.

I don't know that I'll ever escape my golden cage, but I'm not sure I mind all that much.

At least I'm in good company.

Notes

Introduction

1. Zach Seemayer, "'Big Brother' Season 24: Taylor Hale Bullying Drama, Racism, Controversy Explained," *ET*, July 13, 2022, https://www.etonline.com/big-brother-season-24-taylor-hale-bullying-drama-racism-controversy-explained-187149.
2. Taylor Hale (@TheTayMack), "My stomach churns when I think about living in that house without 24/7 live feeds. I am genuinely afraid anyone could have a similar experience to me, and not be believed leaving the house. Sunlight is the best disinfectant. Live feeds are the sun. So no, I'm not watching," Twitter (now X), March 23, 2023, 10:39 a.m., https://twitter.com/TheTayMack/status/1638732278506323970.

Chapter 1: Adaptations

1. *Big Brother*, season 2, episode 30, aired September 20, 2001, on CBS, https://www.paramountplus.com/shows/video/MvygopmT7xtuwW62510_t0AXwEN5Gy4t/.
2. Andy Dehnart, "Former 'Big Brother' Host Ian O'Malley Moved on to a Career in Radio, Film, and Philanthropy," Reality Blurred, September 16, 2007, https://www.realityblurred.com/realitytv/2007/09/big-brother-1-ian_omalley_interview/.

3 Andy Dehnart, "Big Brother 2: Audience Won't Vote; Julie Chen Will Return as Host," Reality Blurred, May 29, 2001, https://www.realityblurred.com/realitytv/2001/05/big-brother-2-big_brother_2_audience/.

4 Paul Römer, "'Big Brother' Executive Producer Speaks Candidly," BigBrother2000.com, August 21, 2000, archived October 18, 2000, https://web.archive.org/web/20001018125558/http://webcenter.bigbrother2000.aol.com/entertainment/NON/article309.html.

5 Michael Peck, "Oh, *Brother*—Not Again," *TV Guide*, January 11, 2001, archived January 25, 2001, https://web.archive.org/web/20010125020600/http://www.tvguide.com/newsgossip/insider/010111c.asp.

6 Ken Tucker, "5 Worst TV Shows," *Entertainment Weekly*, January 24, 2001, archived January 24, 2001, https://web.archive.org/web/20010124001700/http://www.ew.com/ew/features/001222/bestof2000/worsttv.html.

7 "'Big Brother' Creator Wants U.S. Viewers to Get Emotional," Fox Market Wire, February 14, 2001, archived February 22, 2001, https://web.archive.org/web/20010222205202/http://www.foxmarketwire.com/wires/0214/f_ap_0214_26.sml.

8 Paul Römer, "Relationship, Controversy, and Jamie's Letter," BigBrother2000.com, August 28, 2000, archived October 19, 2000, https://web.archive.org/web/20001019021403/http://webcenter.bigbrother2000.aol.com/entertainment/NON/article321.html.

9 "CBS Announces Third and Fourth 'Survivors,'" Zap2it.com, January 9, 2001, archived April 17, 2001, https://web.archive.org/web/20010417005134/http://tv.zap2it.com/news/tvnewsdaily.html?14907.

10 Bill Carter, "'Big Brother' Has Not Been Voted Off CBS," *New York Times*, September 25, 2000, https://www.nytimes.com/2000/09/25/business/media-talk-big-brother-has-not-been-voted-off-cbs.html.

11 "CBS Looks to Shapiro for 'Big Brother' Boost," Zap2it.com, February 21, 2001, archived April 19, 2001, https://web.archive.org/web/20010419004132/http://tv.zap2it.com/news/tvnewsdaily.html?15754.

12 Peck, "Oh, *Brother*—Not Again."

13 Peck, "Oh, *Brother*—Not Again."

14 Laurie J. Flynn, "Faltering TV Show Hits Stride on Web," *New York Times*, September 18, 2000, https://www.nytimes.com/2000/09/18/business/compressed-data-faltering-tv-show-hits-stride-on-web.html.

15 Paul Römer, "Paul Römer Interview Part Three," BigBrother2000.com, September 4, 2000, archived October 18, 2000, https://web.archive.org/web/20001018164819/http://webcenter.bigbrother2000.aol.com/entertainment/NON/article335.html.

16 "Viewer Advisory," BigBrother2000.com, August 15, 2000, archived August

15, 2000, https://web.archive.org/web/20010207151959/http://webcenter.bigbrother2000.aol.com/entertainment/NON/article26.html.
17 Andy Dehnart, "'Web Watchers May Have Revolutionized Reality TV,'" Reality Blurred, September 27, 2000, https://www.realityblurred.com/realitytv/2000/09/big-brother-1-web_watchers_may/.
18 Römer, "Paul Römer Interview Part Three."
19 Römer, "Paul Römer Interview Part Three."
20 Lisa Gandy and Lisa McChristian, "Reality Television Goes Interactive: The Big Brother Television Audience," *The Corinthian* 4 (2002): Article 1.
21 "CBS Looks to Shapiro for 'Big Brother' Boost."
22 Greg Baerg, "Shapiro Examines 'Big Brother's' Web Experiment," Zap2it.com, July 30, 2001, archived August 5, 2001, https://web.archive.org/web/20010805203451/http://tv.zap2it.com/news/tvnewsdaily.html?19619.
23 Ken Tucker, "Sex Has Made 'Big Brother' More Obvious," *Entertainment Weekly*, July 12, 2001, https://ew.com/article/2001/07/12/sex-has-made-big-brother-more-obvious/.
24 Bill Carter, "'Big Brother' Hopes to Engineer an Exit, Then Add a Face," *New York Times*, September 4, 2000, https://www.nytimes.com/2000/09/04/arts/big-brother-hopes-to-engineer-an-exit-then-add-a-face.html.
25 "2001 CBS Big Brother 2 Season Premiere Promo," posted February 7, 2023, by oisfsehgfusd, YouTube, 0:20, https://www.youtube.com/watch?v=wMig4H8NtLU.
26 Susan King, "'Big Brother' Is Emulating Its Big Brother," *Los Angeles Times*, July 5, 2001, https://www.latimes.com/archives/la-xpm-2001-jul-05-ca-18790-story.html.
27 "'Big Brother' Tries to Bore No More," *New York Daily News*, June 21, 2001, https://www.nydailynews.com/2001/06/21/big-brother-tries-to-bore-no-more/.
28 Eric Deggans, "'Big Brother' Tries Again," *Tampa Bay Times*, July 5, 2001, https://www.tampabay.com/archive/2001/07/05/big-brother-tries-again/.
29 Josh Wolk, "'Brother' from Another Planet," *Entertainment Weekly*, July 24, 2001, archived October 6, 2014, https://web.archive.org/web/20141006104659/https://www.ew.com/ew/article/0,,20400144_168642_2,00.html.
30 King, "'Big Brother' Is Emulating Its Big Brother."
31 Ken Tucker, "Sex Has Made 'Big Brother' More Obvious."

Chapter 2: The Evil Doctor

1 *Big Brother*, season 2, episode 15, aired August 7, 2001, on CBS, https://www.paramountplus.com/shows/video/F_Xb76QksYaEASvTXdWcM7_KCeSXoR2G/.

2. John Folsom, "Paging Dr. Will Kirby," *Tomahawk Talk* 81, no. 1 (October 19, 2017), https://issuu.com/fsustomahawktalk/docs/the_tomahawk_talk_volume_81_issue_1/s/5425.
3. *Big Brother*, season 2, episode 1, aired July 5, 2001, on CBS, https://www.paramountplus.com/shows/video/CSF_EmSOf6wyKCpSgVFzYQu6PbZ54ORY/.
4. *Big Brother*, season 2, episode 1.
5. *Big Brother*, season 2, episode 1.
6. David Bloomberg, "*Big Brother 2*, Episode 3: Can Nicole Pull It Out?" Reality News Online, archived August 16, 2001, https://web.archive.org/web/20010816124851/http://www.realitynewsonline.com/article1172.html.
7. Hardy Hill, interview by Taran Armstrong, host, *The Taran Show*, episode 49, Rob Has a Podcast, July 9, 2018, https://robhasawebsite.com/taran-show-49-hardy-hill/.
8. Hill, interview by Armstrong, *The Taran Show*.
9. *Big Brother*, season 2, episode 2, aired July 7, 2001, on CBS, https://www.paramountplus.com/shows/video/tOELoMNRoBHT3kRzt9b8jIvQH5BmOHiW/.
10. *Big Brother*, season 2, episode 3, aired July 10, 2001, on CBS, https://www.paramountplus.com/shows/video/0ZNzICaqlJx5TXyu07dn9ZSF_Ux04PVs/.
11. Bloomberg, "*Big Brother 2*, Episode 3: Can Nicole Pull It Out?"
12. *Big Brother*, season 2, episode 17, aired August 11, 2001, on CBS, https://www.paramountplus.com/shows/video/XXNC8GJZJU3MQ7WKZtRHG2_tC0YWKpIn/.
13. Josef Adalian, "Webcasting of 'Big Bro 2' Shows Net Can Be Profitable," *Variety*, September 27, 2001, https://variety.com/2001/digital/news/webcasting-of-big-bro-2-shows-net-can-be-profitable-1117853311/.
14. Andy Dehnart, "56,026 Paid for Big Brother 2 Feeds," Reality Blurred, September 28, 2001, https://www.realityblurred.com/realitytv/2001/09/big-brother-2-56026_paid_for/.
15. Marshall Sella, "The Electronic Fishbowl," *New York Times*, May 21, 2000, https://www.nytimes.com/2000/05/21/magazine/the-electronic-fishbowl.html.
16. *Big Brother*, season 2, episode 30, aired September 20, 2001, on CBS, https://www.paramountplus.com/shows/video/MvygopmT7xtuwW62510_t0AXwEN5Gy4t/.
17. David Bloomberg, "*Big Brother 2*: The 'Will' Strategy," Reality News Online, archived December 22, 2001, https://web.archive.org/web/20011222005735/http://www.realitynewsonline.com/article1228.html.
18. David Bloomberg, "*Big Brother 2*, Episode 22: Hardy in the Seat of Power," Reality News Online, archived October 31, 2001, https://web.archive.org/web/20011031164107/http://www.realitynewsonline.com/article1271.html.

19. *Big Brother*, season 2, episode 30.
20. *Big Brother*, season 2, episode 12, aired July 31, 2001, on CBS, https://www.paramountplus.com/shows/video/WZMgFhnqfVSkQjfowMid4YYD5P0JNj8t/.
21. *Big Brother*, season 2, episode 22, aired August 25, 2001, on CBS, https://www.paramountplus.com/shows/video/jgpH_mmynLJyWycU7KWpWJpnjhRqrbAP/.
22. "The Creators: John De Mol," posted April 24, 2014, by Ogilvy Asia, YouTube, 15:21, https://www.youtube.com/watch?v=PBwC0LdqXcU.
23. *Big Brother*, season 2, episode 4, aired July 12, 2001, on CBS, https://www.paramountplus.com/shows/video/072A7E86-E980-0136-7D3B-16E06E750647/.
24. "Former BB2 Contestant Krista Suing CBS over 'The Knife Incident,'" Reality TV World, July 3, 2002, https://www.realitytvworld.com/news/former-bb2-contestant-krista-suing-cbs-over-the-knife-incident-440.php.
25. "Former BB2 Contestant Krista Suing CBS over 'The Knife Incident.'"
26. Herman Fuselier, "'Big Brother' May Be Calling on Louisiana Again," *Daily Advertiser*, June 19, 2006, archived June 27, 2006, https://web.archive.org/web/20060627223733/http://www.theadvertiser.com/apps/pbcs.dll/article?AID=/20060619/LIFESTYLE/606190312/1024.
27. O'Sean Aieghlans, "Violence Threatens *Big Brother 2*," Reality News Online, archived December 24, 2001, https://web.archive.org/web/20011224100952/http://www.realitynewsonline.com/article1174.html.
28. Susan Schechter, "*Big Brother*: America vs. Britain," Reality News Online, archived July 26, 2001, https://web.archive.org/web/20011224101639/http://www.realitynewsonline.com/article1175.html.
29. "Evicted 'Big Brother' Member Had Prior Arrests," ABC News, July 16, 2001, https://abcnews.go.com/Entertainment/story?id=103645&page=1.
30. "Evicted 'Big Brother' Member Had Prior Arrests."
31. "Fox: Rockwell's to Blame," *New York Daily News*, April 13, 2000, https://www.nydailynews.com/2000/04/13/fox-rockwells-to-blame/; Bill Hoffmann, "Ex: 'Millionaire' Groom Slapped Me Around," *New York Post*, February 20, 2000, https://nypost.com/2000/02/20/ex-millionaire-groom-slapped-me-around/.
32. Angie Wagner, "Judge Grants Annulment of TV Marriage," *Las Vegas Sun*, April 5, 2000, https://lasvegassun.com/news/2000/apr/05/judge-grants-annulment-of-tv-marriage/.
33. *Big Brother*, season 2, episode 3.
34. *Big Brother*, season 2, episode 26, aired September 5, 2001, on CBS, https://www.paramountplus.com/shows/video/Zet9gPy0ql_0_zs5oipEkSW6tNpknnyI/.
35. *Big Brother*, season 2, episode 29, aired September 18, 2001, on CBS, https://www.paramountplus.com/shows/video/JHA3_LwsNF2AkYMP7UmKORtPHXqkJgiT/.

36 Hill, interview by Armstrong, *The Taran Show*.
37 Brill Bundy, "How Much Do 'Big Brother 2' Guests Know About Terrorist Attacks?" Zap2it.com, September 13, 2001, archived September 17, 2001, https://web.archive.org/web/20010917031536/http://tv.zap2it.com/news/tvnewsdaily.html?20529.
38 Josh Wolk, "'Big Brother' and September 11th's Grim Reality," *Entertainment Weekly*, October 5, 2001, https://ew.com/article/2001/10/05/big-brother-and-september-11ths-grim-reality/.
39 Susan Schechter, "An Open Letter to CBS," Reality News Online, September 13, 2001, archived October 31, 2001, https://web.archive.org/web/20011222053603/http://www.realitynewsonline.com/article1318.html.
40 "Big Brother 2, CBS, and Tragedy: Readers Respond," Reality News Online, September 13, 2001, archived October 31, 2001, https://web.archive.org/web/20011031105413/http://www.realitynewsonline.com/article1321.html.
41 "Big Brother 2, CBS, and Tragedy: Readers Respond—Part 2," Reality News Online, September 13, 2001, archived October 31, 2001, https://web.archive.org/web/20011031110417/http://www.realitynewsonline.com/article1323.html.
42 Bundy, "How Much Do 'Big Brother 2' Guests Know About Terrorist Attacks?"
43 *Big Brother*, season 2, episode 29.
44 Wolk, "'Big Brother' and September 11th's Grim Reality."
45 *Big Brother*, season 2, episode 29.
46 "Reality TV Doing Just Fine, CBS Chief Says," Zap2it.com, November 28, 2001, archived November 29, 2001, https://web.archive.org/web/20011129031852/http://tv.zap2it.com/news/tvnewsdaily.html?22199.
47 Greg Baerg, "Shapiro Examines 'Big Brother's' Web Experiment," Zap2it.com, July 30, 2001, archived August 5, 2001, https://web.archive.org/web/20010805203451/http://tv.zap2it.com/news/tvnewsdaily.html?19619.
48 Brian Lowry, "CBS Defends 'Brother'; Ratings up After Incident," *Los Angeles Times*, July 14, 2001, https://www.latimes.com/archives/la-xpm-2001-jul-14-ca-22146-story.html.
49 Felice Prager, "*Big Brother 2*-aholics Unite!," Reality News Online, archived December 22, 2001, https://web.archive.org/web/20011222025118/http://www.realitynewsonline.com/article1257.html.
50 Andy Dehnart, "Big Brother 3 Contestants Who Even Look at Banner Planes May Be Expelled; Alcohol Rationed, Other Changes Planned," Reality Blurred, July 1, 2002, https://www.realityblurred.com/realitytv/2002/07/big-brother-3-big_brother_3_contestants/.
51 Andy Dehnart, "Shapiro Says Big Brother Concept Is 'Sociologically Intriguing,'" Reality Blurred, July 8, 2002, https://www.realityblurred.com/realitytv/2002/07/big-brother-3-shapiro_says_big/.

52 Hill, interview by Armstrong, *The Taran Show*.

Chapter 3: Influences

1 Brian Lowry, "Watching as 'Big Brother' Watches Them," *Los Angeles Times*, June 27, 2000, https://www.latimes.com/archives/la-xpm-2000-jun-27-ca-45134-story.html.
2 "The Human Experiment: Two Years and Twenty Minutes Inside Biosphere 2," posted September 7, 2016, by Microsoft Research, YouTube, 1:15:06, https://www.youtube.com/watch?v=m1zOYQ9lPwY.
3 "Biosphere 2 Crewmember & Author Jane Poynter Interview," posted September 19, 2006, by bio2news, YouTube, 3:07, https://www.youtube.com/watch?v=bPK05evoFHw.
4 Nick Kanas and Dietrich Manzey, *Space Psychology and Psychiatry* (Springer, 2008), 97–100.
5 Mark Nelson, Kathelin Gray, and John P. Allen, "Group Dynamics Challenges: Insights from Biosphere 2 Experiments," *Life Sciences in Space Research* 6 (July 1, 2015): 79–86, https://doi.org/10.1016/j.lssr.2015.07.003.
6 "The Human Experiment: Two Years and Twenty Minutes Inside Biosphere 2."
7 "The Human Experiment: Two Years and Twenty Minutes Inside Biosphere 2."
8 William J. Broad, "As Biosphere Is Sealed, Its Patron Reflects on Life," *New York Times*, September 24, 1991, https://www.nytimes.com/1991/09/24/science/as-biosphere-is-sealed-its-patron-reflects-on-life.html.
9 *Spaceship Earth*, directed by Matt Wolf, featuring Kathelin Gray, Marie Harding, William Dempster (Impact Partners, 2020).
10 *Spaceship Earth*.
11 "The Creators: John De Mol."
12 John de Mol, "THE BOSS; Radio Days and Reality TV," *New York Times*, June 27, 2001, https://www.nytimes.com/2001/06/27/business/the-boss-radio-days-and-reality-tv.html.
13 Marlene Edmunds, "De Mol Is Reality's Real Thing," *Variety*, July 17, 2001, https://variety.com/2001/tv/news/de-mol-is-reality-s-real-thing-1117802905/.
14 "Het immense vermogen van Talpa-baas John de Mol," Pure Luxe, November 28, 2020, https://pureluxe.nl/2020/11/vermogen-john-de-mol/.
15 "Love Letters (TROS, 2001)het eerste homohuwelijk op TV," posted March 19, 2020, by Meuk TV, YouTube, 1:20:36, https://www.youtube.com/watch?v=3jfO1IJdJKM.
16 Meg Carter, "From the Man Who Gave You Big Brother: Couples in Chains!" *Independent*, September 5, 2000, https://www.independent.co.uk/news/media/from-the-man-who-gave-you-big-brother-couples-in-chains-699141.html.

17. "Endemol Entertainment Holding NV," Encyclopedia.com, accessed February 13, 2024, https://www.encyclopedia.com/books/politics-and-business-magazines/endemol-entertainment-holding-nv.
18. "Big Brother duurste programma ooit," Big Brother 1999, September 7, 1999. https://www.bigbrother1999.nl/big-brother-duurste-programma-ooit/.
19. Ryan Gajewski, "Hollywood Flashback: NBC's Pricey 'Supertrain' Took a Short-Lived Ride," *Hollywood Reporter*, August 4, 2022, https://www.hollywoodreporter.com/movies/movie-news/nbcs-pricey-supertrain-took-a-short-lived-ride-1235190993/.
20. Peter Bazalgette, *Billion Dollar Game: How Three Men Risked It All and Changed the Face of Television* (London: Time Warner Books, 2005), 74-77.
21. "Rolf Wouters—Presenter," Big Brother 1999, October 17, 2011, https://www.bigbrother1999.nl/rolf-wouters-presentator/.
22. "An American Family: Introduction," PBS SoCal, accessed February 13, 2024, https://www.pbssocal.org/shows/thirteen-specials/clip/thirteen-specials-an-american-family-introduction.
23. Matt Schudel, "Craig Gilbert, Creator of 'An American Family,' Called the First Reality TV Show, Dies at 94," *Washington Post*, April 18, 2020, https://www.washingtonpost.com/local/obituaries/craig-gilbert-creator-of-an-american-family-called-the-first-reality-tv-show-dies-at-94/2020/04/18/ea66b34c-7e4e-11ea-9040-68981f488eed_story.html.
24. "Charlie Brooker's Screenwipe—Reality TV Editing," posted March 1, 2007, by Samusek TDS, YouTube, 5:06, https://www.youtube.com/watch?v=BBwepkVurCI.
25. Raymond van den Boogaard, "Zeven werklozen samen op zoek naar een baan," *NRC*, September 28, 1996, https://www.nrc.nl/nieuws/1996/09/28/zeven-werklozen-samen-op-zoek-naar-een-baan-7325941-a591551.
26. Peter Bazalgette, *Billion Dollar Game*, 111.
27. "Project X," Big Brother 1999, accessed February 13, 2024, https://www.bigbrother1999.nl/het-programma/about/project-x/.
28. Jennifer Ringley, interview by Alex Goldman, host, "#5 JenniCam," *Reply All*, podcast, December 17, 2014, https://soundcloud.com/replyall/5-jennicam.
29. "Frequently Asked Questions," JenniCam.org, archived April 20, 1999, https://web.archive.org/web/19990420213308/http://www.jennicam.org/faq/general.html#b.
30. "JenniCam's Jenni on Letterman's Late Show," posted October 27, 2013, by shesnailie, YouTube, 7:20, archived April 15, 2015, https://web.archive.org/web/20150415010936/https://www.youtube.com/watch?v=0AmIntaD5VE.
31. "What Is JenniCam?" JenniCam.org, archived December 6, 2003, https://web.archive.org/web/20031206033013/http://www.jennicam.org/j2kr/concept.html.

32 "JenniJournal," archived August 17, 2000, https:// web .archive .org /web /20000817214014 /http:// www .jennicam .org / -jenni /journal /story .html.
33 Ringley, interview by Goldman, "#5 JenniCam."
34 Ringley, interview by Goldman, "#5 JenniCam."
35 Alex Pham, "Pioneer to Pull Plug on JenniCam," *Los Angeles Times*, December 11, 2003, https:// www .latimes .com /archives /la -xpm -2003 -dec -11 -fi -jenni11 -story .html.
36 Merel van Leeuwen, "Big Brother ziet mij niet," Big Brother 1999, August 4, 1999, https://www.bigbrother1999.nl/big-brother-ziet-mij-niet/.
37 "The Selection," Big Brother 1999, accessed February 13, 2024, https://www .bigbrother1999.nl/het-programma/de-selectie/.
38 Mark Koster, *De Mol: De Machtigste Mediafamilie van Nederland*, (Uitgeverj Balans, 2020), 62.
39 Koster, *De Mol*, 62.
40 "Viewing Figures," Big Brother 1999, accessed February 14, 2024, https:// www.bigbrother1999.nl/het-programma/kijkcijfers/.
41 "Hackers Crack Big Brother Website," Big Brother 1999, September 21, 1999, https://www.bigbrother1999.nl/hackers-kraken-website-van-big-brother/.
42 "Quotes," Big Brother 1999, accessed February 14, 2024, https://www .bigbrother1999.nl/versie-1999/quotes/.
43 "Quotes," Big Brother 1999.
44 Lowry, "Watching as 'Big Brother' Watches Them."
45 "Telefónica to Acquire $5.3B Endemol," CNN Money, March 17, 2000, https://money.cnn.com/2000/03/17/europe/endemol/.
46 "The Creators: John De Mol."

Chapter 4: Community

1 "Big Brother Season 6 Cast Reunites 18 Years After Competing in the Pressure Cooker Competition," posted August 24, 2023, by The Exclusive with Sharon Tharp, YouTube, 1:08:48, https://www.youtube.com/watch?v= jQ0uJ15h1WA.
2 *Big Brother*, season 6, episode 1, aired July 7, 2005, on CBS, https://www .paramountplus.com/shows/video/o_6hxi18zJ1LnvPQd6_nvToRq5Xnk3QU/.
3 *Big Brother*, season 6, episode 1.
4 *Big Brother*, season 6, episode 4, aired July 16, 2005, on CBS, https://www .paramountplus.com/shows/video/txoBCj9_UFkRTw0Git6kpreKnxq0DRGe/.
5 *Big Brother*, season 6, episode 2, aired July 12, 2005, on CBS, https://www .paramountplus.com/shows/video/txoBCj9_UFkRTw0Git6kpreKnxq0DRGe/.
6 *Big Brother*, season 6, episode 2.

7. *Big Brother*, season 6, episode 4.
8. *Big Brother*, season 6, episode 4.
9. "Kaysar Calls James Out!" JokersUpdates.com, July 21, 2005, https://www.jokersupdates.com/archives/bigbrother6usalivefeeds/bbarch072105-071705-072305-P7M.html#1958680.
10. "HOH and Jen Pt 2," JokersUpdates.com, July 22, 2005, https://www.jokersupdates.com/archives/bigbrother6usalivefeeds/bbarch072205-071705-072305-P6M.html#1966047.
11. Susan Schechter, "The Big Brother 3 Live Feeds: A Different Side of the Houseguests," Reality News Online, August 12, 2002, archived October 14, 2002, https://web.archive.org/web/20070426230832/http://www.realitynewsonline.com/cgi-bin/ae.pl?mode=1&article=article2116.art&page=1.
12. Hamsterwatch, "Confessions of a Big Brother Live Feed Watcher," Reality Blurred, June 24, 2015, https://www.realityblurred.com/realitytv/2015/06/confessions-big-brother-live-feed-watcher/.
13. *Big Brother*, season 6, episode 8, aired July 26, 2005, on CBS, https://www.paramountplus.com/shows/video/Evj221hCu07X6dfD5USTzoOAahg0ngfX/.
14. *Big Brother*, season 6, episode 8.
15. "Lisa Donahue." Lisa Donahue Fan Page, Accessed February 28, 2024, https://csnetserver.com/lisadonahue/.
16. Hamsterwatch, interview by Taran Armstrong, February 28, 2024.
17. Hamsterwatch, interview by Armstrong, February 28, 2024.
18. David Bloomberg, interview by Taran Armstrong, February 25, 2024.
19. David Bloomberg, "Big Brother 2: Krista Supporters Strike Back—and Strike Out," Reality News Online, July 10, 2002, archived October 21, 2002, https://web.archive.org/web/20060118071831/http://www.realitynewsonline.com/cgi-bin/ae.pl?mode=1&article=article1275.art&page=1.
20. *Big Brother*, season 6, episode 16, aired August 13, 2005, on CBS, https://www.paramountplus.com/shows/video/A7741843-9F80-D474-0107-16E1690E0B80/.
21. *Big Brother*, season 6, episode 17, aired August 16, 2005, on CBS, https://www.paramountplus.com/shows/video/2l5ygUDjt6Pv7Cfge12RuQMPM87tIanj/.
22. *Big Brother*, season 6, episode 17.
23. *Big Brother*, season 6, episode 18, aired August 18, 2005, on CBS, https://www.paramountplus.com/shows/video/H7HYpjZ8cCcgMYB_XUova_gD_VqQu5pL/.
24. "Kaysar Big Brother 6," Teamkaysar.com, archived May 18, 2007, https://web.archive.org/web/20070518031925/http://www.teamkaysar.com/.
25. "Kaysar Big Brother 6."
26. "Forum Index," Jenvasquezsucks.com, archived February 6, 2006, https://web.archive.org/web/20060206053855/http://www.jenvasquezsucks.com/forum/.

27 "BB6's Jen Vasquez Sucks!," Jenvasquezsucks.com, archived April 27, 2007, https://web.archive.org/web/20070427112701/http://www.jenvasquezsucks.com/forum/viewforum.php?f=1&sid=8fa0881f253ee663f20914ac02599b96.
28 "Best Way to 'Get' Jen…," Jenvasquezsucks.com, archived May 10, 2007, https://web.archive.org/web/20070510233552/http://www.jenvasquezsucks.com/forum/viewtopic.php?t=198&sid=e42674b82ad264503c48c37dc5b96105.
29 "Big Brother Season 6 Cast Reunites."
30 "Big Brother Season 6 Cast Reunites."
31 "Big Brother Season 6 Cast Reunites."

Chapter 5: Twisted

1 Jun Song, interview by Taran Armstrong, March 23, 2024.
2 Brian Lowry, "'Millionaire' Shows Its Age as ABC's Ratings Lead Falters," *Los Angeles Times*, December 1, 2000, https://www.latimes.com/archives/la-xpm-2000-dec-01-ca-59493-story.html.
3 "Outback in Front: CBS Wins Season," E! Online, May 25, 2001, archived June 22, 2003, https://web.archive.org/web/20030622171446/https://eonline.com/News/Items/0,1,8327,00.html.
4 Kevin Downey, "Mercy, It's a Killer of a Midseason," Media Life, January 16, 2002, archived January 18, 2002, https://web.archive.org/web/20040316065316/http://www.medialifemagazine.com/news2002/jan02/jan14/3_wed/news1wednesday.html.
5 *Big Brother*, season 3, episode 27, aired September 12, 2002, on CBS, https://www.paramountplus.com/shows/video/78F6E745-D40E-D185-22C6-38A96C413FD9/.
6 *Big Brother*, season 3, episode 27.
7 Jun Song, interview by Taran Armstrong and Mary Kwiatkowski, hosts, *Big Brother 4 Blockumentary*, podcast, August 2, 2020, https://robhasawebsite.com/big-brother-4-blockumentary-jun-song-interview/.
8 David Bloomberg, "Big Brother 4 to Feature Ex-Spouses!" Reality News Online, June 30, 2003, archived July 28, 2003, https://web.archive.org/web/20030728185919/http://www.realitynewsonline.com/cgi-bin/ae.pl?mode=1&article=article3272.art&page=1.
9 Bloomberg, "Big Brother 4 to Feature Ex-Spouses!"
10 O'Sean Aieghlans, "Big Brother 4 Producers Flirt with Bad Taste," Reality News Online, July 9, 2003, archived August 21, 2003, https://web.archive.org/web/20030821020429/http://www.realitynewsonline.com/cgi-bin/ae.pl?mode=1&article=article3310.art&page=1.

11 *Big Brother*, season 4, episode 1, aired July 8, 2003, on CBS, https://www.paramountplus.com/shows/video/6_alsmeSui9x1tMvnmnCK0svkTVX_R_8/.
12 Song, interview by Armstrong and Kwiatkowski, *Big Brother 4 Blockumentary*.
13 Song, interview by Armstrong, March 23, 2024.
14 Song, interview by Armstrong, March 23, 2024.
15 Don Kaplan, "Out Before It Even Begins—'Big Bro' Boots Brandon for Sneaking Calls," *New York Post*, July 8, 2003, https://nypost.com/2003/07/08/out-before-it-even-begins-big-bro-boots-brandon-for-sneaking-calls/.
16 Song, interview by Armstrong, March 23, 2024.
17 Aieghlans, "Big Brother 4 Producers Flirt with Bad Taste."

Chapter 6: Do Not Assume

1 Hamsterwatch, "Nakomis: 'I Hope You See This, Internet Fuckers! I Hope It Makes You Fucking Happy,'" September 12, 2004, https://www.hamsterwatch.com/091204.shtml.
2 "CBS Promises 'Twisted' Changes and New Rules for 'Big Brother 5,'" Reality TV World, June 24, 2004, https://www.realitytvworld.com/news/cbs-promises-twisted-changes-and-new-rules-for-big-brother-5–2652.php.
3 Wayne Holtz, host, *The Wayne Holtz Podcast*, season 1, episode 1, "Jennifer 'Nakomis' Dedmon of Big Brother," August 7, 2017, https://open.spotify.com/episode/4ZrAGUIG2SooMdbochNMGV.
4 *Big Brother*, season 5, episode 1, aired July 6, 2004, on CBS, https://www.paramountplus.com/shows/video/CDFF1C87-E508–52E8–676B-014193F1CEA2/.
5 *Big Brother*, season 5, episode 4, aired July 15, 2004, on CBS, https://www.paramountplus.com/shows/video/LRS_iM50N1eZFmMPdAt4ZsqNo9vRke59/.
6 *Big Brother*, season 5, episode 13, aired August 5, 2004, on CBS, https://www.paramountplus.com/shows/video/56FE7CE1-F3B4-CB73-F3E5–015562DE08CA/.
7 *Big Brother*, season 5, episode 13.
8 *Big Brother*, season 5, episode 2, aired July 8, 2004, on CBS, https://www.paramountplus.com/shows/video/4uFSyofKYvyRRPyWrhdPj6jgzVL_WBSi/.
9 *Big Brother*, season 5, episode 2.
10 *Big Brother*, season 5, episode 4.
11 *Big Brother*, season 5, episode 2.
12 Hamsterwatch, "Nakomis: 'I Hope You See This, Internet Fuckers!'"
13 Hamsterwatch, "Nakomis: 'I Hope You See This, Internet Fuckers!'"
14 Hamsterwatch, email message to author, March 1, 2024.
15 Steve Rogers and Christopher Rocchio, "CBS Orders an Eighth Season of 'Big Brother' for Summer 2007," Reality TV World, February 2, 2007, https://

www.realitytvworld.com/news/cbs-orders-an-eighth-season-of-big-brother-for-summer-2007—4651.php.
16. Rogers and Rocchio, "CBS Orders an Eighth Season of 'Big Brother.'"
17. "Big Brother Producer Talks About Rigging/Feeds Accusations," posted August 22, 2006, by WebRat1, YouTube, 5:29, https://www.youtube.com/watch?v=B7ArlVXogmQ.
18. Hamsterwatch, email message to author, March 1, 2024.

Chapter 7: The Evolution of Strategy

1. Jason Guy, interview by Taran Armstrong, April 12, 2024.
2. *Big Brother*, season 3, episode 4, aired July 17, 2002, on CBS, https://www.paramountplus.com/shows/video/CeVRvNL5I0CDHdLK0b9dbYW1xpfmZ45s/.
3. *Big Brother*, season 3 episode 4.
4. Guy, interview by Armstrong, April 12, 2024.
5. "Danielle Reyes Personal Profile," CBS.com, archived September 7, 2002, https://web.archive.org/web/20020907211720/http://www.cbs.com/primetime/bigbrother3/houseguests/danielle/index.shtml.
6. "Jason Guy Personal Profile," CBS.com, archived September 7, 2002, https://web.archive.org/web/20020907210525/http://www.cbs.com/primetime/bigbrother3/houseguests/jason/index.shtml.
7. "Jason Guy Personal Profile," CBS.com.
8. Guy, interview by Armstrong, April 12, 2024.
9. Guy, interview by Armstrong, April 12, 2024.
10. Guy, interview by Armstrong, April 12, 2024.
11. Guy, interview by Armstrong, April 12, 2024.
12. Guy, interview by Armstrong, April 12, 2024.
13. Jun Song, interview by Taran Armstrong and Mary Kwiatkowski, hosts, *Big Brother 4 Blockumentary*, podcast, August 2, 2020, https://robhasawebsite.com/big-brother-4-blockumentary-jun-song-interview/.
14. Song, interview by Armstrong and Kwiatkowski, *Big Brother 4 Blockumentary*.
15. Song, interview by Armstrong and Kwiatkowski, *Big Brother 4 Blockumentary*.
16. *Big Brother*, season 7, episode 8, aired July 25, 2006, on CBS, https://www.paramountplus.com/shows/video/gTD5YJJ0gjRQ82UfRsFAqY5H__c7dZHG/.
17. *Big Brother*, season 7, episode 8.

Chapter 8: Controversy

1. Eric Stein, interview by Taran Armstrong, host, *The Taran Show*, Rob Has a Podcast, August 27, 2017, https://robhasawebsite.com/the-taran-show-6-eric-stein-interview/.

2. *Big Brother*, season 8, episode 1, aired July 5, 2007, on CBS, https://www.paramountplus.com/shows/video/uWe9GG9gPv_7ZlF_YhMR_Vu8MnsKJ9V4/.

3. *Big Brother*, season 8, episode 2, aired July 8, 2007, on CBS, https://www.paramountplus.com/shows/video/aPB3CP4LoCLQNblLPol7Ct5jomozQRh1/.

4. Marcy Brown, "CBS Promotes Misogynistic Verbal Abuse to Go On in the Big Brother House," Indybay, August 22, 2007, https://www.indybay.org/newsitems/2007/08/22/18442619.php?show_comments=1.

5. Marcy Brown, "CBS Promotes Misogynistic Verbal Abuse."

6. Andy Dehnart, "NOW Says Big Brother Is 'Completely Out of Control,' Wants Dick Removed from the House," Reality Blurred, August 28, 2007, https://www.realityblurred.com/realitytv/2007/08/big-brother-8-now_dick_removed/.

7. *Big Brother*, season 8, episode 22, aired August 23, 2007, on CBS, https://www.paramountplus.com/shows/video/bWFdnDrA6CWZi95jzaFeK1Y2SbI8YnCq/.

8. Derrik Lang, "Controversial Remarks and a Physical Altercation Fuel 'Big Brother 8,'" *Orange County Register*, August 29, 2007, https://www.ocregister.com/2007/08/29/controversial-remarks-and-a-physical-altercation-fuel-big-brother-8/.

9. Andy Dehnart, "Eric Stays After Amber Explodes; Producers Try to Protect Diary Room Sessions," Reality Blurred, August 10, 2007, https://www.realityblurred.com/realitytv/2007/08/big-brother-8-eric_stays_diary_room/.

10. Lang, "Controversial Remarks and a Physical Altercation."

11. Stein, interview by Armstrong, *The Taran Show*.

12. Stein, interview by Armstrong, *The Taran Show*.

13. *Big Brother*, season 8, episode 1.

14. Stein, interview by Armstrong, *The Taran Show*.

15. Stein, interview by Armstrong, *The Taran Show*.

16. Lang, "Controversial Remarks and a Physical Altercation."

17. Adam Jasinski, interview by Kat Dunn, host, *Conspire Away, B*tches! With Kat Dunn*, podcast, September 1, 2020, https://conspireawaypodcast.libsyn.com/website/adam-jasinski-did-not-win-bb9-fund-an-illegal-drug-operation-spend-4-years-in-prison-and-now-spend-his-life-helping-those-with-addiction-and-mental-health-issues-for-tyler-to-call-old-school-boring.

18. Jasinski, interview by Dunn, *Conspire Away, B*tches! With Kat Dunn*.

19. Jasinski, interview by Dunn, *Conspire Away, B*tches! With Kat Dunn*.

20. Kevin Shelly, "From 'Big Brother' Winner to Drug Felon, Cherry Hill Native Needed a Reality Check," *PhillyVoice*, September 20, 2016, https://www.phillyvoice.com/from-big-brother-winner-to-drug-felon-cherry-hill-native-needed-a-reality-check/.

21 Jasinski, interview by Dunn, *Conspire Away, B*tches! With Kat Dunn.*
22 Jasinski, interview by Dunn, *Conspire Away, B*tches! With Kat Dunn.*
23 Jasinski, interview by Dunn, *Conspire Away, B*tches! With Kat Dunn.*
24 "'Big Brother' Star Fired for 'Retard' Comment," *New York Post*, February 27, 2008, https://nypost.com/2008/02/27/big-brother-star-fired-for-retard-comment/.
25 Salman Rushdie, "Reality TV: A Dearth of Talent and the Death of Morality," *Guardian*, June 9, 2001, https://www.theguardian.com/books/2001/jun/09/salmanrushdie.
26 Peter Bazalgette, *Billion Dollar Game: How Three Men Risked It All and Changed the Face of Television* (Time Warner, 2005), 117.
27 Bazalgette, *Billion Dollar Game*, 182.
28 Bazalgette, *Billion Dollar Game*, 210–211.
29 Bazalgette, *Billion Dollar Game*, 208–209.
30 Bazalgette, *Billion Dollar Game*, 208–209.
31 Bazalgette, *Billion Dollar Game*, 214.
32 Bazalgette, *Billion Dollar Game*, 214.
33 Bazalgette, *Billion Dollar Game*, 218.
34 Bazalgette, *Billion Dollar Game*, 219.
35 Ansbert Kneip, "Der wo President werden soll ," *Der Spiegel*, April 16, 2000, https://www.spiegel.de/politik/der-wo-president-werden-soll-a-7dc05036-0002-0001-0000-000016215220.
36 Bazalgette, *Billion Dollar Game*, 202.
37 Bazalgette, *Billion Dollar Game*, 229.
38 Suzanne Moore, "Jade Goody: A Scorned Celebrity Who Held a Mirror up to Bitter Britain," *Guardian*, August 9, 2019, https://www.theguardian.com/tv-and-radio/2019/aug/09/jade-goody-scorned-celebrity-big-brother-britain-class-prejudice.
39 "The Jane Goody Phenomenon," *Independent*, January 9, 2007, https://www.independent.co.uk/news/people/profiles/the-jade-goody-phenomenon-5542408.html.
40 Stephen Brook, "Shilpa Complains of Racism," *Guardian*, January 18, 2007, https://www.theguardian.com/media/2007/jan/18/bigbrother.raceintheuk.
41 Moore, "Jade Goody."
42 Mark Lawson, "Is It Time to Kill Off Big Brother?" *Guardian*, July 23, 2009, https://www.theguardian.com/media/2009/jul/24/big-brother-television.
43 Lawson, "Is It Time to Kill Off Big Brother?"
44 Daniel Sperling, "Big Brother Live Feed Axe Confirmed by Channel 5," Digital Spy, August 16, 2011, https://www.digitalspy.com/tv/reality-tv/a335457/big-brother-live-feed-axe-confirmed-by-channel-5/.
45 Lucy Williamson and George Wright, "Andrew Tate Charged with Rape and

Human Trafficking," BBC News, June 20, 2023, https://www.bbc.com/news/world-europe-65959097.
46 "Reality TV Star Stephen Bear Guilty of Sex Tape Offences," BBC News, December 13, 2022, https://www.bbc.com/news/uk-england-essex-63911965.
47 "Jeremy Jackson Thrown Out of Celebrity Big Brother," BBC News, January 11, 2015, https://www.bbc.com/news/entertainment-arts-30766963.
48 Mark Lawson, "Big Bother," *Guardian*, July 22, 2002, https://www.theguardian.com/media/2002/jul/22/bigbrother.broadcasting.
49 Annie Yuan, "'Big Brother' Winner Adam Jasinski Sentenced to Four Years in Federal Prison," *Hollywood Reporter*, January 22, 2011, https://www.hollywoodreporter.com/tv/tv-news/big-brother-winner-adam-jasinski-74653/.
50 Yuan, "'Big Brother' Winner Adam Jasinski."
51 Kevin Shelly, "From 'Big Brother' Winner to Drug Felon, Cherry Hill Native Needed a Reality Check," PhillyVoice, September 20, 2016, https://www.phillyvoice.com/from-big-brother-winner-to-drug-felon-cherry-hill-native-needed-a-reality-check/.
52 Shelly, "From 'Big Brother' Winner to Drug Felon."

Chapter 9: The Renaissance

1 Adam Bryant, "CBS Fall TV Shows 2024: The Complete Schedule and Premiere Dates," *TV Guide*, July 21, 2008, https://www.tvguide.com/news/big-brother-brian-36047/.
2 *Big Brother*, season 10, episode 1, aired July 13, 2008, on CBS, https://www.paramountplus.com/shows/video/FqwMFLNiyvw4FHoXCjWEqNTbd0CtMh_3/.
3 *Big Brother*, season 10, episode 1.
4 *Big Brother*, season 10, episode 1.
5 *Big Brother*, season 10, episode 2, aired July 15, 2008, on CBS, https://www.paramountplus.com/shows/video/WAVssicnQsi_cDkChxbISTqqkRCrWyly/.
6 *Big Brother*, season 10, episode 2.
7 "Big Brother Cast: Libra," CBS.com, archived July 18, 2012, https://web.archive.org/web/20120718064935/http://www.cbs.com/shows/big_brother/cast/15602/.
8 *Big Brother*, season 10, episode 13, aired August 10, 2008, on CBS, https://www.paramountplus.com/shows/video/TNjwPAJquALV7yRJSBwrPAyMNfdU7fak/.
9 *Big Brother*, season 10, episode 2.
10 *Big Brother*, season 10, episode 2.
11 "'Big Brother 10' Back with Less Twist, More Scheme," CBS 2, July 8, 2008,

archived July 17, 2008, https://web.archive.org/web/20080808001323/http://cbs2.com/bigbrother/big.brother.cbs.2.766137.html.
12. *Big Brother*, season 10, episode 3, aired July 16, 2008, on CBS, https://www.paramountplus.com/shows/video/TuTp6W4Ga5IiYYzj9uKIND8l_ooPj8yx/.
13. *Big Brother*, season 10, episode 4, aired July 20, 2008, on CBS, https://www.paramountplus.com/shows/video/1_CNOOwEpi6lB_cSkUb_7woNRGquYFIv/.
14. *Big Brother*, season 10, episode 4.
15. *Big Brother*, season 10, episode 4.
16. *Big Brother*, season 10, episode 4.
17. *Big Brother*, season 14, episode 5, aired July 18, 2012, on CBS, https://www.paramountplus.com/shows/video/2259324071/.
18. *Big Brother*, season 10, episode 1.
19. "'Big Brother 10' Back with Less Twist, More Scheme," CBS 2.
20. Dan Gheesling, interview by Taran Armstrong, *The Taran Show*, Rob Has a Podcast, June 15, 2019, https://robhasawebsite.com/taran-show-55-dan-gheesling/.
21. Gheesling, interview by Armstrong, *The Taran Show*.
22. Dan Gheesling, *How to Get on Reality TV: How a Normal Guy Got Cast on Reality TV* (Mist House, 2012), 5–6.
23. Gheesling, interview by Taran Armstrong, *The Taran Show*.
24. Gheesling, *How to Get on Reality TV*, 62.
25. Gheesling, *How to Get on Reality TV*, 65.
26. Gheesling, *How to Get on Reality TV*, 71.
27. *Big Brother*, season 10, episode 5, aired July 22, 2008, on CBS, https://www.paramountplus.com/shows/video/qMro6yhQ8syue5dT8aZsfOQ2PVNiQuI8/.
28. *Big Brother*, season 10, episode 5.
29. *Big Brother*, season 10, episode 13.
30. *Big Brother*, season 10, episode 12, aired August 6, 2008, on CBS, https://www.paramountplus.com/shows/video/UKD67pszVhzrKQprdes2NKMe91gmZZKn/.
31. *Big Brother*, season 10, episode 12.
32. *Big Brother*, season 10, episode 13.
33. *Big Brother*, season 10, episode 13.
34. *Big Brother*, season 10, episode 13.
35. *Big Brother*, season 10, episode 13.
36. William Hammon, "Big Brother 10, August 7: Dan-Freaking-Tastic!" Reality News Online, August 8, 2008, archived August 18, 2008, https://web.archive.org/web/20080818195542/http://www.realitynewsonline.com/cgi-bin/ae.pl?mode=1&article=article8226.art&page=1.

37 *Big Brother*, season 10, episode 14, aired August 12, 2008, on CBS, https://www.paramountplus.com/shows/video/388xhPINiSFCe7NBvr7Hb1q02lXAIlm3/.
38 *Big Brother*, season 10, episode 15, aired August 14, 2008, on CBS, https://www.paramountplus.com/shows/video/ENJber7NizSp57Fbd21yPqZDC2tJPe3P/.
39 *Big Brother*, season 10, episode 21, aired August 28, 2008, on CBS, https://www.paramountplus.com/shows/video/g1bNfUpQK82BWTMxKsifle7t4UZFb3Cc/.
40 *Big Brother*, season 10, episode 19, aired August 24, 2008, on CBS, https://www.paramountplus.com/shows/video/93TZpGw4xg1E5djBdYsGirNKEd0xUFpi/.
41 *Big Brother*, season 10, episode 19.
42 *Big Brother*, season 10, episode 19.
43 *Big Brother*, season 10, episode 20, aired August 26, 2008, on CBS, https://www.paramountplus.com/shows/video/bzEO9Sl8TZFpGau8UDoqaiP9VmJig5Ri/.
44 *Big Brother*, season 10, episode 22, aired August 31, 2008, on CBS, https://www.paramountplus.com/shows/video/1PohCzMAh2fwIJPArr4rwGb_s0Fz9UAc/.
45 *Big Brother*, season 10, episode 20.
46 *Big Brother*, season 10, episode 20.
47 *Big Brother*, season 10, episode 20.
48 *Big Brother*, season 10, episode 21.
49 Matt Richenthal, "Big Brother Recap: Replacement Nominee Roulette," TV Fanatic, August 27, 2008, archived January 4, 2014, https://web.archive.org/web/20140104000353/http://www.tvfanatic.com/2008/08/big-brother-recap-replacement-nominee-roulette/.
50 *Big Brother*, season 10, episode 21.
51 *Big Brother*, season 10, episode 26, aired September 9, 2008, on CBS, https://www.paramountplus.com/shows/video/8CUlqIDju9o5p_lsZq6qx1pjmJF6WI_O/.
52 *Big Brother*, season 10, episode 26.
53 *Big Brother*, season 10, episode 26.
54 "Dan Wins 'BB10' and the $500,000 Top Prize," CBS 2, September 17, 2008, archived September 20, 2008, https://web.archive.org/web/20081201130351/http://cbs2.com/bigbrother/Memphis.Dan.Big.2.819325.html.
55 *Big Brother*, season 10, episode 29, aired September 16, 2008, on CBS, https://www.paramountplus.com/shows/video/BRy__S0ZeghmS60oKsBcWNSLtbjf7LWk/.
56 *Big Brother*, season 10, episode 29.
57 Oscar Dahl, "Exclusive Interview: Dan, Winner of 'Big Brother 10', Part 2," BuddyTV, September 18, 2008, https://www.buddytv.com/exclusive-interview-dan-winner-of-big-brother-10-part-2/.
58 *Big Brother*, season 10, episode 29.
59 "Dan Wins 'BB10' and the $500,000 Top Prize," CBS 2.
60 Gheesling, interview by Armstrong, *The Taran Show*.

Chapter 10: Cancellation

1. Brian Porreca, "'Big Brother OTT': Second Evictee Responds to Accusations of Racism," *Hollywood Reporter*, October 14, 2016, https://www.hollywoodreporter.com/tv/tv-news/big-brother-ott-monte-eviction-938408/.

2. Aaryn Williams, interview by Lara Trump, posted March 23, 2023, by The Right View with Lara Trump, YouTube, 35:38, https://www.youtube.com/watch?v=Ikwknwjtdmc.

3. Andy Dehnart, "Big Brother Already a Cesspool of Racist, Homophobic, and Misogynistic Comments," Reality Blurred, July 1, 2013, https://www.realityblurred.com/realitytv/2013/07/big-brother-15-bb15-racism-homophobia-misogyny/; Ree Hines, "'Big Brother' Rocked by Big Controversy: Racism, Sexism and Homophobia," *Today*, July 3, 2013, http://www.today.com/popculture/big-brother-rocked-big-controversy-racism-sexism-homophobia-6C10523010; Philiana Ng, "'Big Brother 15's' Controversial Houseguests Respond to Losing Their Jobs," *Hollywood Reporter*, September 19, 2013, https://www.hollywoodreporter.com/tv/tv-news/big-brother-15-controversial-houseguests-632350/; Philiana Ng, "'Big Brother 15': Third Houseguest Criticized by Employer over Offensive Remarks," *Hollywood Reporter*, July 6, 2013, https://www.hollywoodreporter.com/tv/tv-news/big-brother-15-spencer-clawson-581328/; Tierney Bricker, "*Big Brother* Issues Disclaimer in Wake of Racial Controversy," E! Online, July 15, 2013, https://www.eonline.com/news/438958/big-brother-issues-disclaimer-in-wake-of-racial-controversy.

4. Ree Hines, "Did a Racist Win 'Big Brother 15'?" *Today*, September 18, 2013, https://www.today.com/popculture/did-racist-win-big-brother-15-4b11196803.

5. "'BB15 Bigotry Supercut,'" posted July 7, 2013, by pronkoforder1, YouTube, 11:48, https://www.youtube.com/watch?v=H3sIaYUxOLs (removed by Endemol USA), archived July 8, 2013, https://web.archive.org/web/20130709175020/https://www.youtube.com/watch?v=H3sIaYUxOLs.

6. Brian Stelter, "Reality Show Contestants Pay a Real-World Price," *The New York Times*, July 8, 2013, https://www.nytimes.com/2013/07/09/business/media/on-big-brother-racial-and-gay-slurs-abound.html.

7. Andrew Wallenstein, "CBS Slaps Disclaimer on 'Big Brother': Beware 'Prejudice,'" *Variety*, July 15, 2013, https://variety.com/2013/tv/news/cbs-slaps-disclaimer-on-big-brother-beware-prejudice-1200562722/.

8. David Kronke, "Racism Alleged, but TV Viewers Not Seeing That Part," *Daily News Los Angeles*, August 6, 2000, archived August 17, 2000, https://

web.archive.org/web/20000817171841/http://www.dailynewslosangeles.com/archives/2000/08/06/lif03.asp.
9. David Kronke, "Racism Alleged, but TV Viewers Not Seeing That Part."
10. Stelter, "Reality Show Contestants Pay a Real-World Price."
11. Andy Dehnart, "Jeff Schroeder Uses Gay Slurs on Big Brother," Reality Blurred, July 14, 2009, https://www.realityblurred.com/realitytv/2009/07/big-brother-11-jeff_gay_slurs/.
12. "Big Brother: Jeff Schroeder's Anti-Gay Tirade," posted July 14, 2011, by LGBTQ Nation, YouTube, 1:58, https://www.youtube.com/watch?v=iUmWV_AJVFw.
13. "Big Brother: Jeff Schroeder's Anti-Gay Tirade."
14. Andy Dehnart, "Lydia Saved, Braden Nominated as Editors Ignore Big Brother 11's Ugliness," Reality Blurred, July 15, 2009, https://www.realityblurred.com/realitytv/2009/07/big-brother-11-pov_braden/.
15. Andy Dehnart, "Braden Evicted After Tie Despite Producers' Pathetic Sanitizing of His Bigotry," Reality Blurred, July 17, 2009, https://www.realityblurred.com/realitytv/2009/07/big-brother-11-braden_out_producers_censor/.
16. Dehnart, "Braden Evicted After Tie."
17. "Big Brother's Braden Defends His Verbal Attack on Lydia," *People*, July 20, 2009, archived July 20, 2009, https://web.archive.org/web/20090720120346/http://tvwatch.people.com/2009/07/17/big-brothers-braden-defends-his-verbal-attack-on-lydia/.
18. Dehnart, "Braden Evicted After Tie."
19. Associated Press, "'Big Brother' Racial Slur Edited Out," *Hollywood Reporter*, July 17, 2009, https://www.hollywoodreporter.com/business/business-news/big-brother-racial-slur-edited-86643/.
20. TY BB (@rizmwimb), "Y'all the tea. Chima snapped! Wow." Twitter (now X), July 25, 2019, 1:21 a.m., https://twitter.com/rizmwimb/status/1154305750728105984.
21. *Big Brother*, season 11, episode 18, aired August 18, 2009, on CBS, https://www.paramountplus.com/shows/video/DPTR41_grq_509rZxVo6tYK8nz7aJBqW/.
22. Associated Press, "Booted 'Big Brother' Contestant Apologizes," *Today*, August 19, 2009, http://www.today.com/popculture/booted-big-brother-contestant-apologizes-1C9403599.
23. Dehnart, "Braden Evicted After Tie."
24. Andy Dehnart, "Why Aren't Ivette's 'Raving Lunatic Racist' Comments and Other Offensive Remarks Airing?" Reality Blurred, September 18, 2005, https://www.realityblurred.com/realitytv/2005/09/big-brother-6-offensive_comments/.
25. Hines, "'Big Brother' Rocked by Big Controversy."
26. Stelter, "Reality Show Contestants Pay a Real-World Price."

27 "BB15 Bigotry Supercut."
28 Ree Hines, "'Big Brother' Contestants Lose Jobs Due to Racist, Homophobic Remarks," *Today*, September 20, 2013, http://www.today.com/popculture/big-brother-contestants-lose-jobs-due-racist-homophobic-remarks-4B11210469.
29 Philiana Ng, "'Big Brother 15' Houseguest Dropped by Agency, Magazine over Offensive Remarks," *Hollywood Reporter*, July 3, 2013, https://www.hollywoodreporter.com/tv/tv-news/big-brother-15-houseguest-dropped-579786/.
30 Philiana Ng, "'Big Brother 15': Another Houseguest Loses Job Over Racial Slurs," *Hollywood Reporter*, July 3, 2013, https://www.hollywoodreporter.com/tv/tv-news/big-brother-15-ginamarie-zimmerman-579843/.
31 Corus Entertainment, "Big Brother Launches Digital Dailies, New Exclusive Content for Season 11 Available on Bigbrothercanada.ca," press release, February 23, 2023, https://www.corusent.com/news/big-brother-canada-launches-digital-dailies-new-exclusive-content-for-season-11-available-on-bigbrothercanada-ca/.
32 *Big Brother*, season 15, episode 8, aired July 14, 2013, on CBS, https://www.paramountplus.com/shows/video/0150FE08-506F-30DA-59FC-DED1B1ED0FF7/.
33 *Big Brother*, season 15, episode 8.
34 "Never saw this before. Jeff Schroeder being homophobic on Big Brother. What the actual f?" Reddit, September 8, 2014, www.reddit.com/r/BigBrother/comments/2fsgm7/never_saw_this_before_jeff_schroeder_being/.
35 "A Peak Behind the Curtain," posted April 10, 2024, by Jeff and Jordan TV, YouTube, 35:12, https://www.youtube.com/watch?v=DrGfbVyqnO4.
36 Williams, interview by Trump, The Right View with Lara Trump.
37 Williams, interview by Trump, The Right View with Lara Trump.

Chapter 11: Cracking the Code

1 Taran Armstrong, host, *We Know Big Brother*, "Alliance Building," Rob Has a Podcast, May 24, 2020, https://robhasawebsite.com/big-brother-alliance-building/.
2 *Big Brother*, season 12, episode 2, aired July 11, 2010, on CBS, https://www.paramountplus.com/shows/video/iWEU46j4idwahWya0vWJFPfOzr9K2BUg/.
3 *Big Brother*, season 12, episode 2.
4 Armstrong, "Alliance Building."
5 "Taran: RHAP Audition Video," posted March 22, 2015, by Taran Armstrong, YouTube, 1:10, https://www.youtube.com/watch?v=QmUE1fMy0es.
6 *Survivor*, season 6, episode 15, "The Reunion," aired May 11, 2003, on CBS, https://www.paramountplus.com/shows/video/3R0OxetT6VntGHhTMf3yT98SvY1vI6w7/.

7. Rob Cesternino, interview by Taran Armstrong, host, *The Taran Show*, Rob Has a Podcast, July 17, 2017, https://robhasawebsite.com/the-taran-show-premiere-episode-with-rob-cesternino/.
8. Rob Cesternino, host, *Rob Has a Podcast*, "The History of RHAP: Rob Cesternino on 10 Years of Rob Has a Podcast," February 10, 2020, https://robhasawebsite.com/rhap-history-10-year-rob-podcast/.
9. Rob Cesternino (@robcesternino), direct message to author, March 26, 2015.
10. Rob Cesternino, email message to author, April 7, 2015.
11. *Big Brother*, season 14, episode 21, aired August 29, 2012, on CBS, https://www.paramountplus.com/shows/video/2274113048/.
12. *Big Brother*, season 14, episode 21.
13. *Big Brother*, season 14, episode 5, aired July 22, 2012, on CBS, https://www.paramountplus.com/shows/video/2259324071/.
14. *Big Brother*, season 14, episode 21.
15. *Big Brother*, season 14, episode 21.
16. *Big Brother*, season 14, episode 21.
17. *Big Brother*, season 14, episode 21.
18. Jarett Wieselman, "'BB14' Stars Break Down the Finale," Yahoo Entertainment, September 20, 2012, https://www.yahoo.com/entertainment/bb14-stars-break-down-finale-173400261.html.
19. Armstrong, "Alliance Building."
20. Armstrong, "Alliance Building."
21. *Big Brother*, season 17, episode 3, aired June 28, 2015, on CBS, https://www.paramountplus.com/shows/video/PA9DL0d73aVkMkvrG_GPewUOLOdNZqzs/.
22. Steve Moses, interview by Taran Armstrong, May 6, 2024.
23. "Big Brother Casting: 'Among Them,'" posted February 17, 2024, by Steven Moses, YouTube, 6:37, https://www.youtube.com/watch?v=siGXdKRniog.
24. Moses, interview by Armstrong, May 6, 2024.
25. Josef Adalian, "Network TV's Ultimate Survivor," Vulture, September 8, 2015, https://www.vulture.com/2015/09/leslie-moonves-on-20-years-at-cbs.html.
26. Moses, interview by Armstrong, May 6, 2024.
27. Dan Gheesling, interview by Taran Armstrong, May 4, 2024.

Chapter 12: The Cookout

1. Greg Braxton, "Black Players Changed 'Big Brother' Forever. Fans Say the Show Can't 'Tiptoe' Around It," *Los Angeles Times*, September 16, 2021, https://www.latimes.com/entertainment-arts/tv/story/2021-09-16/big-brother-the-cookout-julie-chen-moonves.

Notes

2 Tiffany Mitchell, interview by Taran Armstrong, May 25, 2024.
3 Kronke, "Racism Alleged, but TV Viewers Not Seeing That Part."
4 Kronke, "Racism Alleged, but TV Viewers Not Seeing That Part."
5 Mitchell, interview by Armstrong, May 25, 2024.
6 *Big Brother*, season 8, episode 8, aired July 22, 2007, on CBS, https://www.paramountplus.com/shows/video/u1345yjUwMr3Sna6sm1KlmrrznxohB5A/.
7 *Big Brother*, season 8, episode 8.
8 Taylor Hale, interview by Taran Armstrong, May 16, 2024.
9 Kronke, "Racism Alleged, but TV Viewers Not Seeing That Part."
10 Kronke, "Racism Alleged, but TV Viewers Not Seeing That Part."
11 Hugh Ryan, "Real Racism: What Aaryn Gries Reveals About Reality TV," *Daily Beast*, August 25, 2013, https://www.thedailybeast.com/articles/2013/08/25/real-racism-what-aaryn-gries-reveals-about-reality-tv.
12 Ryan, "Real Racism: What Aaryn Gries Reveals About Reality TV."
13 Ryan, "Real Racism: What Aaryn Gries Reveals About Reality TV."
14 Ryan, "Real Racism: What Aaryn Gries Reveals About Reality TV."
15 Vince Dixon, "Big Brother's Diversity Problem by the Numbers," Vince Dixon Portfolio, August 26, 2019, https://vincedixonportfolio.com/2019/08/26/big-brother-diversity-data/.
16 Eric Stein, interview by Taran Armstrong, May 20, 2024.
17 Stein, interview by Armstrong, May 20, 2024.
18 EmpiricalMonarch, "The Bigger Picture: What Big Brother Has Taught Me (About Racism)," Reddit, September 5, 2020, https://www.reddit.com/r/BigBrother/comments/imx4kt/the_bigger_picture_what_big_brother_has_taught_me/.
19 *Big Brother*, season 21, episode 2, aired June 26, 2019, on CBS, https://www.paramountplus.com/shows/video/i39UEUb2SWqfiquzaGMpiLjMxAHY3oB9/.
20 Julia Carter, "Push Me to the Edge: My Survivor Experience," *The Julia Carter* (blog), June 6, 2019, https://thejuliacarter.com/2019/06/06/push-me-to-the-edge-my-survivor-experience/.
21 Carter, "Push Me to the Edge."
22 Carter, "Push Me to the Edge."
23 Kayla Cobb, "CBS Addresses 'Survivor,' 'Big Brother' Racism Accusations," Decider, August 1, 2019, https://decider.com/2019/08/01/cbs-big-brother-survivor-racism-accusations/.
24 Lynette Rice, "*Big Brother* Producer Reprimanded for Racially Insensitive Interaction with Kemi," EW.com, August 1, 2019, https://ew.com/tv/2019/08/01/big-brother-producer-reprimanded-kemi-diary-room/.
25 Rice, "*Big Brother* Producer Reprimanded."
26 Margeaux Sippell, "CBS Execs Respond to 'Big Brother' Racism Accusations

During Fiery Press Session," TheWrap, August 1, 2019, https://www.thewrap.com/cbs-execs-respond-to-racism-big-brother-fiery-tca-session/.

27 Sippell, "CBS Execs Respond."
28 Sippell, "CBS Execs Respond."
29 Sippell, "CBS Execs Respond."
30 Arisa Cox (@arisacox), "There is a reason Big Brother Canada and I are aiming for at least 50% BIPOC on our next cast. BB is a numbers game. If we want every player to have the same chance to succeed, we must evolve past the idea that minorities in the country must remain minorities in the house," Twitter (now X), August 25, 2020, 9:00 a.m., https://twitter.com/arisacox/status/1298289063858974720.
31 Cox, "There is a reason."
32 Ronan Farrow, "Les Moonves and CBS Face Allegations of Sexual Misconduct," *New Yorker*, July 27, 2018, https://www.newyorker.com/magazine/2018/08/06/les-moonves-and-cbs-face-allegations-of-sexual-misconduct.
33 Alex Sherman, "Former CBS CEO Les Moonves Drops Legal Pursuit to Get $120 Million in Severance Pay," CNBC, May 14, 2021, https://www.cnbc.com/2021/05/14/moonves-drops-legal-pursuit-to-recoup-120-million-cbs-severance-package.html.
34 "Black Voices of SURVIVOR Roundtable LIVE—June 24, 2020," posted June 24, 2020, by RHAP: We Know Reality TV, YouTube, 2:15:14, https://www.youtube.com/watch?v=lqJM_05fFuk.
35 "A Petition for Anti-Racism Action by Survivor Entertainment Group," MoveOn, accessed May 28, 2024, https://sign.moveon.org/petitions/a-petition-for-anti-racism-action-by-survivor-entertainment-group-2.
36 "A Campaign for Anti-Racism in the Bachelor Franchise," Change.org, accessed May 28, 2024, https://www.change.org/p/abc-a-campaign-for-anti-racism-in-the-bachelor-franchise.
37 Brice Izyah, interview by Taran Armstrong, May 25, 2024.
38 Izyah, interview by Armstrong, May 25, 2024.
39 CBS, "CBS Sets Target for 50% Representation of Black, Indigenous and People of Color (BIPOC) Across All Casts for Unscripted Series," press release, November 9, 2020, https://www.paramountpressexpress.com/cbs-entertainment/releases/view?id=56315.
40 CBS, "CBS Sets Target for 50% Representation."
41 BB Q&A | Week 10–September 10, 2021, posted September 10, 2021, by RHAP: We Know Reality TV, YouTube, 1:57:09, https://www.youtube.com/live/0e-XIAC_EIg.
42 Mitchell, interview by Armstrong, May 25, 2024.

43 Izyah, interview by Armstrong, May 25, 2024.
44 Mitchell, interview by Armstrong, May 25, 2024.
45 Mitchell, interview by Armstrong, May 25, 2024.
46 Izyah, interview by Armstrong, May 25, 2024.
47 Rashad Grove, "Xavier Prather Makes History as First Black Winner of CBS 'Big Brother,'" *Ebony*, October 4, 2024, https://www.ebony.com/xavier-prather-makes-history-as-first-black-winner-of-cbs-big-brother/.
48 Izyah, interview by Armstrong, May 25, 2024.
49 Jarett Wieselman, "The Anti-Trans 'Big Brother' Houseguest Defends His Comments," BuzzFeed News, September 21, 2017, https://www.buzzfeednews.com/article/jarettwieselman/big-brother-19-cody-unapologetic-about-anti-trans.
50 Mitchell, interview by Armstrong, May 25, 2024.
51 Mariah Espada, "How Big Brother Finally Got Its First Black Winner," *Time*, September 30, 2021, https://time.com/6103015/big-brother-first-black-winner/.

Chapter 13: The Rules of the Game

1 Taylor Hale, interview by Taran Armstrong, May 16, 2024.
2 Hale, interview by Armstrong, May 16, 2024.
3 Hale, interview by Armstrong, May 16, 2024.
4 Taylor Hale, interview by Taran Armstrong; "BB24 Taylor Hale Deep Dive," posted October 5, 2022, by RHAP: We Know Reality TV, YouTube, 6:21:27, https://www.youtube.com/watch?v=jdzo8PIA2QA.
5 Lisa Donahue, interview by Gretchen and Marcellas, hosts *House Calls*, podcast, posted July 28, 2004, Lisa Donahue Fan Page, https://www.csnetserver.com/lisadonahue/mp4/Lisa%20on%20House%20Calls.mp4.
6 Donahue, interview by Gretchen and Marcellas.
7 *Big Brother*, season 3, episode 25, aired September 4, 2002, on CBS, https://www.paramountplus.com/shows/video/sRT1kULBHax2FXQsv8bFW5a6hDxEb9uL/.
8 *Big Brother*, season 3, episode 25.
9 *Big Brother*, season 3, episode 25.
10 *Big Brother*, season 3, episode 25.
11 *Big Brother*, season 3, episode 25.
12 *Big Brother*, season 3, episode 31, aired September 21, 2002, on CBS, https://www.paramountplus.com/shows/video/KJMNY8O73KlPWeZl92EE1kI6ESHDgf9W/.
13 *Big Brother*, season 3, episode 33, aired September 25, 2002, on CBS, https://www.paramountplus.com/shows/video/W5vqeHqgwE_lcQ0KnZmg1vKrJSG6jTTp/.

14 *Big Brother*, season 3, episode 33.
15 *Big Brother*, season 24, episode 2, aired July 10, 2022, on CBS, https://www.paramountplus.com/shows/video/Jdv_M07bM8WiQHqYAEPkq3lzIICp9Uoq/.
16 Hale, "BB24 Taylor Hale Deep Dive."
17 *Big Brother*, season 24, episode 2.
18 Hale, "BB24 Taylor Hale Deep Dive."
19 Hale, "BB24 Taylor Hale Deep Dive."
20 *Big Brother*, season 24, episode 3, aired July 13, 2022, on CBS, https://www.paramountplus.com/shows/video/H5KzIIZY9L6xs8FYJpuJMG8cwMuB_LuU/.
21 *Big Brother*, season 24, episode 4, aired July 14, 2022, on CBS, https://www.paramountplus.com/shows/video/exSIszceNk36YDjrZc0wG1wCGLH1_PX2/.

Chapter 14: The Sword

1 Esther Addley, "Sinisa's Story," *Guardian*, July 26, 2002, https://www.theguardian.com/media/2002/jul/26/bigbrother.broadcasting.
2 Addley, "Sinisa's Story."
3 Addley, "Sinisa's Story."
4 Addley, "Sinisa's Story."
5 Gary Trock, "Ashley Massaro Died of Apparent Suicide After Claiming Years of Depression, Injuries Suffered from WWE Career," Yahoo Entertainment, May 17, 2019, https://www.yahoo.com/entertainment/ashley-massaro-died-apparent-suicide-153853404.html.
6 Eloise Hendy, "How a Long-Forgotten Suicide Helped Define Reality TV Voyeurism," *Independent*, August 5, 2023, https://www.independent.co.uk/life-style/reality-tv-deaths-big-brother-b2386937.html.
7 Eric Margolis, "The Fall of 'Terrace House,'" *New York Times*, July 17, 2020, https://www.nytimes.com/2020/07/17/arts/television/terrace-house-suicide.html.
8 Hendy, "How a Long-Forgotten Suicide Helped Define Reality TV Voyeurism."
9 Kat Pettibone, "Paloma Aguilar Defends Her Behavior on 'Big Brother 24,'" *Us Weekly*, July 27, 2022, https://www.usmagazine.com/entertainment/news/paloma-aguilar-defends-her-behavior-on-big-brother-24/.
10 Steve Moses, interview by Taran Armstrong, May 6, 2024.
11 Moses, interview by Armstrong, May 6, 2024.
12 Moses, interview by Armstrong, May 6, 2024.
13 Dan Gheesling, interview by Taran Armstrong, May 4, 2024.
14 Neda Kalantar, interview by Taran Armstrong, host, *The Taran Show*, Rob

Has a Podcast, September 15, 2017, https://robhasawebsite.com/the-taran-show-9-neda-kalantar-interview/.

15   Kalantar, interview by Armstrong, *The Taran Show*, September 15, 2017.
16   Brice Izyah, interview by Taran Armstrong, May 25, 2024.
17   Taylor Hale, "Monte——'If We Have Something That Nobody Sees and Nobody Knows About, That Would Be Cool,'" Online Big Brother, July 20, 2022, https://www.onlinebigbrother.com/monte-if-we-have-something-that-nobody-sees-and-nobody-knows-about-that-would-be-cool/.
18   *Big Brother*, season 24, episode 9, aired July 27, 2022, on CBS, https://www.paramountplus.com/shows/video/q6PFdKld7n2LDCGToNIu23eKYtECcXdm/.
19   *Big Brother*, season 24, episode 9.
20   *Big Brother*, season 24, episode 9.
21   *Big Brother*, season 24, episode 9.
22   *Big Brother*, season 24, episode 9.
23   Kyle Capener, conversation on *Big Brother* live feeds, July 24, 2022.
24   Capener, *Big Brother* live feeds, July 24, 2022.
25   Taran Armstrong, "BB24 July 24 Live Feed Update | Big Brother 24," posted July 24, 2022, by RHAP: We Know Reality TV, YouTube, 1:25:18, https://www.youtube.com/watch?v=ZVP39mQ_UQk.
26   *Big Brother*, season 24, episode 10, aired July 28, 2022, on CBS, https://www.paramountplus.com/shows/video/vZepLj9DI0cB4Kng5D_lPT5xtGpue41s/.
27   *Big Brother*, season 24, episode 10.
28   *Big Brother*, season 24, episode 10.
29   Izyah, interview by Armstrong, May 25, 2024.
30   *Big Brother*, season 24, episode 35, aired September 25, 2022, on CBS, https://www.paramountplus.com/shows/video/zWjEegAvlvsnnonasYmD_2eRGmtP1O2B/.
31   *Big Brother*, season 24, episode 35.
32   Taran Armstrong, "BB24 September 23 Live Feed Update: Monte Taylor Deep Dive | Big Brother 24," posted September 23, 2022, by RHAP: We Know Reality TV, YouTube, 1:29:18, https://www.youtube.com/watch?v=NhTTtK3Fruo.
33   Taran Armstrong, "BB24 September 22 Live Feed Update: Taylor Hale Deep Dive | Big Brother 24," posted September 22, 2022, by RHAP: We Know Reality TV, YouTube, 1:51:32, https://www.youtube.com/watch?v=Dt32MRXw42k&t=6317s.
34   *Big Brother*, season 24, episode 35.
35   *Big Brother*, season 24, episode 35.

Chapter 15: The Mirror

1. *Big Brother*, season 2, episode 30.
2. Jason Guy, interview by Taran Armstrong, April 12, 2024.
3. Guy, interview by Armstrong, April 12, 2024.
4. Rob Cesternino, interview by Taran Armstrong, May 15, 2024.
5. Taylor Hale, interview by Taran Armstrong, May 16, 2024.
6. Taylor Hale (@TheTayMack), "My stomach churns when I think about living in that house without 24/7 live feeds. I am genuinely afraid anyone could have a similar experience to me, and not be believed leaving the house. Sunlight is the best disinfectant. Live feeds are the sun. So no, I'm not watching," Twitter (now X), March 23, 2023, 10:39 a.m., https://twitter.com/TheTayMack/status/1638732278506323970.
7. Tiffany Mitchell, interview by Taran Armstrong, May 25, 2024.
8. Mitchell, interview by Armstrong, May 25, 2024.
9. Peter Bazalgette, *Billion Dollar Game: How Three Men Risked It All and Changed the Face of Television* (Time Warner, 2005), 99–100.
10. Bazalgette, *Billion Dollar Game*, 99–100.
11. Raph Korine, interview by Taran Armstrong, May 1, 2024.
12. Korine, interview by Armstrong, May 1, 2024.

Acknowledgments

Three years ago, I received a message that started all of this. It was from a literary agent who was familiar with my work and believed that I could be a great writer—if I was interested in trying. Lauren MacLeod, you helped me realize a childhood dream, and I can't imagine having done this without your guidance and support throughout the entire process.

Eleven years ago, another message changed my life—from another person who took a chance on me. I was just a kid right out of college who was way too obsessed with *Big Brother*. Rob Cesternino, you gave me my voice, and you continue to inspire me every day.

Twenty-six years ago, it was my mom who introduced me to *Big Brother*. It became my escape for the next decade. But through it all, the thing I've been able to carry has been your belief that my potential is limitless. Thank you.

I must thank my editor, Kate Roddy, whose enthusiasm for this book went beyond my expectations and never failed to fill me with joy. Liv Turner for coming in clutch to help bring it all home. Emily Janakiram, Kimberly Cook, and Angela Corpus for their hard work marketing the book.

Thanks also must go to John de Mol, Paul Romer, Arnold Shapiro, Alison Groder, Rich Meehan, and the thousands around the globe who have been an essential part of this show's creation for the last two and a half decades.

I am also deeply grateful to each and every one of my friends whose knowledge and experience helped inform so much of this book.

Taylor Hale, who showed us that rules should be broken and could not contain her excitement for me when I told her about this book.

Dan Gheesling, the man who beat *Big Brother* at its own game, and whose faith in my ability to tell a story has propelled me forward as an author.

Tiffany Mitchell, whose master plan left a mark on the show that was too big to ignore and who has always been so generous with her support.

Steve Moses, who promised me we'd work together if we ever ended up playing together. Still holding you to that.

Brice Izyah, the purple-pants badass who helped change the landscape of reality TV.

Eric Stein, who's an actual reality television genius.

Jason Guy, who has taught so many lessons in the school of *Big Brother* strategy.

Jun Song, whose insight has always been as sharp as it is invaluable to me.

Matt Hoffman, the game breaker.

Derrick Levasseur, the undercover mastermind.

Hardy Hill and his jump rope.

Danielle Reyes, who paved the way.

And Neda Kalentar, traitorously charming and smart as hell.

Thank you to every player whose story was a part of this book, and I apologize to every friend or player whose story I didn't tell. I rampaged through the history of this show with a machete, exploring one path of thousands. As a result, there are so many valuable stories left untold.

Thank you to the journalists and prominent voices in this community: Hamsterwatch, Sharon Tharp, David Bloomberg, Andy Dehnart, and many, many more.

Thank you to Raphe Korine and Kevin Jacobs.

Thank you to my partner and my cat for supporting this dream.

Thank you to all of my podcasting cohosts who make the task of reporting on the *Big Brother* live feeds much less lonely.

Thank you to all of my wonderful viewers from the last ten years, whose support has made all of this possible.

And thank you to you, the person who took a chance on this book. I hope you enjoyed it.

About the Author

Taran Armstrong makes a living watching strangers on the internet. He often finds himself being watched by his cat, who has inevitably become the most popular figure in his content. He dreamed one day he'd be an author, and he's not quite ready to wake yet.